Churchill's Thin Grey Line

Other Books by Bernard Edwards

Masters Next to God
They Sank the Red Dragon
The Fighting Tramps
The Grey Widow Maker
Blood and Bushido
SOS – Men Against the Sea
Salvo!
Attack and Sink
Dönitz and the Wolf Packs
Return of the Coffin Ships
Beware Raiders!
The Road to Russia
The Quiet Heroes
The Twilight of the U-boats
Beware the Grey Widow Maker
Death in the Doldrums
Japan's Blitzkrieg
War of the U-boats
Royal Navy Versus the Slave Traders
The Cruel Sea Retold
War under the Red Ensign 1914-1918
The Wolf Packs Gather
Convoy Will Scatter
The Decoys
U-boats Beyond Biscay

Churchill's Thin Grey Line

British Merchant Ships at War 1939–1945

Bernard Edwards

Pen & Sword
MARITIME

First published in Great Britain in 2017 by
PEN & SWORD MARITIME
an imprint of
Pen & Sword Books Ltd
47 Church Street
Barnsley
South Yorkshire
S70 2AS

ISBN 978 1 52671 166 3

Printed and bound in Great Britain
By TJ International Ltd, Padstow, Cornwall

Pen & Sword Books Ltd incorporates the Imprints of Pen & Sword Archaeology, Atlas, Aviation, Battleground, Discovery, Family History, History, Maritime, Military, Naval, Politics, Railways, Select, Transport, True Crime, Fiction, Frontline Books, Leo Cooper, Praetorian Press, Seaforth Publishing, Wharncliffe and White Owl.

For a complete list of Pen & Sword titles please contact
PEN & SWORD BOOKS LIMITED
47 Church Street, Barnsley, South Yorkshire, S70 2AS, England
E-mail: enquiries@pen-and-sword.co.uk
Website: www.pen-and-sword.co.uk

This is for the many who died forgotten in the fog of war

There was no field for gestures or sensations; only the slow, cold drawing of lines on charts, which showed potential strangulation. Compared with this there was no value in brave armies ready to leap upon the invader, or in a good plan for desert warfare. The high and faithful spirit of the people counted for nought in this bleak domain. Either the food, supplies, and arms from the New World and from the British Empire arrived across the oceans, or they all failed.

Winston Churchill

Contents

Preface

The first British casualties of the Second World War occurred on Sunday, 3 September 1939, just nine hours after the conflict opened. They came not from the fighting forces, the Royal Navy, the Army or the Royal Air Force; they were British merchant seamen serving under the Red Ensign in the cargo/passenger liner *Athenia*, torpedoed without warning by U-30 some 200 miles west of Ireland. When the torpedoes struck, two men were killed in her engine room; seventeen other crew members gave their lives to save their passengers.

From that day onwards, until the war ended on 15 August 1945 with the dropping of atom bombs on Hiroshima and Nagasaki, Britain's merchant seamen were in the front line, bringing in the food, fuel and military equipment that saved their country from being crushed under the heel of Hitler's Wehrmacht. In doing so, many of them paid the supreme sacrifice. Figures released by the Registrar of Shipping and Seamen reveal that 2,535 British ocean-going merchant ships were lost in the six-year-long war, and of the 185,000 men and women serving in the British Merchant Navy at the time 36,749 lost their lives, 4,707 others were wounded, and 5,720 ended up in German and Japanese prisoner of war camps. This was a casualty rate of 25 per cent, second only to that suffered by RAF Bomber Command.

This book tells the story of some of those brave seamen, volunteers all, who manned the thin line of grey-painted ships that stretched from horizon to horizon, keeping Britain's vital sea lanes open in the face of a determined and ruthless enemy. Men who, when given the opportunity, fought to defend their ships and the cargoes they carried. Even today, more than seventy years since it all ended, this country is still heavily in their debt.

CHAPTER ONE

Curtain Up – *Athenia* 03.09.39

The *Athenia* sailed out of Liverpool at 4 o'clock on the afternoon of Saturday, 2 September 1939. As she steamed slowly down the River Mersey, her passengers were gathered on deck enjoying the late summer sun, their backs to the dark clouds gathering in the east. War with Germany was then imminent, yet the *Athenia* sailed alone and unarmed. Twenty-four hours later she was sinking, her bottom cruelly ripped open by a German torpedo. The curtain had risen on the Battle of the Atlantic, and it would not fall again for six long, bloody years.

The 13,581-ton *Athenia*, built in 1923 and owned by the Donaldson Atlantic Line of Glasgow, was typical of the medium-sized cargo/passenger liners employed on the North Atlantic run in the days before air travel became available to all. Powered by six steam turbines driving twin screws, she had a service speed of 15 knots, giving her a passage time between Liverpool and Montreal of eight days in average weather. She could never hope to match the big liners in opulence or despatch, but for those on a limited budget and with time to spare she offered good value for money.

On the *Athenia*'s current voyage she had on board 500 Jewish refugees, 311 Americans and 469 Canadians, all anxious to quit Europe ahead of the threatened conflict. She also carried 72 British nationals, some of whom were escaping to more peaceful climes before the balloon went up. Jesse Bigelow, who was returning to Canada with her husband and two children, described the situation:

> Our holidays were not over for another week but I talked my husband into getting an earlier booking on the *Athenia*. There were crowds of people with the same idea and it took hours of standing in line before we managed to get a small cabin on D-deck, down in the bowels of the ship. This turned out to be two berths on one side and two

on the other but no room for trunks or baggage, which were left outside the door . . . I found out that they had to arrange for the accommodation of 200 passengers above the normal total. Temporary bunks were erected here and there and I believe the ship's gymnasium became a dormitory.

Captain James Cook, commanding the *Athenia*, viewed the coming voyage as just another routine crossing. Prior to sailing, he had been warned of possible dangers en route, but nobody, not even the Admiralty, seriously considered the liner would be attacked. Available intelligence indicated that no German submarines had yet left port. In fact, unknown to the Admiralty, Rear Admiral Dönitz, C-in-C U-boats, had moved his headquarters from the Baltic to Wilhelmshaven and in August had ordered his U-boats to take up strategic positions in the North Sea and the Western Approaches. As the sun dropped towards the horizon and the *Athenia* closed the Bar light vessel to drop her pilot, Hitler already had a ring of steel around the British Isles.

One link in that ring was U-30, commanded by 26-year-old Oberleutnant zur See Fritz-Julius Lemp. U-30 was a 745-ton Type VIIA ocean-going submarine, built in 1936 under Hitler's secret rearmament programme known as Plan Z but only now emerging for her maiden voyage. She was equipped with two 6-cylinder MAN diesels and two Brown Boveri electric motors, giving her speeds of 17 knots on the surface and 8 knots submerged, plus a range of 6,200 miles at 10 knots. Her armament consisted of five 21-inch torpedo tubes, four in the bows and one in the stern, with eleven torpedoes, an 88mm deck gun with 220 rounds, and a 20mm anti-aircraft cannon. U-30 had sharp teeth.

The *Athenia* rounded the north of Ireland in the early hours of the morning of Sunday, 3 September and set course to the northwest to pick up the Great Circle route to the Gulf of St Lawrence. Later that morning, while Captain Cook, accompanied by his senior officers, was carrying out his customary Sunday inspection of the accommodation and galleys, Second Radio Officer Donald McRae appeared with a telegram from the Admiralty. The message was brief and to the point: as from 11.00 a.m. that day Britain was at war with Germany. Pre-lunch gins and tonic were postponed, while Cook retired to his cabin to open the sealed orders he had been handed before sailing.

While Captain Cook studied his sealed orders, some 80 miles to the north-west Oberleutnant Lemp was decoding a message he had just received from Wilhelmshaven. It read:

1105/3/9/39

FROM NAVAL HIGH COMMAND STOP

TO COMMANDERS-IN-CHIEF AND COMMANDERS AFLOAT STOP GREAT BRITAIN AND FRANCE HAVE DECLARED WAR ON GERMANY STOP BATTLE STATIONS IMMEDIATE IN ACCORDANCE WITH BATTLE INSTRUCTIONS FROM THE NAVY ALREADY PROMULGATED.

Remaining on the surface, Lemp ordered U-30's bow and stern tubes to be loaded and her deck gun to be made ready for action. Then, with extra lookouts posted, he settled down to await what this first day of the war would bring his way.

Captain Cook, meanwhile, in accordance with his sealed orders, had instructed his officers to clear away the *Athenia*'s twenty-six lifeboats and had commenced zigzagging around his mean course; purely precautionary measures, he assured them. Cook was not unduly worried that his ship might become a target for the new enemy, as under the Prize Rules of 1936, to which Germany was a signatory, attacks on passenger vessels were strictly prohibited. It then only remained for him to reassure his passengers that they were safe. With over a thousand nervous civilians on board, in the unlikely event of anything untoward happening, he had to avoid panic at all costs. Other than that, normal routine was followed: lunch was served, deck games were played, and apart from the frequent changes of course and the extra lookouts, 3 September 1939 was treated as just another routine Sunday at sea.

At sunset, which was about 1845, the *Athenia* was 50 miles south-east of Rockall, with nothing but the broad reaches of the North Atlantic ahead of her. The weather was fine, with only a light breeze, and the sea was calm, except for a long swell, but with the sun already down it was turning cold. Fifteen minutes later, with the night closing in around them, Captain Cook took one last sweep of the empty horizon with his binoculars and decided it was safe to resume a straight course. This being done, he went below to change for dinner.

Had he been aware that his ship was being stalked by a German submarine, Cook would not have left the bridge. Neither he, Chief Officer Barney Copeland, who had the watch on the bridge, nor any of the lookouts had seen the low silhouette of U-30, which had been keeping pace with the *Athenia* at a discreet distance for the past three hours. Before leaving Wihelmshaven, Fritz-Julius Lemp had been warned that British armed merchant cruisers were likely to be on patrol in the northern and western approaches to the British Isles, and now he believed he had found one. The obviously British liner was steaming fast and appeared to have several guns on deck. His suspicions were confirmed when, as darkness closed in, the ship showed no lights, not even dimmed navigation lights. Had she been a passenger vessel, then, in accordance with the Prize Rules, she should have been fully lit. There was no doubt in Lemp's mind that she was anything but a British man-of-war – a legitimate target.

At about 1900 Lemp took U-30 down to periscope depth and manoeuvred into a suitable attacking position, with *Athenia* on his starboard bow. At 1940 he fired a spread of two torpedoes from his bow tubes, and in doing so raised the curtain on the Battle of the Atlantic.

One of Lemp's torpedoes scored a direct hit in the liner's engine room, exploding with a dull thump. The explosion destroyed the watertight bulkhead between the *Athenia*'s engine room and boiler room, allowing the sea to flood into both spaces. It also split open one of the oil feeder tanks, adding to the turmoil as fuel oil mingled with the inrushing sea. But it was in the third class and tourist class dining rooms, directly above the engine room, that the torpedo had its most destructive effect. Passengers enjoying their meal, with no thought of war in their minds, were killed by the blast as they ate. Those who survived rushed to escape but found there was no way out. Both staircases to the upper decks had been demolished. They were trapped by the rising water, and to add to the confusion, all the lights suddenly failed.

Lona Marie Attfield was returning to Canada after visiting relatives in Europe. She spoke of the chaos caused by Lemp's torpedo to *Life* magazine in an interview published on 18 September 1939:

Sunday evening my mother and sister and I had finished our evening meal and had returned to our cabin when at approximately 7.15 p.m. our world was turned upside down by a horrific explosion. We were directed to don our life preservers and proceed to our lifeboat stations. This was nearly impossible as there was utter chaos everywhere with people going in all directions frightened beyond all imagination. Finally we made it to the lifeboat station only to find that the boat was painted fast to the davits. It looked nice but the davits didn't work as advertised. I suddenly realized that it would be a long cold night without proper clothing so I made my way back to the cabin crawling down a broken ladder amidst people seemingly not knowing what to do next. Once in the cabin I gathered our coats and looked around to see if there was anything there that might come in handy if we had to spend the night in a lifeboat. I suddenly saw an apple on the dresser and thought one of us might get hungry during the night. I put it in my pocket and made my way back to the lifeboat station. By now the smell of smoke from the fires was everywhere.

In September 2009, seventy years after the *Athenia* was torpedoed, 93-year-old survivor Barbara Wilson, interviewed by the *Daily Telegraph*, recalled:

I was sitting in the dining room with a young man and his father when the torpedo struck. Some people were knocked to the floor; everything was flying all over the place. I noticed there was a staircase in the distance and I thought I had better try to get to it. It was absolutely hideous because everything was flying all over the place: people, furniture, dishes, everything. Somehow I made my way up the staircase and got up on deck. I stumbled over one man, who was obviously dying. He was stretched out on his back and his eyes were rolling around in a way I had never seen in my life. I knew it must be the last moments for that poor man.

Chief Officer Barney Copeland, who had been relieved for dinner by the Third Officer, wrote in his report:

About 7.45 I was in the saloon when suddenly I felt a very heavy bump underneath on the port side. I immediately went on deck and, whilst going along one of the corridors, I felt another smaller bump. I am sure this second explosion took place in the space between No. 5 main hatches and the hatches of No. 5 hold. The reason I state this is because the beams which weigh about half a ton and the main hatches were blown off, yet the hatches on top of No. 5 hold, which were not nearly so firmly secured nor so heavy, were still in place. This space between the main hatches and the hatches to the hold had been utilized for passenger accommodation.

On arriving on deck, I was informed that we had been torpedoed on the port side. The ship took a list to port of about 6° and all the lights went out (I am sure of this time because I always inspected the ship before 8 o'clock, which was black-out time); the 'Abandon Ship' signal was also being sounded and all lifeboats were being cleared away ready for lowering. I looked over the port side and, at a distance of about half a mile on the port beam I could make out the fore end of a submarine. I could not see the conning tower or after end, as there was a cloud of black smoke practically surrounding her; neither could I see a gun. The submarine disappeared after about two minutes. I am convinced this black smoke came from the submarine because we had not been making any smoke nor was there any fog at the time. The torpedo struck the engine-room near the after bulkhead, which I think collapsed.

What Copeland had witnessed was Oberleutnant Lemp trying to extricate his submarine from an extremely fraught situation. One of the torpedoes fired from the bow tubes had jammed in the tube with its motor still running, and as the torpedo had a timer detonator, U-30 was in danger of being blown apart. Fortunately for Lemp and his crew, they succeeded in withdrawing the torpedo and deactivating its detonator.

The *Athenia* was still very much afloat, and Lemp now attempted to deliver the *coup de grâce* with another torpedo. This missed completely. By the time the miss became apparent, Lemp had consulted his ship recognition books, which identified his victim as either the *Athenia* or her sister ship *Letitia*, of the Donaldson Atlantic Line. Which of the two was revealed minutes later, when U-30's wireless operator intercepted an SOS from the *Athenia*, sent in plain language, giving her name and position. At this stage, even the Germans were not thinking in terms of total war, and in torpedoing an unarmed transatlantic passenger liner Lemp realized he had committed a dreadful mistake, one which might have very serious international repercussions. He decided to slip away and maintain radio silence until the furore died down.

The sea being relatively calm and in spite of her 12° list, all twenty-six of the *Athenia*'s lifeboats were lowered without incident. Chief Officer Copeland supervised the evacuation:

> After the boats were lowered, they were ordered to bear away from the ship. There was no panic at all on board and, as far as any observer could make out, we were carrying out the ordinary 'Abandon Ship' exercises.
>
> Those of the crew who had been employed lowering the boats were then sent for a final search to see that no one was left on board.
>
> Whilst this was going on, I got into the passenger space on the high side, between the No. 5 main hatches and those of No. 5 hold, as previously mentioned. On the low side there was a lot of water, and the bulkheads, woodwork, etc. in the vicinity were all blackened and splintered; and, though we carried no explosives on board, there was a very strong acrid smell, rather like fireworks, which made it very difficult to breathe. There were many bodies lying about there: they were all completely blackened – clothes, faces, everything. I made sure that they were all dead.

There had been numerous replies to the *Athenia*'s SOS, and while Chief Officer Copeland was occupied with the boats, Captain Cook was in the wireless room and in touch with no fewer than six ships. A truly international rescue effort was already under way, with the British destroyers *Electra*, *Escort* and *Fame*, the Norwegian motor vessel *Knute Nelson*, the Swedish motor yacht *Southern Cross* and the American cargo ship *City of Flint* all racing in to help. The nearest, the *Knute Nelson*, was only 40 miles away when, at 11 o'clock that night, the *Athenia* was finally abandoned to her fate, and Captain Cook, the radio officers and all those involved with launching the lifeboats left the ship.

The 5,749-ton *Knute Nelson*, commanded by Captain Carl Anderssen, reached the *Athenia* at about 0200 on the morning of the 4th and immediately began to take on board survivors from the lifeboats. The other ships arrived soon afterwards, and with HMS *Fame* screening for U-boats, the rescue operation continued throughout the night and into the next morning. It was fortunate that the weather held fair, although the swell was heavy, but despite this and the darkness, 1,103 passengers and 315 crew were saved. In all, 93 passengers and 19 crew were lost from the *Athenia,* most of them in three unfortunate accidents that happened during the night. The *Knute Nelson* had taken on board 449 and was manoeuvring to pick up others when, unseen by Captain Anderssen in the darkness, one of the crowded lifeboats got under his stern and was cut to pieces by the Norwegian ship's propeller. Fifty-three passengers, all women, and three seamen died. Later, just as dawn was breaking, a similar accident happened as the *Southern Cross* was taking a lifeboat alongside. The boat capsized after being trapped under the yacht's stern, and another ten people died. Three other passengers also lost their lives when transferring from the lifeboats to the destroyers. One woman who would also have died was saved by the prompt action of Chief Officer Barney Copeland. He explains:

On arrival aboard HMS *Electra* and on going through the list of survivors in my boat, I discovered that one woman was missing. Earlier in the day, she had fallen down a ladder and was suffering from concussion, and I personally had taken her to the Sick Bay unconscious. Whilst we were clearing the boats away, the Nurse had come to me and said she was unable to get this woman out by herself, so I had sent two men to help her – which they apparently failed to do so. I immediately went to the Captain of the destroyer and informed him that there was a woman on board in the *Athenia*'s Sick Bay and asked to be put aboard at once. I was given a boat and we put off to the *Athenia* and went on board with the Bo'sun and one AB. The time was now about 10.30. The Bo'sun and the AB immediately went to the Sick Bay. The door was burst open and the woman was found inside still unconscious. I think the doctor had given her morphia, as her lip had been rather badly damaged and had had to be stitched up. Whilst on board, I looked down No. 5 hatch and noticed the bulk-heads were in a dangerous condition and would not hold out much longer, so we immediately got back into the boat and returned to HMS *Electra* with the woman.

As soon as I got back on board, the *Athenia* sank. The time was now about 11 a.m. Ship's Time.

By the time the last survivor had been taken on board the destroy-ers, U-30 had escaped to the west, well out of range of reprisal. By all accounts, Fritz-Julius Lemp should have then set the air waves on fire with jubilant reports of his conquest; he had, after all, sunk a large British ship, possibly, it could be claimed, an armed mer-chant cruiser. But he now knew that with his first torpedo he had sunk an unarmed passenger liner, almost certainly with heavy loss of life. On the first day of the war he had contravened the Prize Rules. Aware that there were bound to be repercussions in Berlin and around the world, Lemp decided to keep radio silence.

A week later, still having had no communication with Wilhelmshaven, U-30 was 200 miles west of Ireland when she came across the 4,425-ton Glasgow-registered steamer *Blairlogie* blithely making her way unescorted from Portland, Maine to the UK with a cargo of scrap iron and steel. The unarmed British ship was stopped with a fusillade of 88mm shells, three of which scored direct hits on board. Then, in compliance with the Prize Rules, Lemp allowed the *Blairlogie*'s crew to take to the boats, before sink-ing her with a torpedo. When they were clear, he went alongside the boats, handed over a bottle of gin and some cigarettes and wished the survivors *bon voyage* to the nearest shore. To idealists, this was how war should be fought.

Lemp's next encounter came three days later, when the 5,200-ton Belfast steamer *Fanad Head*, on her way from Montreal to Belfast with a cargo of grain, came over the horizon. Again, Lemp adhered strictly to the book, first stopping her with a shot across the bows, then standing back while her crew abandoned ship. He then put a scuttling party of three men aboard the *Fanad Head* and towed her lifeboats clear. However, in his efforts to comply with the rules, the young Oberleutnant lost sight of the fact that his victim had sent out a distress message before she was aban-doned. This had been received by the aircraft carrier HMS *Ark*

Royal which, accompanied by several destroyers, was on anti-submarine patrol 200 miles to the north-east. The carrier immediately launched three Blackburn Skua fighter/bombers, which swooped on U-30 while she was lying stopped on the surface near the *Fanad Head*. Luckily for the U-boat, the Skuas were so close to the water when they dropped their bombs that two of them were hit and brought down by their own shrapnel. Lemp dived in a hurry, leaving his three-man prize crew still aboard the *Fanad Head*, along with another man who had been stranded on the submarine's casings when she dived.

When the only remaining Skua had gone, Lemp re-surfaced and went alongside the *Fanad Head* to pick up his prize crew and the other man, who had swum to the ship. He then backed away, and from a distance of about 500yds sank the abandoned ship with a single torpedo. While he was thus engaged, six Swordfish torpedo bombers from the *Ark Royal* arrived overhead. Lemp crash-dived, but not soon enough to escape the blast of depth bombs dropped by the Swordfish. Two British destroyers then arrived on the scene, and for the next three hours U-30 was subjected to a severe depth charging. She finally limped away with serious damage to her hull and set course for Wilhelmshaven. U-30's first war patrol would warrant no military band playing on the quay when she returned, and no medals would be handed out.

Lemp continued to maintain radio silence on the return passage, and the first Berlin heard about the sinking of the *Athenia* was from BBC news broadcasts. When it became known that twenty-eight US citizens had been lost on the liner, the German High Command feared that the *Athenia* would become the *Lusitania* of the Second World War, with all the adverse publicity that involved. Anxious to avoid repercussions in America, Berlin denied all knowledge of the sinking, declaring that no German submarine had been within 75 miles of the position given. The German Minister of Propaganda, Joseph Goebbels, even claimed that the British had sunk the liner themselves in order to bring America into the war. This was, of course, pure fantasy, but there were those, especially in the United States, who listened to Goebbels and wondered.

When U-30 reached Wilhelmshaven on 27 September she was met by Admiral Dönitz, to whom Lemp admitted he had sunk the *Athenia*. He was sworn to silence, and U-30's log was doctored to expunge all reference to the incident. It was not until the War

Crimes Trials held in Nuremberg in 1946 that the truth came out. By then, Fritz-Julius Lemp was beyond all retribution.

On 9 May 1941, Lemp, then commanding U-110, was involved in an attack on the westbound convoy OB 318. Operating on the surface, he had sunk two British merchantmen and had his sights on a third, when the corvette HMS *Aubretia* came racing in, intent on ramming. Lemp crash-dived, but *Aubretia*'s depth charges so damaged U-110 that she was unable to escape. Caught in the Asdic beams of the destroyers *Broadway* and *Bulldog*, the U-boat was summarily blown to the surface, and her crew set scuttling charges and abandoned her. They were in the water awaiting rescue, when Lemp realized that the charges had not gone off and U-110 was still afloat and in danger of being captured. He was last seen swimming back towards the U-boat, but was not seen again; it is believed he must have drowned.

With U-110 abandoned but still very much afloat, Commander Joe Baker-Cresswell in HMS *Bulldog* put a prize crew on board. The submarine was taken in tow, and her Enigma machine and code books, which were found to be intact, were removed. U-110 sank before reaching port, but her capture was kept a close secret for more than twenty years after the war ended. As far as the Germans were concerned, U-110 had been sunk in battle and her coding equipment had gone down with her. In fact, the Enigma machine and code books had been sent to Bletchley Park and were largely responsible for the cracking of the German U-boat code, with the resultant saving of many ships and lives.

It could be said that in abandoning U-110 Fritz-Julius Lemp had paid in full the debt he incurred by sinking the *Athenia*.

CHAPTER TWO

The Gentleman Pirate –
Royal Sceptre 05.09.39

When Fritz-Julius Lemp sank the *Athenia* without warning, intentionally or not, he was setting the pattern for future German submarine warfare against Britain and her allies. However, at the same time, there were others of his breed out there in the North Atlantic who still believed that the war at sea should be conducted in accordance with the Prize Rules of 1936. These rules emphatically required that the safety of passengers and crew be ensured before a merchant ship was sunk, however impractical that might be in reality. One such believer was 30-year-old Kapitänleutnant Herbert Schultze, who commanded U-48.

U-48, a Type VIIB boat commissioned by Schultze in his hometown of Kiel in the previous April, had sailed from that port on 19 August l939, fifteen days before war was declared. Rounding the north of Scotland undetected by British guardships, she had initially patrolled off the Bay of Biscay, moving north to take up station off the Western Approaches on the outbreak of hostilities.

After forty-eight hours diligently sweeping back and forth across what should have been the throbbing artery of Britain's maritime trade without sighting a single ship, Schultze was beginning to conclude that he was on a fool's errand. Then, at long last, at about 9 o'clock on the morning of 5 September, the masts and funnel of an inbound ship came over the horizon. The boredom of the past few days forgotten, Schultze submerged to periscope depth and waited for the unsuspecting ship to come into his sights.

The Newcastle tramp *Royal Sceptre* was nearing the end of a long and arduous voyage, which had begun in Cardiff three months earlier, when she sailed with a full cargo of coal for Buenos Aires. Owned by Hall Brothers of Newcastle-upon-Tyne, one of the numerous small shipping companies based on Britain's northeast coast, and commanded by 41-year-old Captain James Gair, she was a 4,853-ton steamer built on the River Tyne in 1937. Basic in every respect, she was a typical 'go anywhere, carry anything' ship of her day, having five cavernous cargo holds, on which sat two blocks of accommodation, two masts and a tall funnel.

When U-48 sighted the *Royal Sceptre*, she was homeward bound from the River Plate with a bulk cargo of grain and maize for Belfast. Having left the UK some three months before the declaration of war, she was unarmed and still in her company colours: grey hull, white upperworks and black funnel with the Hall Brothers' insignia. On that clear morning in September 1939 the *Royal Sceptre* presented a very conspicuous target.

Captain Gair and his 32-man crew were all aware that Britain was at war with Germany and conscious that every hour brought them closer to danger, but so far they had not been affected in any way. Normality reigned, with the *Royal Sceptre* being spruced up in preparation for arrival, 'going ashore clothes' being brought out to air and thoughts very much of home. Old habits died hard, but relaxed though the atmosphere might have been, the threat of war was not being entirely ignored. Both lifeboats were swung out ready for lowering should the need arise, extra lookouts had been posted and watches had been doubled on the bridge.

Shortly before noon, the *Royal Sceptre* was 450 miles southwest of Land's End and within three days steaming of Belfast. She was running before a strong southerly wind, with a heavy sea and swell on her port quarter. While this called for extra effort on the part of the helmsman to hold her on course, wind and sea were also giving her a helping hand on this last leg of the voyage.

Chief Officer Norman Hartley had the watch on the bridge with the Third Officer. Both men, having also kept the 12–4 watch during the night, were feeling the effects of lack of sleep. Hartley, sipping his fourth or fifth mug of strong coffee – he had lost count of how many – was reflecting on the morning which, like every other morning since leaving the River Plate, appeared to be passing without incident. The usual string of messages had been coming through on the radio from the Admiralty, but nothing had been said about the sinking of the *Athenia*. All seemed well with the world.

Hartley, contemplating a quick lunch followed by a few hours of blessed sleep, stifled a yawn. His eyelids drooped. Then, suddenly, a commotion 500yds out on the port beam became more than just another breaking wave. As Hartley reached for his binoculars, the conning tower of a submarine broke the surface.

Captain Gair, called from his cabin by the Third Officer, reached the bridge in seconds. He quickly grasped the situation and ordered the helm hard to starboard, at the same time instructing Hartley to pass the word to the engine room for maximum revolutions. The *Royal Sceptre* heeled as she came round under full helm to present her stern to the emerging submarine. Gair, who had been through all this in the Great War of 1914–18, recognized his old enemy, but having no means of fighting back, was going to make a run for it.

The Captain's assessment of the situation was correct. Chief Officer Hartley later gave a very detailed description of the U-boat:

> The colour of the submarine was greenish-grey uniform, and I distinctly noticed below the water line as she sat in the water with her whaleback some 4 feet above the water line, grass at least ½ inch in length, regular along the hull, almost like a streak of paint which was some 2 feet above the water line. The paint was distinctly old, I should say 6 months, but there were patches of newer paint of the same tint which seemed to me to be perhaps put over the old paint perhaps about a month before.
>
> I saw on the conning tower of the submarine, on the side, the figures 48 showing through the paint. It seemed to me that these figures had originally been painted on with a white lead paint which had then been painted over with the greenish grey paint, but had worked through the paint, and these figures were quite plainly read by me . . . In addition to these figures I noticed on the port side of the conning tower, low down and forward, two small plaques or designs; one, the forward of the two, was circular and with a red rim and inside it had a red St George's Cross. The other side was square and red, marked with a red St George's Cross also.

The U-boat had by now manned her deck gun, with obvious intent. And while this was happening, the *Royal Sceptre*, barely two years old and with a relatively clean bottom, was surging ahead as her engineers fed more steam to her powerful 1,450 h.p. engine. In the Dante's Inferno that was her stokehold, firemen, stripped to the waist, hurled coal into the roaring boiler furnaces, and black smoke rolled back from her tall funnel. Unaccustomed to such urgency, the Newcastle tramp, which had the lines of a Thames barge, began to rattle and shake in an alarming way as she worked up to a speed she had never before reached, even on her sea trials.

U-48's first two shells were ranging shots, falling well ahead of the fleeing ship. The German gunners were well trained in their art, however, and even though the U-boat, rolling and pitching in the swell, made a poor gun platform, their 88mm, firing at the rate of a shell every 20 seconds, soon found the range. The defenceless *Royal Sceptre* was quickly bracketed, shells landing in the water all around her as Gair, facing aft and trying to judge the fall of the shot, threw her from side to side under full helm. For those on the bridge of the British ship, so inured to the halcyon days of peace, time stood still as they faced the terrible reality of war.

In his 'shack' below the bridge the *Royal Sceptre*'s radio officer was crouched over his keys tapping out the three-letter emergency signal SSS, code for 'I am being attacked by an enemy submarine'. His frantic calls for help were intercepted by U-48's wireless oper-ator, and Schultze ordered his gunners to concentrate their fire on the fleeing ship's wireless aerials, which were slung between her two masts. The main aerial was quickly shot away, but 'Sparks' immediately switched over to his emergency aerial and doggedly continued to send out his cry for help.

Inevitably, U-48's shells began find their target. The *Royal Sceptre* was soon holed on the waterline, her accommodation was on fire and her decks were littered with wounded men. Although the British ship was doing her utmost to escape, her attacker, with a top speed of 18 knots on the surface, was rapidly overtaking her, shortening the range minute by minute. Captain Gair could no longer ignore the hopelessness of the situation, and as the punish-ment inflicted on his ship continued unabated and the acrid stench of cordite filled the air, he decided the time had come to save the lives of his crew. As yet another shell slammed into the accommo-dation below the bridge, Gair rang the engine room telegraph to 'Stop' and ordered Chief Officer Hartley to sound the 'Abandon Ship' signal. The beat of the *Royal Sceptre*'s engine slowed as her throaty steam whistle signalled her surrender.

On his way aft to the boat deck, Hartley made a brief stop at his cabin to pick up his life jacket and a heavy coat. Then, as he neared the boats, there was an explosion close behind him and shards of red hot shrapnel ricocheted all around him. The navigation bridge had been hit by a shell. Hartley was not then aware of it, but the shell, apart from demolishing the wheelhouse, had killed Captain James Gair as he stood alone on the bridge. From that moment, Norman Hartley was in command of the *Royal Sceptre*.

When Hartley reached the boat deck, he found that both the ship's lifeboats had been lowered to the water and were ready to cast off. The U-boat's gunners were now systematically demolishing the ship, every shell they fired landing with devastating effect. It was time to go.

By now, the starboard lifeboat had left the ship's side, but the port boat was still alongside. Taking one last look around at the doomed, and now deserted, ship, Hartley jumped for the boat's falls and slid down them to join the others in the boat. As soon as he was aboard, the painter was cast off and, as the *Royal Sceptre* still carried some way on her, the boat drifted astern.

It was only when the lifeboat was well clear of the ship that Hartley became aware that he had not been, after all, the last man to leave. A lone figure had appeared on the *Royal Sceptre*'s boat deck waving frantically. It was the ship's radio officer who, true to tradition, had remained at his post until the last minute sending out a distress call. Unfortunately for him, he had stayed too long.

The Chief Officer's boat had no engine, and being the usual heavy wooden ship's boat, was almost impossible to handle under oars, except in a flat calm. Hartley made an attempt to take the boat back alongside, but the rough sea and heavy swell running were too much. Furthermore, the *Royal Sceptre* was still under fire, with shells falling all around her. It had become far too dangerous to approach her. Reluctantly, Hartley allowed the boat to drop astern. He wrote in his report:

> I remained close to the ship, because I thought that the operator would have had the sense to put a ladder over the side and jump into the water, so that we could pick him up. The Wireless Operator, however, waved to the submarine to cease fire, which it did. The submarine then came close to me and told me to go back to the ship and pick up the two men who were still on board. This I did immediately. I rescued the W/T operator, and I asked him

if there was anybody else on board. He said, 'No, only me'. I would have liked to have boarded the ship, the crew, however, were naturally scared of getting the boat smashed up against the ship's side. I did not know that the Captain was missing.

Having rescued the Radio Officer at considerable risk to his boat and its crew, Chief Officer Hartley pulled clear of the ship again. When questioned, the R/O assured him that the SSS signal, along with the ship's position, had gone out, although as he had been using the emergency aerial he had some doubts as to whether the signal had been received. Assuming that this was the case, Hartley decided the best course of action was to remain near the ship and wait for help to come. The *Royal Sceptre* was still afloat, although by now she was little more than a burning hulk.

As his crew lay back on their oars, Hartley saw the enemy submarine approaching his lifeboat again. His report reads:

> The submarine then approached my boat and asked me if I was the Captain. I said, 'No, the Captain is in the other boat', thinking of course that he was. After looking at us for quite a while, he asked me if I had any food. I said, 'Yes, plenty, thank you'. Then he said, 'Have you any water?' I again replied, 'Yes, thank you'. Then he went away from us again. He was away some time, then returned again and said, 'Have you any wounded?' I said, 'We are all quite well here, thank you', and then again he asked if I had any cigarettes, and on my replying, 'No', he said that I could go back to the ship to get some. I said, 'No, thank you. I am safer where I am.'

Having done all he could for those in the lifeboats, Schultze turned his attention to their ship. The *Royal Sceptre*, although on fire and noticeably lower in the water, was showing no immediate signs of sinking, and as there was a strong possibility that British warships were on their way in answer to her distress calls, Schultze was anxious to quit the scene as soon as possible. He had already used up more than half his stock of shells for the 88mm, and he decided he must now sacrifice one of his precious torpedoes to deliver a quick *coup de grâce*. Closing to within 500yds of the *Royal Sceptre*, he fired a single torpedo from his bow tubes. This went home in the crippled ship's engine room, and three and a half minutes later she disappeared beneath the waves, taking the body of Captain James Gair with her. Schultze returned to the waiting lifeboats and assured the survivors that he would send help. U-48 then motored away to continue her patrol.

Riding to sea anchors, the *Royal Sceptre*'s lifeboats remained in position for the next five hours; then, with darkness approaching and Chief Officer Hartley debating whether or not the time had come to set sail for the land, smoke was seen on the horizon to the north-east. An hour later, the British ship *Browning* found them and took them aboard.

The 5,332-ton Lampert & Holt steamer *Browning*, commanded by Captain Thomas Sweeny, bound for South America, had been surprised by U-48 a few hours earlier and stopped with a shot across her bows. Being, like the *Royal Sceptre*, completely unarmed, Sweeny at first considered running away, but knowing all too well that his 20-year-old ship would be hard pressed to make more than 9½ knots, even with her boiler safety valves screwed down, he thought better of it. Lowering his ensign in surrender, he ordered his crew to abandon ship.

Schultze, however, had other plans for the *Browning*. Ordering his gunners to hold their fire, he approached her lifeboats and instructed Captain Sweeny to re-board his ship and go to the rescue of the *Royal Sceptre*'s boats. Sweeny and his crew were immediately suspicious of the German's motives and were reluctant to comply, but when Schultze threatened to blow the as yet undamaged *Browning* out of the water, they agreed to go back. Before they left, Schultze insisted that, after picking up the *Royal Sceptre*'s survivors, Sweeny maintain complete radio silence on his voyage to South America, thereby allowing U-48 to continue her patrol undisturbed. Reluctantly, Sweeny gave his word to keep quiet. It was as though the two captains, Schultze and Sweeny, were engaged in a gentlemanly game of cricket; viewed in the light of the later conduct of the war at sea, this was a bizarre exchange.

Early next morning, Royal Navy destroyers came searching for the *Royal Sceptre* but could find no trace of her or her crew. It was assumed, not without good cause, that she had gone down with all hands, and the Admiralty was informed. This news, following close on the heels of the apparently heartless sinking of the *Athenia*, caused uproar in Britain. Three weeks later, when there was still no news of the fate of the *Royal Sceptre*, the Ministry of Information issued the following statement to the press:

> It is feared that all hope has now to be given up for the officers and crew of the steamship *Royal Sceptre*, sunk by a U-boat on September 6 in a position about 300 miles to the west of Ushant. The crew of the ship were cast adrift in their boats without possible hope of reaching land, a foul act of piracy on the high seas on the part of the German Navy.

On the same day that the press announcement appeared, Winston Churchill, then First Lord of the Admiralty, addressed the House of Commons, saying, 'Many cruel and ruthless acts have been done. There was the *Athenia*, then later the *Royal Sceptre*, whose crew of 32 were left in open boats hundreds of miles from land and are assumed to have perished.'

Coincidentally, even as Churchill was speaking to Parliament, Chief Officer Norman Hartley and the crew of the *Royal Sceptre*, all thirty-two of them, were being landed from the *Browning* in Bahia Blanca, Brazil, after a voyage in which Captain Sweeny, true to his promise to Herbert Schultze, had kept strict radio silence. Hartley later stated:

> During our voyage back to Bahia, I myself listened in to the broadcast from Germany which purported to be a broadcast interview by Capitaine Schultze, commander of a U-boat, and he stated that he had sunk the s/s *Royal Sceptre* having been compelled to do so because she disobeyed his order to stop, and that he regretted the fact that some men were wounded. I say with regard to this, that we received no order to stop other than the two shells fired ahead of the ship, and I further say that the voice which spoke in the broadcast was not the voice of the Commander of the U-boat which sunk us, for he spoke to me in broken English, in a clear tone, but using only phrases which I describe as 'Tourist Guide Book', and his F's were sounded like V's, e.g. He said, 'Have you vood?', and also said, 'Have you vater?', and also he asked 'Have you cigarettes?' In the broadcast it was also stated that the

U-boat had provided assistance for the survivors of the s/s *Royal Sceptre* by intercepting the s/s *Browning* and directing her to our position, and the broadcaster stated that when he arrived the crew of the *Browning* were in their boats and that he said to them, 'Why behave like this. Do you think we are barbarians?' but I have been told by the Master of the s/s *Browning* that no such remark was in fact made to his crew.

After leaving the *Browning*, Schultze continued to cruise in the area, and early on the morning of 8 September met with the British steamer *Winkleigh*. The *Winkleigh*, a 5,055-ton Cardiff tramp owned by W. J. Tatem and commanded by Captain Thomas Georgeson, was inbound from Vancouver with a cargo of grain and lumber. Unarmed, and still in her peacetime colours, she was only 450 miles from Land's End when Schultze brought her up with a shot across her bows. Under the threat of U-48's guns, Captain Georgeson and his crew were ordered to abandon their ship. This they did, but not before an SSS signal had been transmitted.

Once the boats were clear of the ship, Georgeson was ordered to come alongside U-48 and was taken on board for questioning. He later reported that Schultze had greeted him 'very cordially and said he was sorry he would have to sink my ship. He gave me four loaves of bread; then he brought a bottle of schnapps up, taking out a packet of cigarettes, offered me one and put the remainder in my hand.' An astonished Georgeson, who at the very least had expected to end up in a German prisoner of war camp, was then allowed to return to his boat.

Schultze had good reasons for terminating the interrogation of the British captain. Georgeson had revealed nothing of any import, and furthermore Schultze was anxious to be clear of the scene of his conquests before the Royal Navy came hunting for him. In any case, U-48 having been stored for a maximum voyage of thirty days, was now running low on fuel and torpedoes. It was time to go home.

Before leaving, Schultze approached to within 500yds of the abandoned *Winkleigh* and put one of his remaining torpedoes into her engine room. It was a sad sight for those in the lifeboats to see their ship and the cargo they had carried for more than

8,000 miles disappear below the waves. When she had gone, and U-48 had motored away, they were left to contemplate their fate. Fortunately, before nightfall they were found and rescued by the Holland-America liner *Statendam*, and landed in New York a few days later. Meanwhile, Herbert Schultze, well satisfied with his early contribution to Germany's war effort, had set course to the north-east to retrace his steps around the north of Scotland and into the North Sea.

Shortly before noon on the 11th, U-48 had reached a position 150 miles north of Rockall, and was about to come round on an easterly course, when a tall column of smoke was seen on the horizon. This materialized into the 4,869-ton steamer *Firby*, owned by Sir Robert Ropner of West Hartlepool. Commanded by Captain Thomas Prince, the *Firby* was twenty-four hours out of Newcastle, bound for Port Churchill, Hudson Bay in ballast. Anxious to reach the Hudson Strait before the winter ice set in, Prince was taking the Great Circle route and making all possible speed.

Schultze was also intent on reaching his destination without delay, but the meeting with an unarmed and unescorted British tramp was an opportunity not to be missed. When U-48 was within range, he put a warning shot across her bows. Captain Prince's reaction to the threat was instinctive and predictable. Showing his stern to the submarine, he zigzagged away at full speed.

The *Firby*, being in ballast, was high out of the water, and she presented an unmissable target to U-48's gunners. Almost at once their shells began to land, creating havoc on the *Firby*'s decks. She was soon on fire, and with four of his crew already wounded, Prince realized he had no hope of evading his attacker. With a heavy heart, he stopped his ship, lowered his lifeboats and abandoned her.

Approaching the *Firby*'s lifeboats, Schultze called for the ship's captain to identify himself. Prince was still wearing his uniform with four gold bands, so he was unable to hide. He was ordered aboard the submarine, where he was taken below, given a drink, and questioned by Schultze. Like Captain Georgeson before him, Prince had little to reveal. When the U-boat had been first sighted, he had dumped his code books overboard, and other than giving his ship's name and destination, he gave nothing away. Schultze did not press the matter, then gave Prince some bandages and six loaves of bread, before returning him to his lifeboat. In his absence, Prince found that some of the U-boat's crew had dressed the wounds of his injured men, a gesture of compassion he had not expected to see.

Schultze now sank the *Firby* by torpedo, leaving Captain Prince and his men to spend a cold and uncomfortable night in their boats. They were picked up in the early hours of the 12th by the destroyer HMS *Fearless* and landed at Scapa Flow later that day.

There was an interesting sequel to the sinking of the *Firby*. After the war, Captain Thomas Georgeson, late of the *Winkleigh*, was in correspondence with Herbert Schultze, who had sent him some documents he had taken from Captain Prince of the *Firby*. In May 1947 Georgeson received the following letter from the ex-U-boat commander:

Very esteemed Mr Georgeson,

I was very sincerely pleased to have your letter of 8th May, for I learned from it that you and your boy have indeed come safely through this very wicked war. The papers which I send back to you herewith are the only spoil and souvenirs of my U-boat voyages. I send to you willingly for when you stood defenceless on the tower of my boat and had to suffer the cruellest blow that fate can deal to a sailor, it pained me inwardly to act so. Your pain at the war between our two peoples was at that hour also my pain. The torpedo which I shot at the *Winkleigh* was fired with a sad heart. Perhaps you felt then that as men, we were not against each other. Afterwards I sank many more fine ships, but have never been happy about this. No sailor can be glad about sinking a ship.

The German people are now in a state of fearful necessity which seems to us almost hopeless, unless the differences between East and West can be bridged over in a reasonable and peaceful manner.

The hopes of many Germans in this respect are directed to the far seeing political ability of the English Government administration which has stood the test of centuries, and they hope your Government will succeed in giving Europe a reasonable and humane peace.

I close this letter with best wishes for your own well being and for the well being of your family.

I should be glad if you remember our meeting at that time in the Atlantic in its human aspect, and I remain with a handshake,

Yours respectfully,

Herbert Schultze, who was known in the U-boats as 'Vati' (Daddy) Schultze because he took very good care of his crew, was indeed a 'gentleman pirate'. Others who came after him were not cast in the same mould.

CHAPTER THREE

The Honeymoon Continues –
Cheyenne 15.09.39

On 3 September 1939, when Britain declared war on Germany, her vital sea lanes were already compromised. Two weeks earlier, eighteen of Admiral Dönitz's U-boats, the paint barely dry on their hulls, had slipped out of Wilhelmshaven under the cover of darkness to take up strategic positions in British waters. The English Channel being heavily patrolled by ships of the Royal Navy, they had been forced to take the longer route to the Atlantic, via the north of Scotland, running submerged during the day and on the surface at night. Maintaining strict radio silence at all times, they had avoided detection. Detailed off to guard the South-Western Approaches to the Channel were two Type VII boats, U-29 and U-53, commanded respectively by Otto Schuhart and Ernst-Günter Heinicke, both experienced *Kriegsmarine* officers.

Schuhart and Heinicke reached their designated patrol area some 350 miles to the west of Land's End on 28 August, and from then on had been keeping a discreet watch on passing shipping. Patrolling at periscope depth by day and submerged at night, it was frustrating work for the young men who manned these boats. They had come with their blood up, prepared for war, yet they were forbidden to do more than enter details in the log of each ship seen, of which there was a steady stream, inward and outward. This unnatural situation prevailed until midday Berlin time on Sunday, 3 September, when the dogs of war were unleashed. Then, suddenly, there was nothing. The horizon was empty, except for the occasional British destroyer trailing her smoke across the as yet untroubled waters. Frustration turned to dismay.

For the next five days the two U-boats each played their own separate game of hide-and-seek with the Royal Navy. Then the disappointments of the past weeks were swept away by a surge of adrenaline, and for U-29 at least, the war finally opened. On the afternoon of 8 September she sighted the British motor tanker

Regent Tiger, inbound with 10,600 tons of petroleum and 3,400 tons of diesel oil. Unarmed and unescorted, the tanker was easy meat, being stopped with a warning shot across her bows, after which ship and cargo were sent to the bottom by a single torpedo.

It was all so easily done, and for Otto Schuhart and his men the long wait must have seemed worthwhile. However, the *Regent Tiger* proved to be a false dawn, and another five days passed before the next opportunity presented itself. This turned out to be the British ocean-going salvage tug *Neptunia* of just 789 tons gross. She was on her way out from Falmouth to assist a British destroyer damaged in a collision off the south coast of Ireland while escorting the small westbound convoy OB 3. The destroyers HMS *Vansittart* and HMS *Walker* had collided, *Walker* being seriously damaged and unable to proceed under her own steam.

Contrary to Schuhart's expectations, the tug was to prove no docile conquest. When he put a warning shot across her bows, instead of heaving to as expected, *Neptunia* presented her stern to the U-boat and steamed away at full speed, her radio setting the ether alight with frantic distress calls. Schuhart gave chase, but it was not until the tug was hit by several shells that she was stopped and abandoned by her crew.

Fearful that the *Neptunia*'s calls for help might bring down the wrath of the Royal Navy on U-29, Schuhart tried to finish off the tug quickly with a torpedo, but this exploded prematurely, as did a second. What should have been a relatively swift and easy operation was now turning into a time-consuming and expensive farce.

Schuhart resorted to his deck gun again, but the stubborn little ship was still reluctant to go down. After the expenditure of several more shells, the *Neptunia* at last gave up the ghost, catching fire and sinking. U-29 then made off before retribution appeared on the scene.

Next day, U-29 was idling on the surface 180 miles south-west of the Fastnet Rock, when her luck at last took a turn for the better. Over the horizon came the 3,481-ton tanker *British Influence*, nearing the end of a 6,500-mile passage from the Persian Gulf with 12,000 tons of diesel and fuel oil. Having been almost a month at sea, with very little contact with the outside world, the crew of the *British Influence* were totally unprepared for the reality of war when U-29's shells began to fall around them. Ordered by

Schuhart to take to the boats, they complied, then watched bewildered as their ship was finished off with a torpedo.

It may have been the sight of the British seamen huddled in their lifeboats that reminded Otto Schuhart of his duty under the Treaty of London, which was to deliver the crew of his victim to a place of safety, and he now went to ridiculous lengths to comply. First firing distress rockets, he then stood by the tanker's lifeboats for the next five hours waiting for a suitable rescue ship to come, even though he was aware that the *British Influence* had broadcast an SOS and that the rescue ship might well be a British destroyer.

Fortunately for U-29, the Royal Navy must have been busy elsewhere, and the only ship that came to investigate the British tanker's predicament was the 5,444-ton Norwegian motor vessel *Ida Bakke*. The neutral-flag cargo ship, commanded by Captain Anton Zakariassen, had been passing on her way to the US via Panama when she saw U-29's rockets go soaring into the sky. However, as soon as he became aware of the U-boat on the surface near the lifeboats, Zakariassen turned tail and ran. Schuhart gave chase, not to sink the Norwegian but to bring her back to take on board the survivors. Captain Zakariassen was of course not aware of Schuhart's intentions, and as the *Ida Bakke* was a 16-knot ship, the chase was prolonged.

When the *Ida Bakke* was finally caught and stopped, Schuhart managed to persuade Zakariassen that it was his duty to take the *British Influence*'s survivors to a place of safety, and this the Norwegian did, landing them at Baltimore on the south coast of Ireland on the 15th. The *Ida Bakke* then continued her voyage to Panama, but a few hours after leaving Baltimore, her wireless operator picked up a distress message from the British tanker *Cheyenne*, then sinking 150 miles west-south-west of the Fastnet. Her untimely demise was U-53's opening contribution to Germany's war on British shipping.

The Anglo-American Oil Company's 8,825-ton motor tanker *Cheyenne*, British flagged, British manned and commanded by Captain Hugh Kerr, was bound from Aruba to Swansea with 12,600 tons of benzine. She was only thirty-six hours from the Bristol Channel when U-53 surfaced and challenged her. Instinctively, Captain Kerr called for maximum revolutions and turned stern-on to the U-boat. Although at best the *Cheyenne* could only manage 12 knots, nearly an hour went by before U-53 caught up with her. Captain Kerr described the chase:

When the submarine realized what we were doing he fired one shot, which fell short. We ordered all men under cover and still carried on, keeping him astern, and he immediately opened fire, keeping up repeated fire straddling the ship. This went on for fifty minutes. They fired in all about 20–25 rounds. I carefully watched the speed of the submarine, hoping that we might outdistance her, as by this time we were doing 12 knots, but in the course of half an hour I realized that the submarine was gaining at the rate of about 4 miles an hour, estimating his speed at anything between 15 and 17 knots. He ceased firing for about ten minutes and then fired a volley of about five rounds, one at each beam and the last three dropping about 100 yards ahead. We realized then he had our length and as we were loaded with benzine, and not wishing to sacrifice life, and as nothing was appearing in sight which would account for assistance, we stopped the engines. This was about an hour after the submarine fired the first shot. The first shot was intentionally wide.

What followed should have been an example of how, in an ideal world, the war at sea would be fought. Having taken the way off his ship, Captain Kerr sent his men to their boat stations, and when they were assembled, wearing life jackets as in any routine boat drill, the *Cheyenne's* lifeboats were swung out ready for lowering.

Meanwhile, U-53 had closed to within a mile of the tanker and was also hove to. She then waited patiently while the *Cheyenne's* crew lowered their boats to the water and abandoned ship in good order. Unfortunately, although the weather was fair at the time, during the operation one of the lifeboats capsized and six men were drowned.

When the remaining boats had rowed clear, Heinicke moved in closer and taking careful aim, put a torpedo into the *Cheyenne's* No. 4 cargo tank, just forward of the bridge. Captain Kerr, observing the destruction of his command from the stern of his lifeboat, later wrote:

There was very little explosion, though a large column of water and benzine went up and when this subsided we could see the port side of the vessel blown right out with ragged plates. He waited about ten minutes, and as the ship didn't show any signs of sinking, he fired a second torpedo which struck more or less in the same position. There was a small explosion and a column of water and the ship appeared to have broken her back. The bow and stern both came out of the water, the bow appearing to fall over towards the stern, and the bow finally broke away and both parts continued to float. The submarine watched developments for about 15 minutes or so, and then came over to the boats, and enquired if everyone was all right or anyone hurt, or if anyone required anything, and having assured him that everything was all right, he asked for the Master and for my papers, but I assured him that I hadn't any. He asked me why. I said I had no time to get any papers; although I had them in my bag. And then he asked me, 'Why did you try to escape?' I said, 'Self-preservation', or something of that kind. He then said, 'You made me lose 25 rounds of ammunition.'

In a footnote to his report to the Admiralty, Captain Kerr stated that while he and his crew were abandoning ship under the guns of the enemy submarine they saw what appeared to be a British sloop or patrol boat approaching from the east. He described her as being 'painted grey with a very short and very thick funnel and a well sloped bow, stern well sloped away with cruiser stern. She had two short masts and, beam on, her bridge was higher than the funnel and appeared very narrow.'

As the unidentified vessel approached at speed, Kerr assumed that the Royal Navy was coming to his rescue, but then watched open-mouthed as she steamed past, completely ignoring their obvious plight. He then recollected that for three nights past his wireless operator had heard short plain language transmissions in Spanish on an unusual wavelength, and as Spain was neutral, he assumed the stranger must be a Spanish patrol boat.

It seems most likely that the ship seen by Kerr was either a Spanish Navy sloop – the description fits – or an Irish fishery protection vessel. Given that she had surprised a German U-boat in the act of sinking a British ship, it may well be that the neutral vessel did not want to get involved and had consequently made herself scarce.

The patrol boat was barely out of sight, when a would-be rescue ship arrived on the scene. She was the 7,016-ton Union Castle cargo liner *Rothesay Castle*, commanded by Captain Ernest Furlong and inbound to Glasgow from the USA. She had received the *Cheyenne*'s distress calls and was hurrying to help, but sighting the U-boat on the surface, Captain Furlong, having come this far without molestation, had second thoughts and steamed away at full speed. Heinicke, desperate to get the survivors off his hands, gave chase. The *Rothesay Castle*, however, had a service speed of 16 knots, and with a little encouragement from the bridge her engineers produced an extra knot. Realizing he had little hope of overhauling the British ship, Heinicke returned to the *Cheyenne*'s lifeboats. He informed Captain Kerr that he had been in contact with the eastbound German passenger liner *Köln* and that she would pick them up. He set course to the west and told the boats to follow him. With visions of a German prisoner of war camp looming, Kerr was reluctant to agree, but he had no other option.

Both lifeboats were under oars and sail, but the wind was fitful and light, and the U-boat was soon out of sight. Kerr followed in her wake for about four hours, at which point smoke on the horizon indicated that U-53 was returning. Heinicke informed Kerr that the *Köln* had refused to pick up survivors and was continuing on her voyage, but that he would tow the *Cheyenne*'s boats to within sight of the Irish coast to ensure their rescue. While the tow was being discussed, the Campbell-class destroyer HMS *Mackay* came over the horizon and opened fire on the stationary U-53 with her 4.7s.

HMS *Mackay* had been with the westbound convoy OB 3 when two other destroyers, *Vansittart* and *Walker*, were in collision. *Walker* was so badly damaged that she was unable to proceed under her own steam and had radioed for help. This was the call the salvage tug *Neptunia* had been answering when she met her end at the hands of Otto Schuhart's U-29.

U-53 was so engrossed in trying to sink the wreck of the *Cheyenne* that she failed to see the approach of HMS *Mackay*. She had only just succeeded in setting the forward section of the wreck on fire when she found herself on the receiving end of the destroyer's guns, whose first shells fell within 100yds of the submarine. More shells followed, and Heinicke was forced to crash-dive. *Mackay* followed up with a few depth charges, but U-53 escaped without damage.

Having landed the crew of the *British Influence* at Baltimore, Co. Cork, the Norwegian motor vessel *Ida Bakke* had resumed her passage to Panama, but she had been only a few hours at sea when she was once again called upon to play the Good Samaritan. On the afternoon of the 15th she picked up distress calls from the *Cheyenne*, then being fired on by U-53. Captain Zakariassen immediately increased speed and headed for the position given.

By this time, with HMS *Mackay* out of sight in pursuit of U-53 and with darkness closing in, Captain Kerr and his men faced the prospect of a long and uncomfortable night in their open boats. They were more than delighted when the *Ida Bakke* appeared. Twenty-four hours later, they too had been landed at Baltimore, where they joined the crew of the *British Influence* to await transport to the UK. In the meantime, HMS *Mackay* had completed what Ernst-Günter Heinicke had begun, using her guns to send to the two broken halves of the *Cheyenne* to the bottom, along with what remained of her cargo of benzine. In the opening days of the war, U-29 and U-53 had thus already denied their enemy 24,000 tons of precious fuel. The first round had gone to the U-boats.

During the night that followed, the two U-boats in question received orders to search for Convoy OB 3, whose escort force had been seriously depleted, firstly by the disabling of HMS *Walker* and then by the diversion of HMS *Mackay* to the aid of the *Cheyenne*. On the afternoon of the 17th, while carrying out a sweep for OB 3 some 350 miles west of Cape Clear, U-53 sighted an unescorted merchant ship on an easterly course. She was the 5,193-ton Newcastle-registered *Kafiristan*, homeward bound from Cuba with 8,870 tons of sugar. Heinicke stopped her and then sank her with a torpedo and gunfire. Six of the British ship's crew died in the attack.

It had been another easy victory for Ernst-Günter Heinicke, but he was still trying to fight the war by the book, and under the Prize Rules he was now responsible for the safety of twenty-nine survivors in two lifeboats. His dilemma was solved by the appearance of the US-flag *American Farmer*, which came in sight en route to New York with passengers and cargo. Heinicke stopped her and ordered her to take the *Kafiristan*'s survivors on board. Under the threat of U-53's guns, the neutral American complied. This humanitarian gesture almost cost Heinicke dear. While the survivors were boarding the *American Farmer*, a flight of three British

Fairey Swordfish torpedo bombers swooped out of the clouds and attacked the surfaced U-boat with bombs and machine-gun fire.

Fortunately for Heinicke, his lookouts were fully alert, and he was able to crash-dive before the attacking Swordfish did any real damage. However, in the rush to submerge, some of U-53's gunners were left on the casings and they drowned as the U-boat went down. The British planes were from the 25,000-ton aircraft carrier HMS *Courageous*, which was on anti-submarine patrol nearby, and they had been flown off in answer to the *Kafiristan*'s urgent radio calls for help. Due to his insistence on adhering to the Prize Rules, Heinicke had taken a risk too far, and U-53 was lucky to have survived the surprise attack.

Two of *Courageous'* four-destroyer screen had also been sent to the defence of the *Kafiristan*, leaving the carrier dangerously exposed, a situation of which Otto Schuhart in U29 was quick to take advantage, although the meeting of the two enemies was purely by chance. U-29, still casting around for Convoy OB 3, was running at periscope depth when an aircraft was sighted circling low down. The biplane was identified as a Fairey Swordfish, which had a short range; and as the nearest British airfield was over 500 miles away, Schuhart correctly assumed that a British aircraft carrier must be somewhere close by. Remaining at periscope depth, he continued searching, and at 1800 smoke was sighted on the horizon. Within the hour, Schuhart had *Courageous* in his sights.

It so happened that as U-29 approached within torpedo distance of the carrier she had turned into the wind to land the Swordfish returning from their mission to protect the *Kafiristan*. The huge 786ft-long carrier, standing high out of the water and virtually hove to, was a target not to be missed, and when Schuhart fired a spread of three torpedoes, two of them went home in her engine room. She capsized and sank in fifteen minutes, taking with her 518 of her crew of 1,520.

Ernst-Günter Heinicke commanded U-53 for only two patrols, in which he sank only two ships, the tanker *Cheyenne* and the *Kafiristan*. In each case he made every effort to abide by the Prize Rules, particularly in the treatment of survivors. For his diligence he was relieved of his command in December 1939 and sent to serve under Korvettenkapitän Helmuth von Ruckteschell in the commerce raider *Widder*. The move proved to be a culture shock for Heinicke, since Von Ruckteschell was notorious for not taking prisoners. U-53, then under the command of Korvettenkapitän Harald Grosse, was sunk off the Shetland Islands on 24 February 1940 by the destroyer HMS *Gurkha*. U-29 had a more successful career, sinking another nine Allied ships before being taken out of active service early in 1941. She spent the rest of the war in the Baltic as a training boat.

By the time the first month of the war came to an end, British shipping had received a severe mauling at the hands of Dönitz's U-boats. Thirty-three British merchantmen had fallen to their torpedoes, a total of 153,000 tons gross. And it would get worse, much worse.

CHAPTER FOUR

The Gloves Come Off –
Abukir 28.05.40

In the late spring of 1940, for the first time in her long existence, Great Britain came face to face with humiliating defeat. The British Expeditionary Force, which had crossed the Channel 300,000 strong, confident it would put a swift end to Hitler's dream of world domination, was in full retreat.

On 10 May 1940, after eight months of the 'Phoney War', during which both sides had bombarded each other with propaganda leaflets and verbal insults from the safety of their respective bunkers, Hitler had finally let loose his dogs of war. Eighty German divisions, eight of them armoured, supported by squadrons of fighters and dive-bombers, rolled across the frontiers of Holland and Belgium. Little Belgium fought gallantly but was quickly overwhelmed; Holland, bombed and shelled into submission, surrendered within five days.

British and French troops advanced into Belgium in an attempt to stem the German advance, but lacking modern armour and short on air cover, they were outclassed and outfought. By the 20th of the month, with the encircling pincers of the German armies closing on them, the Allies were in headlong flight to the coast. As May drew to a close, Winston Churchill, now Prime Minister, authorized a plan, codenamed Dynamo, for the evacuation of the remnants of the BEF from the beaches of Dunkirk and Nieuwpoort. It was into this confused maelstrom that the small British steamer *Abukir* sailed.

The *Abukir*, under the command of Captain Rowland Morris-Woolfenden and with a British crew of twenty, weighed in at a mere 689 tons; she was in many ways reminiscent of John Masefield's 'dirty British coaster', complete with a 'salt-caked smokestack' that belched forth black smoke on the rare occasions that she reached her top speed of 8 knots. She had been built on the River Tyne in 1920 for the London & Channel Islands Steamship

Company, who had named her *Island Queen* and employed her in the cargo/passenger trade between Southampton and Jersey for the next fourteen years.

In 1934 the *Island Queen* was sold to Monroe Brothers of Liverpool and renamed *Kyle Queen*. A year later, bought by the Pharaonic Mail Line of Alexandria, she left British waters for the Mediterranean. She was registered under the British flag, but was in fact owned by the Egyptian Government, who named her *Abukir* after the bay where Nelson so roundly trounced the French in 1798. For the next five years she operated a service between Alexandria and ports in the Eastern Mediterranean and Red Sea.

It was a complicated background for an uncomplicated little ship that boasted just two cargo holds, four derricks, a few very basic passenger cabins and a 97 h.p. coal-fired steam engine. She was not 'dirty' in the true sense of the word; rust-streaked, perhaps, but she was twenty years old and sorely in need of a coat of paint. Nevertheless, she served her new owners well, going about her business in unhurried but reliable fashion.

When war broke out in Europe, the *Abukir* was rudely snatched away from her Mediterranean idyll and found herself back in the cold, often turbulent English Channel, where she had begun her voyaging twenty years earlier. She had been requisitioned by the Admiralty, who put her under the management of the General Steam Navigation Company of London to serve as a supply carrier for the BEF in France. As a concession to war, her wheelhouse was encased by concrete slabs, and a single Lewis machine gun, a relic of an earlier war, was mounted on her upper bridge to ward off marauding enemy aircraft.

When she sailed out of Southampton on the afternoon of Saturday 25 May 1940, the *Abukir* had on board a cargo of biscuits and flour for the British Army, to be landed in Ostend. For Captain Woolfenden and his crew this promised to be just another all too familiar trip up through the Dover Strait as far as the North Goodwin light vessel, across to the West Hinder to pick up a Belgian pilot at the Akkaert Buoy, and into the welcoming arms of the breakwaters of Ostend. This involved an easy twenty-four hours steaming, a night alongside in Ostend discharging and back to Southampton for Tuesday morning. They had done it so many times before that it had become pure routine. Rumours were flying around that 'things were happening' on the other side, but nobody told the men of the *Abukir* that they were sailing into the mouth of hell.

Leaving the Solent and entering the Dover Strait, it soon became apparent to Captain Woolfenden that all was not as it should be. Where he had expected to meet the usual chaos of criss-crossing fishing boats and ferries and to be engaged in a hair raising game of 'dodgems' with ships of all flags and sizes inbound and out-ward bound, he found only empty sea. Two British MTBs hurried by on some unknown mission, but they completely ignored the *Abukir*. It was not until he was abreast the North Goodwin, and about to alter course to cross the line of sandbanks that bisect the Dover Strait, that Woolfenden was made aware of the dangerous situation into which he was sailing. A British examination vessel on patrol hailed the coaster to warn her that the port of Ostend was under siege and had been closed to all shipping for some days. Woolfenden was advised to return to Southampton. He gave some thought to the matter, but decided that if the situation in Ostend was as bad as he had been told, then the British Army urgently needed the cargo he carried. The *Abukir* continued on course.

It was still light when the *Abukir* neared the Akkaert Buoy, where the Ostend pilot was usually to be found, and Woolfenden was not surprised to find that the pilot cutter was off station. Ahead, 15 miles or so, the breakwaters of Ostend were clearly visible, but an ominous pall of black smoke was hanging over the port. However, it was a straight run in, and Woolfenden decided to go in at slow speed, hoping to pick up a harbour pilot at the entrance. Again, he was disappointed.

Second Officer Patrick Wills-Rust takes up the story:

> We got through the piers without a pilot and did not know where to go. There was nothing in the harbour. Presently a motor launch came along with a very excited pilot on board who said he would take us in, but that we should never get out. The Captain wanted to turn the ship round so as to be able to get out quickly when the Germans arrived, but the pilot would not do this. We berthed between a French sloop which had no armament and one other English coaster, the *Maquis*. We were asked to move, as the boilers of the ship astern of us were likely to blow up.

When safely moored in another berth, Captain Woolfenden assessed the possibility of landing his cargo. No one had come aboard to explain the situation, and the quay was in complete darkness. He left Chief Officer Lewis Evans in charge of the ship and went ashore. There he could find no sign of life. Most of the buildings were in ruins, still smoking from the last air raid, and it was soon obvious that the port had been abandoned.

While Woolfenden was ashore, German bombers arrived overhead and stick after stick of bombs came raining down. There appeared to be little opposition; just a single anti-aircraft gun was firing back. Dodging from cover to cover, Woolfenden finally ended up in a ditch with a party of British soldiers. With the bombs crashing down all around them and the air filled with choking smoke, the officer in charge, Lieutenant Harris, explained to Woolfenden that the advancing Germans were only a few miles outside the town and that he and his men had retreated all the way from the Belgian frontier and were desperately seeking a passage back across the Channel. He advised Woolfenden that it would be pointless to land his cargo, as it would almost certainly fall into German hands. Furthermore, he strongly recommended that the *Abukir* waste no time in quitting the port.

Now appraised of the true situation, Captain Woolfenden returned to the *Abukir* with Lieutenant Harris and his men in tow. As they were mounting the gangway, the German bombers came back, and once more the silence of the deserted port was shattered by the crash of exploding bombs as the high-flying JU 88s emptied their racks. Some bombs fell dangerously close to the moored coaster; so close that Woolfenden decided it would be wise to take cover in some nearby woods until the raid was over. To try to defend the *Abukir* with her Lewis gun and the rifles of Lieutenant Harries and his men would have been only a suicidal gesture, so she was left to her fate.

Miraculously, the *Abukir* survived the bombs unscathed, and half an hour later, when the German bombers had flown away, Woolfenden led his men back aboard and made preparations to leave the port. There was no pilot available, and all navigation lights on the breakwaters were out, but the moon had risen which, combined with the fires in the port, gave sufficient light to see the way out. Woolfenden decided to sail without a pilot.

The first mooring ropes were about to be cast off when an Army despatch rider skidded to a halt alongside the ship. He carried word from Admiral Sir Roger Keyes to Captain Woolfenden that the *Abukir*'s cargo of food was urgently needed ashore and should be landed without delay.

This was a request Rowland Woolfenden could not ignore, and as it was obvious there would be no help from the shore, it was down to the ship to discharge her own cargo. It is written into the Articles of Agreement of all British merchant ships that, when absolutely necessary, i.e. for the safety of the ship, the crew must discharge or load cargo. When this was put to the *Abukir*'s crew, who were by now more than anxious to get away from bomb-ravaged Ostend, they volunteered to a man. Officers and ratings turned to, opened the hatches, manned the derricks and began discharging.

Second Officer Rust wrote in his report:

> There were no stevedores about and no one else who would unload the goods. We unloaded ourselves and Dutch and Belgian soldiers gave us a hand. We were bombed continually during the unloading and had to go and hide in the woods. Lorries came and took the goods to the front. After 36 hours we had unloaded most of the cargo, except some flour at the bottom.
>
> There was another air raid and the ship astern of us, the *Diamond*, was hit. The Captain said we must get out tonight. That afternoon we received a message from Sir Roger Keyes saying that they were evacuating Bruges and that he was coming with us.

Admiral of the Fleet Sir Roger Keyes, later to become Head of Combined Operations, was then liaison officer to King Leopold of the Belgians. His British Mission was the only credible authority left in Belgium and was organizing the evacuation of the remnants of the BEF left in Bruges, along with any civilian refugees that could be got out. The Germans were at the gates of the town, and time was of the essence.

Within the hour, in a lull between air raids, the refugees came streaming through the dock gates led by a party of British troops, exhausted after fighting a rearguard action all the way from the Belgian/German border. They were taken on board the

Abukir, along with fifteen German prisoners of war they had picked up along the way, a small number of RAF aircrew and ground personnel, some Belgian servicemen, six priests, forty or fifty women, including a party of nuns from the British convent in Bruges, and a group of British schoolgirls. When they were all on board, a collection of lorries, motor cycles and staff cars belonging to the troops were swung aboard and stowed in the holds.

The embarkation was carried out with German bombers overhead, and panic was never far below the surface. When the *Abukir* was ready to sail, her limited accommodation was packed and her decks crowded. There was no count made of the numbers, but it is believed the coaster had at least 250 souls on board.

Second Officer Rust's report continues:

> We were waiting for nightfall, and at 8.55 p.m. we received a message from Sir Roger Keyes to say that he would not come and that we were to get out. When dark came we set out, the air raids were terrible. I think they thought we had Sir Roger Keyes on board and wanted to kill everybody. The weather was in our favour with very low clouds. We decided to cut across for the North Goodwins. Planes were all over us and so we sent out an SOS 'Aircraft attack!'

The bombers followed the *Abukir* out through the breakwaters and into the open sea. Miraculously, none of them scored a hit on the crowded little ship, but it was nearing midnight before they gave up and flew away. It was only then that Captain Woolfenden left the bridge. He had been on his feet for more than forty-eight hours and was completely exhausted. Leaving Second Officer Rust in charge, he went down to his cabin, hoping to catch an hour's sleep. The low cloud had disappeared with the German bombers, and the moon had risen, conveniently lighting the way for the fleeing *Abukir*.

At about 01.15 on the 28th, while nearing the West Hinder light vessel, Rust saw what appeared to be the periscope of a submarine about 500yds off the *Abukir*'s starboard beam. Seconds later, he saw the track of a torpedo heading straight for the ship. Ordering the helm hard to starboard to comb the track of the torpedo, Rust dived for the voice pipe and called the Captain to the bridge.

The torpedo was running down the starboard side of the ship, missing by only a few feet, when Woolfenden reached the bridge. He immediately turned stern-on to the reported periscope and began to zigzag away. The Captain later said that he had also seen a periscope, but it must have been a trick of the light. The *Abukir*'s attacker was in fact the German E-boat S-34.

When it had become clear to the German High Command that the Allies were planning to evacuate the remnants of their beaten armies from the beaches of Dunkirk, a flotilla of nine motor torpedo boats, or *Schnellboote*, was transferred from Norway to Borkum Island. These shallow-draught MTBs were ideally suited for operations in the shoal-strewn waters of the southern North Sea and the Dover Strait. Powered by three Daimler-Benz diesels developing 6,000 h.p., giving them a speed of 40 knots, they were highly manoeuvrable and able to dash in, deliver their torpedoes and escape before their victim had time to retaliate. They were considered to be the perfect weapon to deal with the small craft expected to be used to evacuate the British and French troops. S-34 had fired the first shot.

S-34, commanded by Oberleutnant-zur-See Obermaier, was of 100 tons displacement and armed with two 21-inch torpedo tubes, a 20mm cannon and two 9mm machine guns. She carried a total complement of twenty men. Only a few days previously, along with the other boats of her flotilla, she had been moved from Borkum to a base at Den Helder on the coast of Holland, and she was on her first patrol from there.

Twenty minutes after narrowly escaping Obermaier's first torpedo, the *Abukir* had reached a position 5 miles east of the West Hinder light vessel. Still zigzagging, she was keeping within the buoyed channel through the sandbanks that divide the northern end of the Dover Strait. Captain Woolfenden was holding his breath and silently praying that he had thrown off his pursuer. Then, without warning, a torpedo streaked out of the darkness to port and shot across the coaster's stern. It was another very near miss.

Still unable to identify his assailant, Woolfenden ordered smoke floats to be dropped, but as the canisters were going over the stern he sighted what he believed to be a submarine on the surface some 300yds off the port bow. Having no gun on board of any real account, Woolfenden put the helm hard over, intent on ramming.

It was a brave gesture born of desperation, for the little *Abukir* was far too slow to turn, and Oberleutnant Obermaier, guessing his opponents intentions, took advantage.

Second Officer Rust takes up the story again:

> The submarine drew abeam of us and let fly with two torpedoes. One missed us and went across our stern. The other hit us amidships in the engine room. There was a terrific smash and everything was pandemonium on deck. The wheelhouse collapsed on top of me and I was trapped by the concrete slabs which had fallen on me and pinned me to the deck. I think the ship sank in about 30 seconds, after breaking in two.
>
> Although I was trapped, I could see everything over my head. The stern burst into flames and I saw flames forward. I could see the water coming up and coming over my head. The ship hit the bottom and turned over, the debris was thrown off me and I was released and came to the surface. I was more or less dazed and could hardly breathe, but I can remember the submarine's searchlight and the sound of the machine-gunning, and I saw people being shot in the water. When I picked up the Mate later he had a bullet hole right through the head.
>
> The next thing I remember was two sailors floundering around me. I got them onto a hatch which was floating about. I got hold of a piece of wood and swam about to see what was happening. I blew a whistle and shouted to the people to keep calm and not to waste their strength. While this was going on I heard the Captain's voice calling, 'Is that you, Rust?' The Captain said we must do what we could to save people. There was plenty of wreckage about for them to hold on to, but they gave up and would not hold on. When daylight came I was clinging to a piece of wood which I think was the top of the chart house.
>
> I saw two fellows in the water and swam over to them, one of them was badly wounded – he was one of the Air Force pilots. He had a compound fracture in both legs, his pelvis was broken and he had a big hole in his back. I got a hatch and managed to get him out of the water.

It was later learned that Captain Woolfenden had been thrown into the forward cargo hold by the force of the exploding torpedo and had sustained two broken legs and a broken collar bone. Yet his first thoughts were for his passengers.

The two airmen Second Officer Rust gone to help were RAF Wireless Operator LAC Dear and Air Gunner AC 1 Stanhope, whose aircraft had been damaged and forced to land at Ostend. They, and three others of the Wellington's crew, had joined the refugees boarding the *Abukir.*

LAC Charles Dear later related his story:

> The ship's Mate had made his cabin available to us. This was a small single-berth cabin totally inadequate for four persons – Stanhope had remained on deck – I therefore decided to vacate this somewhat overcrowded situation and join him, leaving S/Ldr Glencross, Plt Off Cameron and Sgt. Parkhouse in the cabin.
>
> A short while later when standing at the stern rail, I saw the tracks of two torpedoes approaching, one missed the stern by a few feet and I vividly recall looking down at it as it passed. The second torpedo did not miss, and slammed into the *Aboukir* amidships.
>
> My next recollection was of being an awful long way under water and came to the surface near drowning. Fortunately, there was some floating debris nearby which I eagerly clung to. Meanwhile the *Aboukir* had completely disappeared.
>
> Strangely, I do not remember any noise, no cries for help, no machine guns, no engines – complete silence. Contrary to some other reports.
>
> Sometime later, I saw a piece of wreckage in the distance offering greater safety than the inadequate piece of flotation I was clinging to. Kicking off my flying boots I swam to what proved to be the top of a deck cabin. From this I learned a lesson, always take your life raft with you since the deck cabin was further away than I had reckoned, and fully clothed was almost beyond my capability.
>
> On reaching the raft I found Stanhope, a member of the ship's crew and an RAF officer (Ian) already on board.

> I cannot recall that we had a lot to say to each other. Sitting in the cold water up to one's waist was hardly conducive to any form of banter. We simply had to bear it and await rescue.

That rescue came at daybreak on the 28th, and happened by pure chance.

The attack on the *Abukir* had been so sudden, and she had gone down so quickly – in less than half a minute, witnesses said – that her wireless operator had no time to get away an SOS. Other than the seagulls who circled noisily over the wreckage, no one was aware of the loss of the ship. It was sheer luck – or Divine intervention, as some would have it – that as the sun lifted from the horizon four British destroyers appeared from the north-east, steaming in line astern and heading for the North Goodwin.

HMS *Anthony*, *Codrington*, *Javelin* and *Grenade*, their decks crowded with men saved from the beaches of Dunkirk, where Operation Dynamo was in full swing, were heading for Dover. *Codrington*, under the command of Captain George Stevens-Guille DSO, OBE, RN, already had over 800 on board, but she stopped, dropped her boats and began the rescue.

Of the estimated 250 souls aboard the *Abukir* when she left Ostend, *Codrington*'s boats found just thirty-two survivors in the waters near the West Hinder light vessel, including the injured Captain Rowland Morris-Woolfenden, Second Officer Patrick Wills-Rust, two nuns and a handful of RAF personnel. They had been in the water for six bone-chilling hours and were all suffering from exposure. Chief Officer Lewis Evans, Chief Engineer Harry Lawrence and twelve others of the *Abukir*'s crew of twenty-one had been lost with their ship. The bodies of some of the missing were washed ashore on the beaches of France, Belgium and the Friesian Islands in the ensuing months.

HMS *Codrington* landed her pathetic human cargo in Dover later on the 28th. Next day, she returned to Dunkirk and over the following nine days brought back another 4,600 troops, thereby playing a vital role in Operation Dynamo. When Dynamo came to an end, on 4 June 1940, a total of 338,226 British, French and Belgian soldiers had been brought back to Dover to carry on the fight from British soil.

Several of those who survived the sinking of the *Abukir* described how S-34 turned her searchlight on those struggling in the water and deliberately machine-gunned them. It may be that Oberleutnant Obermaier was under orders to wage total war on those who had escaped, hopefully to fight another day, but it was still an act of sheer barbarism which cost the lives of many innocent women and children. This was one war crime of the many committed by the Germans in the years to come that was overlooked at Nuremberg.

CHAPTER FIVE

Second Time Unlucky – *Clan Macphee* 16.08.40

Birkenhead in wartime was not a sight to inspire the poets: row upon row of drab terraced houses, blackened gaps still smouldering where the Luftwaffe's bombs had fallen a few days earlier, smoking chimneys, clanking trams, pubs with no beer. What man in his right mind would not long to leave all this for the open sea and the touch of a warm tropical sun?

So ran the thoughts of Chief Officer Harry Chadd, standing by on the forecastle head as the tugs eased the *Clan Macphee* out of Vittoria Dock and into the West Float to await the tide in the river. She was a deep-loaded ship, full to the hatch tops with cargo for South Africa and beyond, and the tugs were having difficulty handling her.

It was just after 6 o'clock on 13 August 1940, a fine summer's evening marred only by the stench from the turgid waters of the dock stirred into life by the threshing propellers of the straining tugs. In Chadd's experience, unberthing from Birkenhead docks was always a long drawn out process, and he was aware that it might be well into the night before he was relieved of his vigil at the anchors. Due on the bridge to take up the watch at 4 o'clock in the morning, there might be little sleep for him this night. But after that, the long, relaxing sea passage to the Cape was something to look forward to.

The 6,628-ton *Clan Macphee*, one of the more elderly units in the fleet of Cayzer Irvine of London and Glasgow, better known as Clan Line Steamers, having first wetted her keel as far back as 1911, had already survived one world war and was now actively involved in another. Part-loaded in Glasgow, she had completed in Birkenhead, and was bound for South and East African ports to discharge. From there she would steam north to India, to Bombay and the fragrant Malabar Coast to pick up a cargo of tea and jute for London. This was an itinerary the ship had followed so many times in her long career that it was said she knew the way without recourse to charts or compass. Commanded by 46-year-old Captain Thomas Cranwill, the *Clan MacPhee* carried a total complement of eighty-seven, of whom sixteen were British officers and the rest Indian ratings, Lascars from the Ganges Delta. This mix of crew was, by arrangement with the Indian authorities, the norm for most British ships trading regularly with India. It undoubtedly exploited a form of cheap labour, but the Lascars were by tradition good seamen, and it provided work for many villages in the Sunderbans where there had been none before.

As anticipated by Chief Officer Chadd, the sun was far below the horizon before the *Clan Macphee* cleared the docks and entered the River Mersey. By the time she dropped her pilot off the Bar light vessel, the long summer twilight had turned to darkness, and the North Channel beckoned.

Next morning, near the entrance to the Firth of Clyde, the *Clan Macphee* joined ships from the Bristol Channel, the Clyde and East Coast ports, to form Convoy OB 197. When complete, the convoy consisted of fifty-three merchantmen, mostly British, bound for ports in North and South America, West Africa and the Cape of Good Hope. Only two escorts were provided, the 21-year-old destroyer HMS *Mackay* and the newly-commissioned corvette HMS *Heartsease*. In retrospect, this seems hardly adequate, but in those early days of the war the U-boats, restricted in range, were said to be active only in the western and south-western approaches to the British Isles. The theory was that convoys were required only to get the ships clear of these danger zones. However, OB 197's depleted escort was in no small way the result of the Royal Navy's loss of so many ships in the recent evacuation of the BEF from Dunkirk. Also, it seems, the Admiralty was not yet fully aware that the U-boats had recently moved house to bases further south which gave them a decided advantage over a much depleted Royal Navy

When France surrendered in June 1940, Admiral Dönitz immediately began preparations to move his U-boats from Kiel to ports on the French coast of the Bay of Biscay. Brest, Lorient, La Pallice and La Rochelle were all easily defended and offered direct access to the North Atlantic. Lorient, which had been a major French naval base, was a valuable acquisition, as it offered far better dockyard facilities than Kiel. More importantly, perhaps, the U-boats would no longer have to negotiate the hazardous 450-mile passage around the north of Scotland, thereby increasing their operational time in the Atlantic by at least a week.

All went well for OB 197 until the morning of 16 August when, unknown to Captain George Stevens-Guille, Senior Officer Escort in HMS *Mackay*, the convoy acquired an unwelcome shadow.

Since their early success in sinking the liner *Athenia* within hours of the outbreak of war, Fritz-Julius Lemp and U-30 had sunk a total of eleven ships, totalling 38,741 tons gross. In addition, they had damaged the 31,000-ton battleship HMS *Barham*, putting her out of action for six months. And to pile success on success, Lemp had sown a minefield off the Bar light vessel, at the entrance to the Mersey, which reaped another five Allied ships of 27,540 tons.

It was fitting then that U-30 was the first boat to be transferred to Biscay, sailing from Lorient on 5 August on her eighth war patrol. Four days later, in the North-Western Approaches, she sank the 5,779-ton Swedish motor vessel *Canton*, inbound from Calcutta to Liverpool with a cargo of pig iron and produce. The following week was barren, then at dawn on the 16th she sighted OB 197. Lemp radioed Lorient, reporting a large convoy apparently poorly defended.

Back in Lorient, installed in his new headquarters at Kerneval, Dönitz contacted two other boats patrolling in the area, U-46 and U-48, and ordered them to join U-30 in a joint attack on OB 197. Meanwhile, Lemp would continue to shadow the convoy. This, in effect, was the first trial of Dönitz's long-advocated pack attack strategy.

U-46, a Type VIIB, was slightly larger than U-30, and had a history marred by early lack of success. Commissioned in November 1938, she had carried out six war patrols under the command of Herbert Sohler without sinking, or even damaging, a single enemy ship. Sohler had been relieved of his command in May 1940 and replaced by the more experienced Engelbert Endrass. On his first patrol in U-46, Endrass reversed the boat's poor record by sinking the 20,000-ton British armed merchant cruiser *Carinthia*, and followed up this kill with another four ships totalling 16,000 tons. Now Endrass was back at sea and hungry for more Allied tonnage to add to his already impressive score.

U-48, another Type VIIB of pre-war build, was on her sixth war patrol and her first under the command of Hans Rudolf Rösing.

On the outbreak of war, with Herbert Schultze in command, she had already been on station in the North Atlantic and was soon to earn a place in the record books. On her first five patrols she sank no less than 112,470 tons of Allied shipping, earning for Schultze the Knight's Cross. Thirty-five-year-old Rösing, who had assumed command prior to her sailing on her sixth patrol in May 1940, was a long-serving naval officer who had spent much of his time in surface ships, culminating with command of the motor torpedo boat S-15. He had transferred to U-boats in 1933.

When Fritz-Julius Lemp first sighted OB 197 he was taken aback by the sheer size of the convoy. He counted more than fifty ships, steaming in ten columns abreast and covering at least 10 square miles of ocean. When a closer inspection revealed that this huge armada was defended by only two escorts, Lemp was even more amazed. In retrospect, such a state of affairs was indeed unbelievable, but it was inevitable given the overstretched condition of the Royal Navy at the time. Dunkirk had taken a heavy toll of the destroyers and smaller craft needed for convoy work, and those remaining were thinly spread across a dozen or more different war zones, each with their own particular demands. The handy little corvettes, specifically designed as convoy escorts, had begun to arrive, but not in sufficient numbers to meet the demand. Captain Stevens-Guille was doing his utmost to provide cover for OB 197 with the two ships of his command, but it was nowhere near enough. *Mackay* and *Heartsease* were diligently sweeping the perimeter of the convoy with Asdic, and their lookouts were painstakingly alert, but they failed to detect the three U-boats as they moved in.

Rösing in U-48 was first to strike, at about 10.00 a.m., emptying his bow tubes at one of the outriders of OB 197, the 2,325-ton Swedish steamer *Hedrun*. Only one torpedo found its target, striking the small ship squarely amidships. The *Hedrun*, on passage from Swansea to Newport, Rhode Island with a cargo of coal, sank in just three minutes. Eight of her crew were lost, including the Master and his wife.

When the *Hedrun*'s distress rockets went soaring skywards, *Mackay* and *Heartsease* made a show of force by dropping depth charges, but this gained the convoy only a short respite. The U-boats came back again at noon, U-46 setting her sights on the 6,189-ton Dutch motor vessel *Alcinous*. The *Alcinous*, outward from Liverpool to Cape Town and the Far East with general cargo, was fortunate in that Endrass's torpedo went home in her forward hold. She was down by the head, but showed no signs of sinking. Her crew stayed with her, and less than an hour later she was making full speed to rejoin the convoy. Meanwhile, the U-boats had withdrawn, presumably to reload their tubes.

At 1600 OB 197 was roughly 120 miles west-south-west of Rockall, and Captain Stevens-Guille, who had orders to disperse the convoy when at the extreme range of the U-boats' operational area, decided that it was safe for the merchantmen to go their own separate ways. This decision, though necessary, was premature, but there were so many convoys to screen, and so few escorts available.

Captain Thomas Cranwill, of the *Clan Macphee*, who for some time had been unhappy about the vulnerability of the convoy, heaved a sigh of relief when the Convoy Commodore hoisted the signal to disperse. He immediately rang for full speed and hauled around to the south-west. Surging ahead at her best 12½ knots, the *Clan Macphee* was soon pulling away from the other ships. Ahead lay 6,000 miles of empty ocean in which the U-boats had no place.

An hour later, Cranwill had lost sight of the other ships and, with the weather deteriorating rapidly, he judged it was safe to cease zig-zagging and set course due south for the Cape. At that time he was totally unaware that only half a mile out on the *Clan Macphee*'s port side U-30 was hidden beneath the waves and Fritz-Julius Lemp was at his periscope, watching and waiting for the opportunity to strike. At 1730, in full daylight, Lemp gave the order to fire the bow tubes.

Chief Officer Harry Chadd was on the bridge of the *Clan Macphee*:

> I saw no splash of water, or any flame. However, there was some smoke with a peculiar smell. We were hit right in the centre of the engine room on the port side between No. 1 and 2 tanks, about 200ft from the bow.

Lemp's torpedo caused extensive damage to the ship on her port side from the funnel aft. No. 4 lifeboat and the bridge jolly boat had both gone, blown clean over the side. The engineers' accommodation was completely wrecked, as was the crew's accommodation aft. But the most serious blow had fallen on the engine room, which was laid wide open to the sea. All those below on watch were killed instantly, and many died in the accommodation above. Such was the extent of the damage that it was clear the *Clan Macphee* could not remain afloat for long.

Chief Officer Chadd relates what followed:

> We immediately gave the order to abandon ship. The men allotted to No. 4 boat all piled into Nos. 3 and 6 boats, which of course made too many for them to carry. I ordered them out, but even at the point of the gun they refused to leave the boat, and so I started to pull them out. I afterwards learned that they had some idea that I wasn't going to permit them into any boat.

Panic followed on panic as the *Clan Macphee* started to founder. Chadd's report continues:

> The ship was going down rapidly, in fact we only had 8 minutes altogether from the time the torpedo struck us until she sank, and so we made haste to load the boats. As we were lowering one of the port boats the davits broke and the boat capsized, landing on top of the men who had been thrown into the water. There were no more boats on the port side, so I crossed over to the starboard side where I saw the Captain's boat, which is No. 5, already lowered. However, apparently they had lowered it too fast and it had been flooded. It only contained 6 men and it drifted away. At this juncture the ship suddenly dipped by the bow and eventually sank on an even keel.
>
> Only No. 3 boat was got away without any incident and this of course was filled to capacity. The Captain, myself, and several others of the crew threw rafts over the side, and I managed to reach one together with the Wireless Operator and Gunner.

What befell Captain Cranwill is not known, but it seems he must have gone down with his ship, along with his Chief Engineer John Robertson, Third Engineer William Innes, Carpenter George Bain and forty of the *Clan Macphee*'s Lascar crew, the majority of the latter having been lost in the panic to get the boats away.

Those who survived the sinking were fortunate in that another ship was following close astern. She was the

Hungarian-flag *Kelet*, a steamer of 4,295 tons built in 1913 for the Hain Steamship Company of London as the *Tregarthen*, and now owned by the Neptun Sea Navigation Company of Budapest. The *Kelet* had also just left OB 197 and was on her way to the Gulf of Mexico in ballast. She should not really have been enjoying the doubtful security of the convoy, as Hungary was then a member of Hitler's Axis – a reluctant one, perhaps, but as Germany had the might to crush her easily at any time, she had little choice but to cooperate. However, the *Kelet*, apparently unsure of her status in wartime, was still in her peacetime colours and had a large Hungarian flag painted on each side of her hull.

The *Clan Macphee* was still afloat when the *Kelet* sighted her, although she was obviously in a sinking condition and her boats were seen to be in the water. When one of those boats capsized, the *Kelet*'s national status became an irrelevance; following the unwritten law of the sea, she went to the rescue of the survivors. One of her crew, Seaman Alwis, who spoke English, later wrote down his recollections of the incident:

> I saw a vessel in the distance. There were a lot of men swimming about in the water around her, and then I saw a lifeboat capsize throwing more men into the water. There were many natives.
>
> Our Captain gave the order to don our lifebelts, and then we proceeded to where these men were and picked up as many survivors as we could. The task was made very difficult because of the bad weather but we managed to pick up quite a number. One boat which was flooded came alongside our vessel. There were a number of dead men in the bottom and only two survivors. Our Chief Officer and some of the crew went to pick up another 5 men and just then we saw a submarine which came over to our ship. I don't know what passed between the Captain and the Commander of the submarine but it soon went away.

There is no record of which U-boat approached the *Kelet*, but it seems safe to assume it was U-30 and that Fritz-Julius Lemp came to some agreement with the Master of the Hungarian ship to make no move against the *Kelet*, so long as she took care of the *Clan*

Macphee's survivors. This was Lemp showing his humanitarian side, and it suggests that for some at least the conflict at sea was still a 'gentleman's war'. Chief Officer Chadd's statement confirms this:

> The *Kelet*, which was one of the stragglers of the convoy, had by this time picked up the crew of the overloaded boat, and any other survivors they could see. We were also taken on board, and almost as soon as on board, which was about 1½ hours after the attack, I saw the submarine surface. He immediately spotted the flooded boat containing 6 men, and went over to it. He apparently spoke to the Steward [Chief Steward James Patterson], asking him where the Captain was and the name of our vessel. I doubt if there was any other conversation because before the Steward arrived alongside the *Kelet* he died. One other man died, and two were drowned in trying to board the *Kelet*, leaving only two natives in the boat, who said the commander of the submarine spoke English.
>
> The Commander, having spoken with the 6 men, came over to the *Kelet*, and told the Captain about the men in the flooded boat, and then went away. When the flooded boat arrived alongside, probably due to inexperience in getting aboard a vessel during rough weather, two of the men were drowned whilst trying to climb the ladder. There were two dead men in the boat. They did not appear to have any injuries, so probably died from shock, so there were only two survivors out of the six men.
>
> The submarine was a dark grey colour, and I think was of the U25/26 type. The conning tower, which was raked, was set well aft, and had a gun standing quite close to it. I should think the submarine was about 270ft long. She was very fast and when she left us she picked up to a speed of about 17 knots.

The *Kelet* was then about 320 miles from the nearest land, the Outer Hebrides, and Chadd discussed with her Master the possibility of returning to the east to land him and his fellow survivors. The Hungarian captain was not willing to take the risk of going back into the danger zone, but eventually a compromise was reached by which he agreed to land the survivors in the Azores, a destination which would involve little deviation from his route to the Gulf of Mexico.

At dawn on 19 August the *Kelet* had reached a position 650 miles due west of Land's End. In the previous sixty hours since leaving the scene of the attack on OB 197, the passage towards the Azores had been without incident, and the weather was steadily improving. She was now nearing the outer limits of the U-boats' hunting grounds and would have been safe – had not one of Dönitz's the few long-range boats crossed her path.

U-A, built in Kiel in 1938 for the Turkish Navy, was of 1,200 tons displacement, almost twice the size of the Type VIIs that stalked the sea lanes further east. Designed to be used as a mine-layer, she was well armed with six torpedo tubes, four in the bow and two in the stern; she had a 105mm gun built into the fore end of her elongated conning tower, and a 25mm anti-aircraft gun aft. But it was her range, 15,000 miles at 10 knots, that gave her the advantage over the Type VIIs. She was a submarine for distant waters.

Under the command of Kapitänleutnant Hans Cohausz, another long-serving officer of the *Kriegsmarine* who had been in U-boats since 1935 and had also served on Dönitz's staff, U-A had sailed from Kiel on this, her first war patrol, on 6 June 1940. Since then she had roamed far and wide, from Iceland to West Africa, sinking firstly the British armed merchant cruiser *Andania* in the Denmark Strait and most recently the Greek tramp *Aspasia* off Madeira. Cohausz was heading for northern waters again when he encountered the *Kelet* steaming determinedly for the Azores. Chief Officer Chadd described the meeting:

> On the morning of 19th August at about 4.25 a.m. I heard a shot fired across our bows, and I came up on deck just in time to intercept a message from a submarine, which was about 3 miles away on our port side, asking for the ship's papers to be sent over. The Captain of the *Kelet* hadn't been able to read the message so I translated it for him, whereupon he sent a boat over with the Chief Officer in charge. The weather was fine at the time, and when the boat went over to the submarine it was broad daylight, being about 6 a.m.

The *Kelet's* boat returned to the ship, after which Cohausz signalled the Hungarian to approach the U-boat at slow speed. When they were within hailing distance, he ordered the *Kelet* to lower her boats and abandon ship. Any arguments about nationality were obviously not going to yield results, and as U-A had her guns trained on the unarmed merchantman, the *Kelet's* crew, along with the forty-one survivors from the *Clan Macphee*, took to the boats. For the second time in less than seventy-two hours Harry Chadd found himself climbing into a lifeboat. He wrote in his report:

> There were only two lifeboats and two dinghies, so the Captain instructed me to throw the rafts over the side for the natives. We took plenty of provisions and I went into the starboard boat which was lowered by that time. The Captain went and collected instruments, etc. from the chartroom, and he came back after 15 minutes. His last act on board the *Kelet* was to hoist the Hungarian flag.
>
> We pulled away from the ship, and we saw the submarine dive. Whilst below the surface he fired a torpedo into the port side of the *Kelet* right amidships, which hit the boiler room. We saw the track of the torpedo, and then there was a sheet of flame. However, the *Kelet* did not sink, but kept on an even keel.

Chadd saw the U-boat suddenly surface on the port side of the stricken ship and move around to her starboard quarter. Then, from close range, she began systematically demolishing the *Kelet* with a barrage of shells from her big gun. Broken and on fire, the elderly ship finally keeled over and sank.

The German submarine cruised amongst the wreckage for a while; then, apparently satisfied with her work, she made off in a north-westerly direction at full speed. When she was out of sight, the pathetic collection of boats and rafts bearing the survivors from the *Kelet* came together. A head count revealed that another six of the *Clan Macphee's* crew had lost their lives with the Hungarian ship, leaving just thirty-five of her original complement of eighty-seven still alive.

After some discussion of their predicament, the Master of the *Kelet* suggested that they set a course for Spain or Portugal, some 650 miles to the south-east, but Harry Chadd had somewhere closer in mind, namely the west coast of Ireland. In the end they agreed to go their own separate ways.

Chief Officer Chadd later reported:

> The Captain went off steering in a far more easterly direction than I did. He was two points on my bow and appeared to be making for the Channel.
>   I attached one raft to my boat and the other was towed by the dinghy. We fixed up a sail, and rowed too, but after 24 hours we had only made about 10 miles. I realized that it was hopeless to try and carry on like that so I told the 11 natives on the raft that we would have to part and look for assistance. We divided all our provisions and I sailed across from there keeping as much to the nor'ard of E.N.E. as I could.

Chadd's lifeboat made good progress throughout the rest of the day, but towards evening the weather deteriorated sharply, with the wind freshening up to gale force and generating a rough sea. The boat was constantly awash, and continuous baling became necessary. This continued day and night for the next five days until, at about 0900 on the 24th, smoke was sighted on the horizon ahead.

The 948-ton Norwegian collier *Varegg* had had a regular run carrying coal from the UK to France until that fateful summer of 1940 when French resistance collapsed. She was then assigned to bring pit props from Lisbon, and joined Convoy OG 41 on 29 June for the passage to Portugal's west coast. Unfortunately for her but, as it turned out, to the advantage of Chief Officer Chadd and his fellow survivors, the *Varegg* was unable to maintain convoy speed and was left behind. Two days after leaving OG 41, she was about 400 miles west of Ireland when her lookouts saw something on the water. It was the *Kelet*'s boat containing the men of the *Clan Macphee* who had survived the double sinking earlier in the month.

The *Varegg* arrived in Galway on the morning of 22 August. Among the fortunate thirty-five survivors of the *Clan Macphee*'s original complement of eighty-seven men was one who had now lost his ship on three occasions since the outbreak of war eleven months earlier. David Murray, who had been captain's steward on the liner *Athenia* when she was sunk within hours of war breaking out, had joined the *Clan Macphee* after a short survivor's leave; now, in addition, he held the dubious distinction of having been twice robbed of his ship by Fritz-Julius Lemp's U-30.

CHAPTER SIX

The Jolly Boat –
Anglo Saxon 21.08.40

On Wednesday, October 30th, a ship's boat containing two men came ashore on the island of Eleuthera. The men were discovered lying on the beach in an advanced state of exhaustion by a farmer named Martin who was working in a field nearby and had seen the boat approaching. He obtained help and the men were removed to the Governor's Harbour and the resident Commissioner reported the circumstances to the Colonial Secretary at Nassau, who issued instructions for their removal to the hospital in Nassau by aeroplane. The Chief Medical Officer went with the plane from Nassau and they were brought back and placed in hospital the next day. Although in a very weakened and emaciated condition, every hope is entertained of a rapid recovery.

Report from the office of the Colonial Secretary at
Nassau, Bahamas, October 1940.

The story behind these events began three months earlier and 3,000 miles away in the upper reaches of the Bristol Channel, where the London-registered steamer *Anglo Saxon* had arrived in Newport, Mon. with a full cargo of steel from America.

The 5,596-ton *Anglo Saxon*, built in Sunderland in 1929 when the world was in the grip of a severe economic depression, was a typical 'workhorse' of her day, a coal-burner, blunt in the bow and broad in the beam. Owned by Lawther, Latter of London, she had known lean times in her early days, chasing cargoes to the far corners of the globe, often for little return. But she had survived, and now, with Britain at war, she was never without a cargo, always on her marks and being hurried in and out of port to meet the voracious demands of war.

Commanded by 53-year-old Captain Philip Flynn, the *Anglo Saxon* carried ten officers, three petty officers, twenty-six ratings and a Royal Marine gunlayer, the latter supplied by the Admiralty along with a 4-inch anti-submarine gun of ancient vintage and a brace of machine guns that may well have seen service in the trenches of Flanders in 1914–18. During the coming voyage, Marine Francis Penny would have the unenviable task of forming and training guns' crews from amongst the *Anglo Saxon*'s hands, most of whom, being fiercely independent merchant seamen, might well resent this interference with their normal watch-keeping routine.

Early on the morning of 6 August 1940, while the RAF prepared to do battle with Hitler's Luftwaffe, the *Anglo Saxon* emerged from the pall of dust hanging over Newport's coal hoists sagging under the weight of a full cargo of 'best Welsh'. She was bound for the coaling station at Bahia Blanca, 6,000 miles deep in the South Atlantic. Powerful tugs eased her into the locks, and by the time the sun was halfway to the yardarm, she was butting into a rising south-wester.

Coal, even 'best Welsh', is one of the dirtiest of cargoes to carry. The loading process, whereby coal is dumped from a great height into the holds, ensures that every exposed inch of decks and superstructure ends up coated with a thick layer of black dust. Once the *Anglo Saxon* was at a discreet distance from the land, it was up to Boatswain Tom Maher and his deck crew to sluice down with hoses and make the ship presentable for her next call, Milford Haven at the mouth of the Bristol Channel. It was back-breaking work, guaranteed to cure the hangovers acquired in the dockside pubs of Newport the previous night, but by the time the *Anglo Saxon* anchored in Milford Haven just before dark, she had regained some of her dignity.

There was now a short respite while the *Anglo Saxon* was joined by several other ships from Bristol Channel ports, and late on the 8th a rendezvous was made south of the Smalls Rocks with ships from Liverpool and the Clyde. When formed up in nine columns abreast, Convoy OB 195 consisted of twenty-seven merchantmen, escorted by the destroyer HMS *Vanoc* and the Flower-class corvettes *Geranium* and *Periwinkle*.

Four days later, when 700 miles west of Land's End, the convoy dispersed and the merchantmen were left to go their own separate ways, some turning south for West Africa and the Cape, others continuing west to North America. The *Anglo Saxon* was alone in heading for South America, and she soon found herself with an empty horizon on all sides.

On the evening of 21 August the *Anglo Saxon* was approaching the Tropic of Cancer, and in the opinion of Captain Flynn and his officers she was well out of reach of the enemy. She had ceased to zigzag, normal watches were being kept, with just one lookout in the bows at night, and the guns were manned only when an exasperated Marine Penny was putting his largely uninterested recruits through their paces.

On the bridge, Third Officer Walter Murray had the watch, with 21-year-old Able Seaman Roy Widdecombe at the wheel. The wheelhouse was in complete darkness, apart from the soft glow of the dimmed compass binnacle light, and the only sounds to disturb the tranquillity of the night were the steady beat of the *Anglo Saxon*'s engine and the click of the wheel as the helmsman eased the spokes to keep her on course. A light north-easterly breeze and just enough swell to give the ship a lazy, almost soporific roll completed the magic of the night.

In the wireless room abaft the bridge, Second Radio Officer Roy Pilcher listened with half an ear to the distant bursts of atmospherics, the only sound to disturb the ether that night. If there were any other ships about, then they were not advertising their presence. Below the bridge, in his cabin, Captain Philip Flynn was relaxing in his armchair with a book. Right aft, in the crew messroom, voices were raised as steaming hot mugs of cocoa were passed around. The talk was of the delights of South American ports, where the wine flowed free and every girl was a Hollywood beauty. The war seemed so remote that it was not even discussed.

For the average British merchant ship – and the *Anglo Saxon* might be so classed – radar was still a distant pipe dream. The horizon was limited to the range of the 'Mark 1 Eyeball', and on a dark night such as this its range was negligible. No one could have been aware of the terrible danger that lay ahead.

Masthead lookouts aboard the German commerce raider *Widder* had spotted the *Anglo Saxon* some 10 miles astern while it was still light and, keeping out of sight, she had kept station on the unidentified ship until darkness fell. Now she was about to pounce.

The auxiliary cruiser *Widder* ('Ram'), otherwise known as *Hilfskreuzer 21*, was of 1929 vintage, having been built in Kiel for the Hamburg Amerika Line, who christened her *Neumark*. She was a 7,851-ton fast fruit carrier designed for service between Hamburg and the West Indies, and this trade she had plied until being requisitioned by the *Kriegsmarine* on the outbreak of war in 1939. She had undergone an extensive conversion, which included new 6,700 h.p. steam turbines, giving her a top speed of 14.8 knots and an endurance range of 34,000 miles without refuelling. Her armament consisted of six 5.9-inch and one 3-inch gun, four 21-inch torpedo tubes and an impressive array of smaller calibre cannon and machine guns. She also carried two Heinkel 114 reconnaissance seaplanes.

Appointed to command the newly-commissioned *Widder* was 49-year-old Kapitän zur See Hellmuth von Ruckteschell, a former U-boat commander in the First World War. In German naval circles his was seen as a controversial appointment, von Ruckteschell being described as a 'complex, religious and cultured man, with an artistic nature and a passion for classical music' and 'moody, introspective and difficult to like'. He was also known to suffer from chronic migraine and stomach problems. Hellmuth von Ruckteschell did not appear to be the ideal man to command a ship of war, not least a commerce raider briefed to sail alone.

The *Widder*, disguised as a neutral Swedish merchantman, emerged into the North Atlantic at the end of May 1940 to embark on her new career. She had the element of surprise and found instant success, sinking six Allied ships totalling 41,000 tons gross in her first two months at sea. It was obvious that she would never match the success of Dönitz's U-boats, but she posed a serious threat, which the Royal Navy, with so few ships in the area, could not hope to meet.

As he closed on the unsuspecting *Anglo Saxon*, von Ruckteschell was aware that he had less than twenty minutes to act before the moon rose and revealed his presence. He would have to strike swiftly and ruthlessly to cripple his victim before she was able to take flight. At 2008, having closed the range to 2,500yds, he opened fire with every gun that could be brought to bear.

The effect was instantaneous and catastrophic, the *Widder*'s first salvo of 5.9-inch shells scoring a direct hit on the *Anglo Saxon*'s poop, completely demolishing it. The British tramp's 4-inch gun, yet to be fired in anger, was blown over the side, and with it went any chance she might have had of defending herself. Ammunition in the ready-use locker was set on fire and began to explode, adding to the chaos.

Directly below the poop, in the crew messroom, where seconds before there had been the rattle of mugs and the buzz of relaxed conversation, men lay dead and dying, while the flames crackled and danced around them.

Having dealt the first crippling blow, the *Widder* now closed to within 500yds and raked the helpless merchantman with her machine guns and 20mm pom-poms, at the same time continuing to pump high explosive shells into her. As a result, the *Anglo Saxon* and many of those aboard her were literally shot to pieces. A number of men had reached the boat deck, but the two lifeboats were reduced to matchwood in their davits as they attempted to lower them. The deck was littered with bodies.

Roy Widdecombe, who had managed to extricate himself from the blazing ruins of the wheelhouse, found Captain Flynn's lifeless body slumped against the port bulwark. The Captain had been shot down while he was in the act of throwing overboard the ship's code books and secret papers. Surrounded by devastation and death, Widdecombe suddenly felt very alone and helpless. Fortunately, at this point he was joined by Chief Officer Barry Denny, who appeared to be one of the few survivors. The two men looked around for a means of escape.

In addition to her lifeboats, the *Anglo Saxon* carried two small jolly boats, one on each side of the bridge. These 18ft boats, normally used for painting ship or communication with the shore in sheltered waters, were still intact. With great difficulty, for the jolly boats were heavy wooden craft, Denny and Widdecombe succeeded in swinging out the port side boat and lowered it to the water.

By this time one of the *Widder*'s shells had destroyed the *Anglo Saxon*'s main boiler, and the ship was slowly losing way through the water, allowing the two survivors to board their small boat safely. Before they cast off they were joined by five others, namely Second Radio Officer Roy Pilcher, Third Engineer Lionel Hawks, Marine Francis Penny, Second Cook Leslie Morgan and Able Seaman Robert Tapscott. Three of the late arrivals were injured: Pilcher's left foot had been smashed by shell splinters, Penny had bullets in his right arm and leg and Morgan had been shot in the right foot. These seven men, none of them in very good shape, were all that remained of the *Anglo Saxon*'s crew after von Ruckteschell's guns had done their work.

Crouching down out of sight below the gunwales, the survivors allowed the jolly boat to drift away from the glow cast by their burning ship. As they receded into the darkness of the night they saw the raider steaming in circles and raking the water with tracer, presumably bent on eradicating all evidence of her night's work. And as they watched, the *Widder* administered the *coup de grâce* to the *Anglo Saxon* by torpedoing her. The poor broken ship keeled over and sank amid a cloud of steam and smoke, and the German raider then made off to the east at speed.

As was his right, Chief Officer Denny had assumed command of the jolly boat, and it was his decision to stream a sea anchor and await the coming of dawn before making any move. It was a long night, and when daylight finally came, just after 0500 on the 22nd, the seven men found themselves completely alone on an empty ocean. They had hoped for other survivors, a lifeboat or life-raft, but there was nothing; only a few pieces of charred wreckage marked the grave of the *Anglo Saxon* and, presumably, that of the thirty-four other men who had sailed in her.

Those who were left now looked to their future. A check of the boat's contents showed that it was equipped with mast and sail, six pairs of oars, a sea anchor, a box of distress flares, matches, a canvas boat cover, a compass, an oil light and a small medical kit. By way of sustenance, the boat's lockers contained a tin of ship's biscuits, 18lb of tinned mutton, and eleven tins of condensed milk. There was also a 4 gallon keg of fresh water.

Even with only seven men in the boat, and with strict rationing imposed, it was obvious to Denny that these supplies would be inadequate for the prolonged voyage facing them. When the *Anglo Saxon* was attacked she had been in the region of 850 miles west of the Canaries. As Chief Officer Denny, an experienced navigator, was well aware, sailing eastwards was out of the question. The prevailing winds in the area were north-easterly, and they were under the influence of the North Equatorial Current, which flowed west at between 10 and 20 miles a day. The only choice open to them was to head west, taking advantage of wind and current. Unfortunately, the nearest land to the west was 1,600 miles away in the West Indies. Given the best of good luck, and fair weather all the way, the seven men could look forward to at least two months at sea. It was a daunting prospect, but there was no other way. Denny put it to his fellow survivors, sugaring the pill by assuring them that they would almost certainly be picked up by a passing ship within a few days. There was no argument. The sail was hoisted and course set to the west.

The first day passed well enough, but the wind was fitful, and most of the little progress made was by virtue of the current. Once under sail, Denny used his limited knowledge of first aid to clean and dress the wounds of the injured. Radio Officer Roy Pilcher's foot had been smashed by gunfire, while the wounds of 2nd Cook Leslie Morgan and Marine Penny were less serious. The jolly boat's first aid kit contained only the bare medical essentials, bandages, lint, antiseptic powder and iodine, with which Denny did the best he could.

Chief Officer Denny was now keeping a log with the stub of pencil and some scraps of paper he had found. The entry for the following day reads:

> August 23rd, Friday. Wind E.N.E. 3. Slight sea, slightly confused easterly swell, partly cloudy. Half a dipper of water per man 6 am also half a biscuit with a little condensed milk. Sighted a vessel showing no lights at 11 pm. Showed sea flare. She cruised around but was of the opinion she was a raider as she was heading N.N.E. We were about 100 miles from our original position. Kept quiet and let her go off.

Denny was wise to exercise caution, for these were remote waters, and it is more than likely that the ship sighted was the *Widder* searching for another victim. These thoughts he kept to himself, and despite the disappointment, morale in the boat remained high. Three days later, Denny's log showed that, even in the face of a deteriorating supply situation, it remained so:

> August 26th, Monday. Bosun bird flew overhead. Sun rose at 6.25 a.m. A.T.S (Ship's time). Becalmed, occasional fitful gusts. Glaring sun rays. Bale out 24 buckets daily. 6 a.m. Issued meat rations out from day previous wrapped

in canvas, little taken, half a dipper of water per man, little drop of condensed milk, spirits of whole crew keen, no murmur from wounded men. Hoping to sight vessel soon but praying for squalls and a decent wind. During a.m. Medical treatment given by 3rd Engineer and myself. W/T operator's left foot which is badly crushed bathed with salt water for an hour and last linen bandage applied, well covered up but swelling badly. 2nd Cook's right foot swollen badly, ankle badly strained with bullet wound just above ankle, bathed with salt water and well bandaged. Gunlayer's right forearm washed first in fresh water, then iodine applied and bandaged. All day long blinding sun's rays and cloudless, becalmed. During afternoon First Officer, 3rd engineer, gunlayer, A.B.'s Widdecombe and Tapscott dipped their bodies in water overside, taking care to keep their faces out of the water, result greatly invigorating. Rations still half a dipper of water per man at 6 a.m. And 6 p.m., only eat half a biscuit per day, no need for more, and a little condensed milk, the boiled beef kept in canvas still good and the fat is appreciated. Although the W/T is weak, everyone else in good spirits and very cheerful. Keeping two watches, one myself other 3rd engineer, two A.B.s four on and four off. Having no nautical instruments or books on board can only rely on the compass and stars at night. Trusting to make a landfall in the vicinity of Leeward Islands, with God's will and British determination. 10.30 p.m., wind freshening from eastward, skimming along fine at about 5 knots.

And a day later:

August 27th, Tuesday. Wind E.N.E. 3 to 4, partly cloudy, no rain yet. 6 a.m. ration given, half a dipper of water, no one felt hungry. Managed to give each man a cigarette made out of newspaper and half a can of tobacco, but only 8 matches left so this luxury will soon be stopped. On port tack heading S.W. True making about four knots and throughout the night, held a lottery in evening as to who gave nearest date of being sighted or making landfall. Sun set 6.42 p.m. A.T.S.

The reality was that no one, not even Chief Officer Denny, really knew where they were or how much longer it would be before they reached land or were picked up. By the time the sun went down on the 27th, the jolly boat had been under sail on a westerly course for five and a half days, and although they had been becalmed some of the time, it is safe to assume they had been averaging at least 2 knots. In that case, the survivors would have covered less than 300 miles, and thus they still had another 2,000 to go. Denny, having spent fifteen years at sea, much of it keeping watches on the bridge of a ship, must have been aware of their situation, yet his log continued to err on the optimistic side. Then, on 1 September, having been becalmed all the previous day and night, the tone of that log changed. He wrote:

> September 1st, Sunday. During Saturday night crew felt very thirsty, boiled mutton could not be digested and some felt sick, doubled the water issue that night. 6.15 a.m. Half a dipper of water per man and same in p.m. Wind S.S.W. 2, slight northerly swell, steering west true. W/T Op. Failing slowly, hope to see something soon. 8 a.m. W/T Operator R.N. Pilcher passed peaceably away. Committed his body to the deep with silent prayer.

Another two days went by, then the handwriting in the boat's log changes. Able Seaman Roy Widdecombe had taken over, and the entries were brief and to the point:

> Sept. 3rd, Tuesday. One dipper of water per man at 7 a.m. And again in evening. Things going from bad to worse, 1st Mate, who wrote this diary up to this point, going fast. Good breezes from E.S.E.
>
> Sept. 4th. Everybody very much weaker. The Mate is going fast now. 1.30 p.m. Sunday, Penny very much weaker, slipped overboard. From 10 p.m. Tonight 14 days out, tried to make the Leeward Islands, Porto Rica, Hayti, but the German raider given none the right to take a sextant, chronometer, extra water, tin fruit or bottled fruit, no rum or brandy for wounded crew. Evidently intended to smash all lifeboat gear to kill all inquiry, but we got the small gig, seven of us, by wind somewhere in vicinity of Leeward Islands.

At this point, Widdecombe seems to be drifting into the realms of fantasy; the boat was then nowhere near the Leeward Islands, probably nearly 2,000 miles to the east. The log continues, but with only a single entry on occasional days:

Sept. 5th. Chief Mate and 3rd Engineer go over the side. No water.

Sept. 9th. 2nd Cook goes mad and dies. Two of us left.

Sept. 12th. A cloud burst gave us water for 6 days.

Sept. 20th. Rain again for four days. Getting very weak but trusting in God to pull us through.

Sept. 24th. All water and biscuits gone but still hoping to make land.

With these poignant words the jolly boat's log closes. Only Robert Tapscott and Roy Widdecombe were left alive. They had no food and no water, and no hope left. They lay across the thwarts of the boat and waited for death.

Five weeks later, on 30 October, the *Anglo Saxon's* jolly boat, weather-stained and barnacle-encrusted, was cast ashore on the tiny island of Eleuthera in the Bahamas, having sailed and drifted a total of 2,544 miles in seventy days. Of the seven who had survived the guns of the *Widder*, only the two Welsh ABs Robert Tapscott and Roy Widdecombe remained alive. During the concluding days of their epic voyage they had subsisted on scraps of seaweed and a single flying fish, with only the occasional shower of rain to slake their raging thirst. At one point they were so desperate that they drank the alcohol out of the boat's compass. How they remained sane throughout all those harrowing days without hope is beyond comprehension.

When their boat grounded on the sandy shore of Eleuthera, Tapscott and Widdecombe were so weak and emaciated that they were very near to death. A local beachcomber found them and they were taken to hospital in Nassau, where their lives hung in balance for some weeks. Roy Widdecombe was the first to recover, and in February 1941 he joined the British cargo liner *Siamese Prince* in New York to sail for home. He was destined never to see his native Wales again: on 17 February, when she was only twenty-four hours out of Liverpool, the *Siamese Prince* was torpedoed by a U-boat and sank, taking all on board with her, Roy Widdecombe included.

Robert Tapscott's recovery was more prolonged. It was summer 1941 before he was released from hospital in Nassau. From there, perhaps wishing to hit back at those who had subjected him to such a terrible ordeal, he went to Canada, where he joined the Canadian Army. In 1943 he returned to sea and served throughout the rest of the war, but the horrors of those seventy days spent in an open boat still haunted him. In 1963, then forty-two years old, he took his own life. So died the sole survivor of the forty-one men who manned the *Anglo Saxon*.

The *Widder* sank only two more ships after the ill-fated *Anglo Saxon*, bringing the total for her first sortie into the Atlantic to ten ships of 58,644 tons. This was considered by the German General Staff to be a poor return for the effort required to keep the raider at sea. When she returned to her home port of Brest on 31 October 1940, the *Widder* was withdrawn from active service and became a repair ship for the German Navy in Norway. She was seized by the Royal Navy at the end of the war and sold to Greek owners, ending her days as a world-wide tramp. In 1955 she ran on to rocks near Bergen and was declared a total loss.

After leaving the *Widder*, Helmut von Ruckteschell took command of the commerce raider *Michel*, in which he continued to use the same tactics as he had in the *Widder*, attacking lone ships at night and smothering them with gunfire, with the express purpose of killing or maiming the crew before they had a chance to react. In 1947 von Ruckteschell faced a British Military Court charged with the indiscriminate killing of Allied merchant seamen. He was found guilty and sentenced to ten years in gaol. He died in prison in Hamburg in September 1948, aged fifty-eight.

A sad footnote to this chapter illustrates the appalling treatment meted out to the British merchant seamen of the day by those who should have known better. It was written in 2003 by the adopted son of an unnamed seaman serving in the *Anglo Saxon* when she was sunk:

> When news that the ship was missing became known, my mother's allowance from the shipowners was stopped immediately – apparently the usual practice at that time. After some delay, she was given a temporary payment (presumably by some government department) until the ship's fate was confirmed. This derisory payment consisted of 22 shillings and 6 pence per week (about £1.12 in today's money) and 5 shillings (25 pence) for me. My

grief-stricken mother was ordered to appear, with me, before a committee of 'greybeards' – to be told that my adoption was not considered 'legal enough' (although it had been done through a solicitor) and there would be no allowance at all for me – even worse, she would be required to pay back the temporary allowance of five shillings per week. At some time in all this I learned for the first time that I was adopted. She and my lovely Dad – who had just been killed in the service of his adopted country – had cared for me since I was about 12 days old – and this was the unbelievable treatment handed out by the greybeards. My mother was devastated.

CHAPTER SEVEN

A Tramp Hits Back –
Newton Pine 13.12.40

The 4,212-ton *Newton Pine*, owned by John Ridley, Son & Tully of Newcastle-upon-Tyne, had served the charter market for fifteen years. Her outward cargoes had mostly been coal from South Wales; once in the cross-trades, she carried anything her agents could lay their hands on to any destination required. It had been hard work, often involving heavy bulk cargoes carried over great distances, and inevitably she was showing a few wrinkles. There had never been much time for maintenance, and now her paintwork was visibly cosmetic, covering up years of rust, and her well worn triple-expansion steam engine coughed and spluttered when pushed. Built for 9½ knots, she was more comfortable at a steady 8.

When, on 27 November 1940, the *Newton Pine* sailed out of the River Plate with a cargo of grain from Buenos Aires for Liverpool, the southern summer was at its height. The air was dry and pleasantly warm, the sky overhead a seamless blue. It was a far cry from Newcastle on a cold wet November afternoon, Captain Charles Woolner reflected, as viewed the world from the bridge.

Passing Montevideo harbour and approaching the pilot station at the mouth of the river, the *Newton Pine* was within sight of the half-submerged wreck of the scuttled German pocket battleship *Graf Spee*, a grim but cogent reminder of the world she was returning to. Further north, where the U-boats held sway, ships were going down at the rate of 100 a month. The weeks spent in Buenos Aires, where that war was only a tiny black cloud on the far horizon, had dimmed the memories.

As the wreck of the German warship slid past to starboard, Charles Woolner gave a thought to the *Newton Pine*'s sister ship, the *Newton Beech*, sunk by the *Graf Spee* soon after the outbreak of war. The two ships, both built in Sunderland, had been launched within weeks of each other. Fortunately, none of the *Newton*

Beech's crew had been harmed, and all were later rescued by the Royal Navy when the prison ship *Altmark* was forcibly boarded in Norwegian waters. That, Woolner reflected wryly, was when the war at sea was still a relatively civilised business. Since then, things had gone downhill rapidly.

While the *Newton Pine* had been languishing in Buenos Aires, the Battle of the Atlantic had changed tenor. Gone were the German gentleman sailors who commanded the surface raiders and the early U-boats, to be replaced by the hard men of the *Kriegsmarine*. The war at sea had degenerated into a fight to the death between Dönitz's U-boats and Britain's merchantmen, and a very one-sided fight at that.

As the winter of 1940 drew near, the U-boats, although few in number, perhaps only nine or ten at sea at any one time, were operating from their new bases in the French Biscay ports and could therefore spend considerably longer at sea. The Royal Navy, on the other hand, stretched to its absolute limits, was struggling to provide a credible defence for the increasing number of convoys crossing the Atlantic.

The problem was highlighted by the fate of two convoys in October 1940. Firstly, the slow convoy SC 7, consisting of thirty-five merchantmen carrying some 200,000 tons of food, timber, steel and ore, which set out from Sydney, Nova Scotia on 5 October. The convoy's sole escort was the 14-knot sloop HMS *Scarborough*, armed with a single 4-inch gun and a rack of depth charges. Three days out from Sydney, SC 7 ran into a fierce Atlantic storm, in the midst of which it was attacked by a pack of seven U-boats. Twenty of the thirty-five merchant ships were sunk, and two others suffered serious damage, while 141 men lost their lives.

Following hard on the heels of SC 7 was the fast convoy HX 79, which had sailed from Halifax on the 8th. Comprising forty-nine ships and escorted by two armed merchant cruisers, HX 79 overhauled SC 7 and in doing so sailed right into the arms of the same U-boat pack that had savaged the slow convoy. At this point, the AMCs escorting HX 79 had been ordered to another convoy, leaving HX 79 completely undefended. In response to the attack on SC 7, no fewer than eleven destroyers, corvettes and armed trawlers were racing out from the Western Approaches, but they would arrive too late to save HX 79. Twelve more ships and their precious cargoes were lost, and another 88 merchant seamen found watery graves. In all, the two convoys had lost a total of 32 ships, plus a quarter of a million tons of cargo and 229 men.

The inflicting of such heavy casualties on two convoys by just seven U-boats, none of which were themselves even damaged, was considered by Berlin to be a major victory – which, indeed, it was. The 'Night of the Long Knives', as it became known among the U-boat men, encouraged Admiral Dönitz, who now also had twenty-six Italian submarines based in Bordeaux at his disposal, to try his fortunes further afield. He turned a predatory eye on the West African port of Freetown, where Allied ships bringing cargoes from South America and the Cape were assembling to form convoys for the voyage north. It was time to send his U-boats south.

Having dropped his sea pilot at the mouth of the River Plate, Captain Woolner put the *Newton Pine* on a north-easterly course, and as she lifted easily to the first of the long Atlantic swells, he opened the sealed orders handed to him by the British consul in Buenos Aires. His first reaction to the single typewritten page of instructions was one of resigned disappointment. The Admiralty's orders were explicit: instead of proceeding direct to the North Channel, as he had anticipated, he was to call at Freetown and there join a convoy for the remainder of the passage north. On paper, this would involve no more than an extra half day's steaming at the most, but Woolner feared the *Newton Pine* might well languish for weeks in the West African hell-hole waiting for the convoy to form. This would put paid to the slim hope he and his crew had cherished of a quick passage home, possibly arriving in time for Christmas.

The Admiralty's orders made no mention of any increased threat from U-boats in the North Atlantic but, reading between the lines, this was implied. The *Newton Pine* was well armed for a British merchant ship at that stage of the war, having both a 4-inch anti-submarine gun, and a 12-pounder. However, other than Gunlayer Frederick Morgan, a merchant seaman who had spent time at an Admiralty gunnery school, the guns were manned by ordinary crew members, none of whom had had any serious gunnery training. Woolner had insisted on regular drills while at sea, but at best his men were only amateur gunners. Furthermore, in order for them to have any real effect on the outcome of an attack, the U-boat would have to be on the surface, a most unlikely scenario.

The first two weeks of the passage north from the Plate passed without incident, and in good weather. Then, when the *Newton Pine* was crossing the Equator, a radio message was received from the Admiralty advising Captain Woolner of a U-boat reported to be in his vicinity. Woolner was not unduly perturbed by this warning, but as a precaution he posted extra lookouts and began zig-zagging during daylight hours. The 4-inch gun on the poop was kept manned day and night.

On the afternoon of 13 December the *Newton Pine*, then 2° north of the Equator and 650 miles south-west of Freetown, was trailing her smoke across a flat calm ocean. The ship was quiet, the afternoon siesta was over, and the rattle of cups in the officers' pantry signalled that afternoon tea was on its way.

Chief Officer John Davidson, who was in his cabin preparing to go on watch at 1600, heard a shout from the bridge, and the ship suddenly heeled to port as the helm was put hard over. Davidson ran for the bridge, arriving in the wheelhouse at the same time as Captain Woolner. A breathless Second Officer explained that he had been writing up the log and had gone out on to the starboard wing of the bridge to read the thermometer, when he saw a disturbance in the water about 1,500yds away on the quarter. At first he had thought it was a frolicking porpoise, then he saw a track of bubbles heading straight for the ship and immediately ordered the helm hard to port.

As the *Newton Pine* presented her stern to the danger, the torpedo passed close along her starboard side, clearly visible below the surface. It broke surface two or three times, then when about 1,500yds ahead of the ship it disappeared. Captain Woolner took charge of the bridge, rang for emergency full speed and steadied the ship on a course of 315° to keep her stern-on to the unseen U-boat.

The *Newton Pine* was now in an extremely dangerous situation. Alone on an empty ocean 650 miles from the nearest land, she was being stalked by an invisible enemy, an enemy against which she had very little in the way of defence. Submerged and out of sight, the submarine needed only to bide her time until she was in position to fire another torpedo, while Woolner could do no more than make a run for it, hoping to sight and dodge the missile when it came. Should the U-boat surface, she would have twice the speed of the *Newton Pine* and superior armament manned by highly trained men. In her defence, the British tramp had only her 4-inch, which with the exception of Gunlayer Morgan was in the hands of rank amateurs. The next few hours, until darkness wrapped her cloak around them, would be crucial.

Woolner's next action was to order his wireless operator to send a message to all ships warning of the presence of an enemy submarine in the area. It was while he and Chief Officer Davidson were in the chartroom compiling the message that the ship was rocked by a heavy explosion.

Both men rushed out into the wing of the bridge to see shells bursting in the water astern and a surfaced submarine clearly visible about 4 miles on the port quarter. The 4-inch on the poop was already manned and loaded, and Woolner gave the order to open fire. He then manoeuvred the ship to keep the enemy right astern, thus presenting the smallest possible target. And so the battle began.

Captain Woolner later described the action:

> The first shells from the submarine fell about 1,000 yards short. I think he was on his maximum range and using his speed to overtake us and get on the target, and then turn off slightly to keep at a safe distance, but to hold us in range. The shells from the submarine were gradually creeping up about 50 yards at a time until they were about 50 yards under our stern.
>
> We made 2 or 3 increases of deflection 2 right until I reached 20 right and our shots were falling in line and blotting out the target. The enemy submarine had now got very accurate range, straddling the ship either side of the engine room. The submarine appeared to have twin guns as the shots always came in pairs; I think the guns were mounted on the fore part of the conning tower. When the submarine got close to us he opened up independent firing and I decided to alter course to starboard to try to spoil the enemy's range and deflection. The alteration was made 60° to starboard. I ceased firing, steadied the ship, and opened fire again, lifting the range another 200 and the deflection a further 2 right. The enemy shots now landed over the ship about 50/150 yards off the port bow. Our first shot landed on the target, blotting out the

submarine with smoke and spray. Our next shot again completely blotted out the conning tower, and the submarine ceased firing immediately. The submarine appeared to take a heavy roll and then re-appeared showing only half the conning tower out of the water for several seconds and then disappeared. The man in the crow's nest reported that the submarine re-appeared slightly two or three times, disappeared and was not seen again from the mast-head. Our gun's crew kept closed up and ready for another half hour, after which the tube was extracted, and the gun kept loaded.

We had prepared smoke floats, and immediately after the enemy had disappeared from view a smoke float was dropped over astern to conceal our movements, and when it was well alight, giving a good screen, we set course of 315°, making a detour in that direction as long as the smoke lasted, but the submarine never re-appeared. It was a very clear moonlit night, but I am perfectly confident the submarine had gone.

Altogether we fired 22 rounds at the submarine and the action lasted thirty minutes. I am convinced that we hit the submarine with two shells, the first on the waterline or slightly below, bursting his side tank, and the second one hit in the vicinity of the gun and the ammunition hatch filled with the roll of the submarine.

On a lighter note, Woolner added:

During the action the Donkeyman [senior engine room rating] went along the deck and saw the Cook on his hands and knees beside a white pail under cover of the A/A gun screen. He was handing cups of tea to the men on the gun platform. Suddenly the Cook crawled away and the Donkeyman followed him to see what was the matter. The cook rushed to the galley, opened the oven door, and then said, 'Thank God, the bread's alright for tomorrow.'

I should like to speak very highly of the whole crew; they are very enthusiastic and efficient, and the discipline was very good. The gun's crew used their knowledge of gun drill exercised during the voyage to very good effect.

Thanks to the refusal of Captain Woolner and his dedicated crew to surrender to the guns of a vastly superior enemy, the *Newton Pine* reached Freetown safely on 16 December. There she lay at anchor for six days while other ships came in from the south and south-west to form Convoy SLS 60, which finally set off for the north on 22 December.

SLS 60 was made up of eleven merchant ships sailing completely unescorted. Ahead of them lay a voyage of 2,969 miles, nineteen days steaming at the convoy's speed of 6½ knots, much of it through areas not yet threatened by U-boats perhaps, but an extremely hazardous undertaking nevertheless.

The voyage did not begin well, for within hours of sailing from Freetown the tanker *British Premium*, carrying 8,000 tons of crude oil from Abadan, was straggling astern with engine problems. She was out of sight of the convoy when, on the afternoon of Christmas Eve, she was found by U-65 and sunk with two torpedoes. Thirty-two of the tanker's crew died with her.

The identity of the submarine the *Newton Pine* crossed swords with is to this day in doubt, but it seems most likely that it was U-65. The Admiralty thought likewise, basing their premise on an entry in U-65's log which read as follows:

13 December 1940: Steamer in sight. Moved forward. Steamer turns 45 dgs cutting across shortly before torpedo, target missed. Attempted torpedo from shallow angle. Steamer appeared to spot torpedo as it turns suddenly in order to use side guns. Surfaced for artillery engagement as I suppose that steamer was broadcasting. Fired approx. 30 times. 2, possibly 3, hits. Steamer moves slowly when hits approach 100m. Turns away, stops firing. Observation of hits too unsafe. Steamer is broadcasting with directional transmitter but we can pick it up. Freetown repeats SOS on all wavelengths then transmits a 4 digit coded FT report of 7 groups. During the night lively bustle. The FTs were partly repeated on 600m by Ascension. SOS was transmitted about ten times. *Newton Pine* uses smoke screen and despite energetic attempts disappears from sight.

U-65, a Type IXB long-range boat, commissioned in Bremen in February 1940 by Kapitänleutnant Hans-Gerrit von Stockhausen, had sailed from Lorient on 15 October and was the only Axis submarine confirmed as being in the Freetown area at the time of the attack on the *Newton Pine*. She had been ordered south by Admiral Dönitz to 'test the waters' before other U-boats were sent to harass northbound convoys.

Von Stockhausen had been a month at sea and was near the Equator when he found his first target on 15 November. She was the Asiatic Steamship Company's 5,618-ton *Kohinur*, bound from the Bristol Channel to Alexandria with military stores. One torpedo fired from periscope depth was sufficient to sink her. A few hours later, U-65 torpedoed the Norwegian tanker *Havbør* which, coincidentally, was engaged in picking up survivors from the *Kohinur*. The tanker caught fire, and twenty-eight of her crew perished, along with thirty-one survivors from the *Kohinur* who died when the oil on the water caught fire.

U-65 went on to sink five more Allied merchantmen, bringing giving her total score under the command of Hans-Gerrit von Stockhausen to twelve ships sunk of 66,764 tons. On 10 January 1941 she returned to Lorient, where von Stockhausen was promoted to Korvettenkapitän and awarded the Knight's Cross of the Iron Cross. After a three-month-long refit in Lorient, she sailed again in April 1941 with Kapitänleutnant Joachim Hoppe in command. On 28 April she was depth-charged and sunk off Iceland by the destroyer HMS *Douglas*.

These subsequent events proved beyond doubt that the Admiralty's conclusions regarding the identity of the attacker claimed to have been sunk by the *Newton Pine* were wrong. However, so convinced were they of the integrity of Captain Woolner's report that they took the unprecedented step of awarding prize money to a merchant ship. The sum awarded to Woolner and his crew was not disclosed, but it will have been substantial.

It is interesting to note that in his report to the Admiralty Captain Woolner said, 'I think the submarine was an Italian of the BALILIA class. It had a very long conning tower, with a square cut fore part, and two guns mounted at its forward base.' At that time, of the twenty-six Italian submarines based in Bordeaux under the control of Admiral Dönitz, the only one known to be operating in the Atlantic was the *Comandante Faà di Bruno*. She was similar in size and appearance to U-65, except that she had a noticeably long conning tower, forward of which were mounted two 100mm (3.9″) guns.

The *Comandante Faà di Bruno* sailed from Bordeaux on 31 October 1940 with orders to patrol the Allied convoy lanes to the south of Iceland. An article written after the war by the retired Admiral Attilio Duilio Ranieri of *Regia Marina Italiana* throws some light on her fate:

> On the 31st October, 1940, the FAA DI BRUNO departed for its first, and unfortunately only mission in the Atlantic, patrolling west of Scotland. It was assigned the zone between 57° 20′ N and 58° 20′ W, west of the meridian 20° west. It should have re-entered on the 5th January 1941.
>
> After the departure all contacts with the boat were lost. The causes of its loss are still unknown. The enemy could have sunk it, but it could also have succumbed to a breakdown, possibly due to the rough sea, which in that season plagues the North Atlantic; or due to an internal fault, such as the explosion of hydrogen gas from the batteries. We do not even know if the boat ever reached the assigned patrol area.
>
> Based on British documentation, in the post-war period it was possible to attribute the sinking of the FAA DI BRUNO to the British destroyer HMS HAVELOCK, which reported having attacked, on November 8th in position 56° 01′ N, 17° 50′ W, a submerged submarine and having seen broken off pieces, air bubbles and fuel emerge.
>
> Later, and considering the events reported by the HAVELOCK had happened in a zone very distant from that which the FAA DI BRUNO would have crossed, a more accurate study of the positions and the events indicated that the boat attacked by the British vessel was the Smg. MARCONI. From this attack the MARCONI escaped almost unharmed.
>
> Therefore, it is not even possible to define when this boat was lost and we have to conceal its loss under the generic and bureaucratic label 'lost on an undefined date between October 31st 1940 and January 5 1941'.

The *Faà di Bruno* was also claimed by the two destroyers HMCS *Ottawa* and HMS *Harvester*, who reported that they had sunk her in a joint action 250 miles west of Fastnet on 6 November 1940. This claim further confuses the *Newton Pine* story, and makes Captain Woolner's description of the submarine he fought a gun duel with all the more puzzling. Could it be that the *Faà di Bruno* had strayed so far from her assigned patrol area? If so, then what of U-65's log entry which named the *Newton Pine*?

In 1941 the *Newton Pine* was sold to the Graig Shipping Company of Cardiff, and despite all the efforts of the U-boats, German and Italian, to put an end to her activities, she continued to ferry cargoes across the Atlantic. She appeared to be unsinkable, until on 3 October 1942 she sailed from Loch Ewe with Convoy ONS 136, westbound to Halifax, Nova Scotia in ballast.

When about 250 miles south of Iceland, ONS 136 ran into a storm of such intensity that its ships, battling against hurricane force winds, mountainous seas and squalls of rain, were soon in total disarray, several straggling astern out of sight. One of them was the *Newton Pine*, then under the command of Captain Evan Owen Thomas.

Alone and struggling to even make steerage way, the ageing tramp was sighted by U-410, commanded by Kapitänleutnant Kurt Sturm. At 1025 on the 15th Sturm fired one torpedo which missed; but his second torpedo, fired five minutes later, went home in the *Newton Pine*'s after hold which, being empty, soon filled, dragging her under within a few minutes.

Miraculously, in view of the weather, two lifeboats got away from the sinking ship with twenty or thirty survivors on board. Sturm claimed to have brought the boats alongside U-410 and interrogated the survivors, which given the weather at the time seems unlikely. Whatever happened, the *Newton Pine*'s boats were never seen again, presumably capsized and sunk by the heavy seas. Captain Thomas, thirty-nine crew and seven DEMS gunners were lost.

Captain Charles Woolner, who died in 1984 aged 96, remained fully convinced that his gunners had sunk an enemy submarine, which he identified as being Italian. His claim was authenticated by the Admiralty's award of prize money. But which submarine really fought the gun duel with the *Newton Pine*? The entry in U-65's log confirms that she had been involved in a fight with a British merchant ship, which von Stockhausen named as the *Newton Pine*, but U-65 was certainly not sunk, nor was there any official report of serious damage, although she did spend an unusually long time in Lorient after the patrol in question. As to the *Comandante Faà di Bruno*, an article written for the Canadian magazine *Northern Mariner* in 1991 by Fraser M. McKee does throw some light on her fate:

> The Italian Navy at first ascribed her loss as 'unknown', but in immediate postwar assessments, Roskill credited her loss to HMS *Havelock* on 8 November. But for that to be correct, the boat would have been one hundred miles off track, and at any rate she had been missing for quite some time prior to that date. On 6 November the merchantman *Melrose Abbey* was attacked on the surface by a submarine's gunfire, called for help, and *Ottawa* and *Harvester* arrived shortly thereafter. They fired on the still surfaced U-boat, *Ottawa* getting away five salvoes before the target dived. After a short hunt, a target was located, and *Ottawa* made four attacks with twenty-one depth charges. Underwater explosions were heard, and some oil came to the surface, but no identifiable debris. And in those days of too few escorts, the attacking destroyers could not afford to wait for more certain material to surface. Their attack, it turns out, was almost exactly on the dead reckoning course for the *Faà di Bruno*'s patrol area. But the hard-nosed Admiralty Assessment Committee at that time had felt that there was 'insufficient evidence to credit a destruction'. *Havelock*'s later attacks, they judged, were the more likely, and at first she got the credit. But a search of postwar Italian records soon showed that *Havelock* had attacked the Italian *Marconi*, which although somewhat damaged reached home and recorded the exact time and date of that attack.

CHAPTER EIGHT

Return to War – *Otaio* 28.08.41

In the summer of 1940 the future of Britain as a free nation hung in the balance. All continental Europe lay under the heel of the German dictator and his allies, and only Perfidious Albion remained defiantly unconquered. But her wounds were many and deep. The cream of her Army, the British Expeditionary Force, some 394,000 strong, sent to stem the German advance, had escaped from the beaches of Dunkirk, rescued by the Royal Navy and a bizarre collection of small boats cobbled together at the last moment. More than 300,000 men had returned, but they were demoralized and without much of their arms and equipment.

Massed on the other side of the Channel were 130 German divisions, ten of them armoured, backed by 3,000 bombers and 1,500 fighters of the Luftwaffe, while hundreds of barges and landing craft were waiting in French ports within easy reach of Britain's southern coast.

Only one last obstacle remained to be overcome before Hitler gave the word for Operation Seelöwe ('Sealion') to be launched – supremacy in the air must first be established. And as the Luftwaffe outnumbered the RAF by two to one, this seemed achievable. On 31 July, in a conversation with Admiral Raeder, Hitler was reported as saying, 'If after eight days of intensive air war the Luftwaffe has not achieved considerable destruction of the enemy's Air Force, harbours and naval forces, the operation will have to be put off until May 1941.' The Führer's worst fears were realized, and the Battle of Britain is inscribed forever in history as a decisive victory for the few of the RAF.

As the end of the summer of 1940 drew near, and Hitler realized that his plans for invasion were going badly wrong, he turned his wrath on Britain's cities and their infrastructure. The 'Blitz' began on 7 September, its initial target being London's East End and its busy docklands.

Saturday, 7 September 1940, a fine, warm day, was drawing to a close as the Luftwaffe opened Operation Loge ('Lodge'), designed to cripple London's docks. In the Royal Group of docks work had finished for the day, hatches were being covered and dock workers were streaming out of the gates, when the sirens set up their mournful wail. They signalled the start of the first mass daylight raid of the war: 250 German bombers, with a large fighter escort, had penetrated the RAF's defensive ring, and the sky over London reverberated to the drone of unsynchronized engines.

The bombs rained down without let-up, right through until the early hours of the 8th. More than 400 civilians died that night, and another 1,600 were seriously injured. The docklands took the brunt of the attack, and fires raged amongst the wharves and warehouse from Tower Bridge to Woolwich. The bombers came back on two further consecutive nights for more of the same. In all, 21,000 tons of shipping was sunk and eighteen ships totalling 83,336 tons were damaged and put out of action for many months. And this was at a time when Britain's very survival depended on her merchant shipping.

Among the ships damaged in the London Blitz was New Zealand Shipping Company's 10,298-ton refrigerated motor vessel *Otaio*. Built by Vickers-Armstrong at Barrow-in-Furness in 1930, the *Otaio* was a smart, twin-screw ship on a regular run carrying general cargo out to Australia and New Zealand, returning with frozen meat. Badly damaged by bombs, her next move was into the repair yard. A ship of her calibre would be sorely missed.

In fact, it was not until August 1941, eleven months later, that the *Otaio* was back at sea again, her scars healed and her holds crammed with general cargo and military stores, along with a sizeable quantity of mail for Australia. In command was 41-year-old Captain Gilbert Kinnel, who carried with him a British crew of seventy. The *Otaio* sailed from Liverpool on the morning of 23 August 1941, dropped her pilot at the Bar light vessel around noon, and before nightfall she joined Convoy OS 4, which was then forming up in the North Channel. It was a lengthy rendezvous, with ships arriving not only from the Mersey but also from Milford Haven, the Clyde and East Coast ports.

When complete, OS 4 comprised thirty-five merchantmen sailing in eight columns abreast, escorted by six destroyers, four sloops, an AA ship and a special service vessel which carried two reconnaissance seaplanes. A rescue ship was also in attendance. The convoy made an impressive sight in the gathering dusk, its forest of funnels trailing smoke from horizon to horizon. The unusually strong escort was deemed necessary now that Dönitz's U-boats were well established in their new bases in the Biscay ports. Being so much closer to the convoy routes, they were exacting a very heavy toll on Allied shipping.

OS 4 would follow the usual itinerary, dispersing off Freetown when it was considered the risk from U-boats was minimal. Before that, once it was considered safe to do so, a number of ships with destinations on the other side of the Atlantic would detach to go their own separate ways; the *Otaio* being one such. Her first port of discharge was Melbourne, to which she was routed via Curaçao and the Panama Canal. A long haul lay ahead of her, a minimum of six weeks at sea, but with the United States of America still neutral, she had the consolation that for much of the time she would be in waters not yet penetrated by the U-boats. In the event that she was unfortunate enough to encounter one of the German commerce raiders said to be lurking in southern waters, she was considered capable of giving a good account of herself. Powered by two Doxford diesels giving 1,884 nominal h.p., she had a service speed of 16 knots, with a few more knots in reserve, and could probably outrun any adversary. Furthermore, she carried a 4-inch and a 12-pounder, both mounted aft, enough armament to give her a fair chance in a running fight.

It may well have been summer in the North Atlantic, but the weather was not in a summer mood. As soon as the convoy left the shelter of the North Channel it ran straight into a roaring Force 9 westerly, with mountainous seas and blinding rain squalls. The deep-laden merchantmen were soon in trouble, plunging head-on into the crested Atlantic rollers. The convoy speed, which had been set at 7½ knots, dropped to a mere crawl.

OS 4 was not alone in this turbulent Atlantic wasteland. Not many miles over the horizon to the north-west were three inward bound convoys, so bunched up together by the prevailing weather that they were all but merging into one huge armada. Suddenly the sea between Iceland and the west coast of Ireland was therefore awash with choice, slow-moving targets, and Admiral Dönitz was quick to take advantage.

Homing in on the eastbound convoys was a pack of eight U-boats, led U-557, commanded by 26-year-old Ottokar Paulssen. Wedged in the conning tower of U-557, with rain and spray streaming from his oilskins, Oberleutnant Paulssen was on his second war patrol in command, and with only one ship sunk to show for his efforts he was beginning to lose heart – and this horrendous weather could be the straw that broke the camel's back.

The voyage had begun to go wrong at an early stage. Sailing from Lorient on 13 August, U-557 had been only twenty-four hours at sea when engine problems had forced her to return to port. She sailed again five days later, and had been battling the elements ever since. Herbert Werner, one of U-557's watch officers, wrote after the war:

> As we approached the northern region the sea rose higher: cold spray and foam and a slashing wind mauled me during my watch on the bridge. Visibility quickly dropped from 16 miles to 4. The typical North Atlantic weather caught up with us once again. U-557 beat the waves head-on and listed strongly in the long breakers as the chase went into its second day.
>
> Alarrrmmm! It was exactly 1730.
>
> The boat tilted immediately and submerged fast. Paulssen, racing into the control room, called into the tower, 'Exec, what's the matter up there?'
>
> Kern [First Watch Officer Oberleutnant Kern] replied through frozen lips, 'Destroyer bearing thirty, distance four thousand metres.'
>
> As soon as the Chief had the boat under control, the soundman reported that high-pitched propellers were slowly disappearing; we had not been detected. The operator made another discovery: 'Wide sound-band port ahead. Must be a convoy.'
>
> We had run into the starboard flank of an unreported convoy. Paulssen ordered the crew on battle stations and the boat on periscope depth. The scope revealed nothing, so the Captain brought us to the surface.
>
> As soon as the tower was clear, we rushed through the cascading waves onto the platform. Visibility was only two miles. A thick layer of clouds hung just above the boiling sea. We immediately pushed after the source of the sound band. Forty minutes later we again sighted an escort and quickly outmanoeuvred her. The sea, rolling

from west to east, drove us violently ahead as huge, long waves lifted our boat at her stern and carried her forward high on their crests.

Quite by chance, Paulssen had stumbled on OS 4. He immediately reported the convoy to Lorient, who then ordered him to shadow it while the other U-boats were called in.

On the bridge of the *Otaio*, bracing himself against the shock-like motion of the ship as she met the Atlantic rollers bow-on, Captain Gilbert Kinnel silently cursed the powers that condemned him to stay with this rapidly disintegrating convoy. Allowed to go her own way, the *Otaio* would by now have been well to the south, and probably in much more comfortable weather. However, Kinnel grudgingly accepted that, for the time being at least, he was better off under the protection of OS 4's destroyers and sloops. Meanwhile, with the convoy barely making 5 knots in the gale, it would still be some time before the magic 20° West was reached and the threat of the U-boats diminished. Kinnel looked forward to the parting of the ways. At that time, no one in the convoy was aware that they were being shadowed by U-557, with seven others of Dönitz's hastily gathered together pack rapidly homing in on Paulssen's signals.

Captain Kinnel wrote in his report:

> We proceeded without incident until about midnight on the 25th/26th, when we heard depth charges exploding. The weather at the time was bad and misty. In the morning we noticed that several ships were missing but at the time we did not know whether they had straggled or not.

The commotion Kinnel had heard during the night had been OS 4's escorting ships hunting U-557 after she had carried out an opportunistic and highly successful attack. Approaching the convoy unseen shortly after midnight, Paulssen had fired a spread of four torpedoes at the jumbled mass of shipping.

U-557's first torpedo went home with devastating effect in the hull of the 4,414-ton Norwegian motor vessel *Segundo*. Sailing in ballast for Curaçao, the *Segundo*'s empty No. 2 hold was blown wide open to the sea, and she sank in just seven minutes. Seven men went down with her, the remaining twenty-seven of her crew being snatched from the raging sea by the sloop HMS *Lulworth*.

Two of Paulssen's torpedoes, knocked off course by the severe weather, missed completely, but the fourth found another target. She was the 6,303-ton British steamer *Saugor*, owned by James Nourse of London and bound Calcutta with a cargo of general, including twenty-eight aircraft for the RAF. She also went down with a rush, fifty-nine of her crew of eighty-two being lost. The remaining twenty-three were picked up by the rescue ship *Perth*.

Having emptied his bow tubes, Paulssen retired to reload, returning to the attack an hour later. His target then was Hain Line's 4,736-ton steamer *Tremoda*, bound for the Cameroons in the Gulf of Guinea. She did not sink at once, but was so badly damaged that she was abandoned by her crew, twenty-one of whom were picked up by the Free French sloop *Chevreuil*.

U-557, then still the only one of the pack to have located the convoy, came back for more at 0230 on the 27th, sending to the bottom Hall Brothers' 4,954-ton *Embassage*, along with her cargo of military equipment destined for West Africa. Only three of her crew of forty-two survived.

In just two hours of that storm-racked night Ottokar Paulssen had outwitted all the frantic efforts of OS 4's considerable escort force and had released all his pent-up frustration by inflicting serious damage on the convoy. Four ships and 20,000 tons of cargo, much of it military equipment and stores, had been consigned to the deep, and 136 men and one woman, the wife of the Chief Officer of the *Segundo*, had lost their lives.

Paulssen reflected in later life:

> During those moments between life and death, I pictured the seamen on their doomed vessels – riding the huge waves holding on to life rafts. I felt sorry for those courageous men who had to suffer and go down with their ship; it was a terrible ending of a hopeless struggle. I could understand why the British seamen persisted; they were fighting for the very existence of their country. But I was bewildered by the stubbornness of the captains and crews from foreign lands. Why did they continue sailing for the British, defying our torpedoes and the growing ferocity of the battles?

The daylight hours of the 27th were relatively quiet, except for the arrival overhead of one of the Luftwaffe's Focke-Wulf Kondors. The big four-engined reconnaissance bomber circled menacingly out of range of the convoy's guns for a while, but did not attempt to attack. All the time, the plane's wireless operator was signalling an accurate position of the convoy to the searching U-boats.

When darkness closed in again, the weather still had not relented, and with ships finding it impossible to keep station, the convoy was now scattered over many miles of the ocean. Captain Kinnel of the *Otaio* commented, 'Even the Commodore ship was not in station, and we had to alter course to get out of his way.'

By early afternoon on the 28th the weather was at last showing signs of moderating, and some semblance of order was being restored to the convoy, which was back up to 7½ knots. Although there remained more than 100 miles to steam before the limit of 20° W was reached, at this point the Commodore decided that the time had come for those ships not continuing on to Freetown to go their own separate ways. The signal to disperse was hoisted.

No one was more relieved than Captain Kinnel to see the flags breaking out from the Commodore's yardarm. He immediately began to increase speed and altered course to the south-west. Two other ships, the *Fresno Star*, bound for Buenos Aires, and the tanker *Donnacilla*, also for Curaçao, followed suit. Unfortunately, as the *Otaio* drew away from the other ships she unwittingly ran into the path of U-558 which, alerted by Lorient, was searching for the convoy.

U-558, another Type VIIC, commissioned in Hamburg seven months earlier, was on her third war patrol and had yet to put her torpedoes to good use. In command was 27-year-old Kapitänleutnant Günther Krech, who had been with her since she first sailed down the Elbe. Although he had joined the *Kriegsmarine* in 1933, Krech did not have a great deal of experience in submarines. After three years in surface ships, attaining the rank of Leutnant zur See in October 1936, he had been seconded to the staff of the Luftwaffe, returning to the *Kriegsmarine* to begin his U-boat training on the outbreak of war. There followed a year as First Watch Officer with Joachim Schepke in U-100, graduating to command when he commissioned U-558. Her first two war patrols in the Atlantic had yielded no dividends. When the deep-loaded 10,000-tonner, sailing alone and unescorted, hove in sight, Krech approached cautiously, intent on his first kill.

Captain Kinnel, greatly relieved at being released from the strictures of the convoy, was anxious to put as much distance between himself and the other ships as soon as possible. However, in view of the weather prevailing, he was careful not to increase speed too quickly and risk damage to the ship. Calling for ten revolutions at a time, he brought the *Otaio* up to 12¼ knots, at which speed she seemed to ride the seas fairly comfortably. Lookouts had been posted at every vantage point around the ship, eleven men in all, but not one of them saw Krech's torpedoes coming.

Captain Kinnel's report states:

> I was just going into the chartroom when at 1440 GMT (28th) in position 52° 16' N 17° 50' W the ship was struck by a torpedo on the port side abreast of No. 5 hold, about 430 ft from the stem, followed about 7 to 8 seconds later by a second torpedo in the engine room on the port side, below No. 4 boat, about 300 ft from the stem. The sea at the time was rough with a heavy westerly swell, wind was WNW force 6–7, weather was cloudy with occasional squalls and visibility was only moderately good. We were making a speed of approx. 12¼ knots on course 225°.
>
> The first explosion sounded muffled but the second explosion was more of a crack. A large column of water was thrown up, and we later found No. 4 boat full of water. No flash was seen except by one of the engineers who escaped from the engine room. He stated that he saw a flash in the engine room and that a fire was started immediately. This engineer was slightly burned. He happened to be on the top platform of the engine room when the ship was struck. There was a nasty smell, which I was unable to localise: it may have been from our cargo.

The engineer referred to by Captain Kinnel was probably the *Otaio*'s Sixth Engineer, who had been working on the top platform when the torpedo exploded below him. So quickly did the engine room flood that he found himself swimming for his life. The others on watch below had no escape. Third Engineer David Watson, Ninth Engineer Lachlan Ferguson and the two greasers, Thomas Borlase and Walter Francis, all lost their lives.

When Krech's second torpedo hit and the sea poured into the engine room, the *Otaio* took a very heavy list to port. The port engine had been completely destroyed, and with the starboard engine still going ahead, the ship swung round on to an easterly heading. The wind and sea, then being on the starboard side, exacerbated the list, so that the doomed ship went over almost on to her beam ends. To add to the catastrophe, all power failed, and the ship was plunged into total darkness. The wireless room, located at the after end of the bridge, had been completely wrecked, but it was possible to get away an SOS with the emergency transmitter. Distress rockets were also fired from the bridge.

The plight of the *Otaio* was now so dire that Captain Kinnel could no longer hope to save her; and even though he realized that, with the ship listing so heavily and seas mountainous, abandoning her would be no easy operation, he gave the dreaded final order.

Things went wrong right from the start. When the after starboard boat was being lowered with two men in it, the Carpenter, who was working the gravity brake, let it go at a run. The boat hit the water and was immediately lifted high by a wave, unhooking the forward fall. It was hanging upended when the next wave lifted it again, unhooking the after fall. The boat and its two terrified occupants drifted away into the teeth of the storm.

Captain Kinnel described the next sequence of events:

> I went over to the port side of the boat deck and saw No. 2 forward port boat safely out and lowered into the water. This boat remained alongside with a good many men in it, some more descended the ladder and completed the complement. I then went to No. 4 after port boat. The explosion had smashed the port accommodation ladder and the railings above it, and while in the process of lowering No. 4 boat the ship rolled and the steel gallows of the gangway swung out, catching the inboard bilge of this boat and causing it to trip. Some of the men managed to scramble back on board but others were tipped into the water as the heavy swell lifted the boat and unhooked one of the falls and the boat capsized. (I did not actually see this accident as I was attending to the rafts at the time.) The forward port raft was safely launched with the Chief Officer and a member of the crew on it, but the after port raft had been smashed by the explosion at No. 5 hold.

> The Chief Officer should have been in charge of No. 2
> boat but the Chief Engineer took charge of the boat in his
> absence. The two starboard rafts could not be released
> as they had become jammed, no doubt due to the rough
> weather we had experienced during the last two days.

When he had seen everyone who was still alive clear of the ship,
only then did Kinnel look to his own safety. One lifeboat was still
alongside the ship, and he was able to board it by sliding down
one of the lifelines. When the boat cast off, Kinnel looked back at
his ship to see that she was settling rapidly by the stern, her after
well deck already awash.

Fortunately for the survivors, the *Otaio*'s SOS had been picked
up by the escorts of OS 4, and HMS *Vanoc* came looking for them.
When they were aboard the destroyer, a count was made which
revealed that of the *Otaio*'s crew of seventy-one thirteen were
missing. Four were known to have died in the engine room, the
others being lost when abandoning ship. The *Otaio* was seen to
sink later that afternoon.

CHAPTER NINE

Beyond Capricorn –
Kirkpool 10.04.42

The great white bird had been following them for days, skimming the tops of the long South Atlantic rollers with only the occasional lazy flap of its outstretched wings to keep it aloft. There were some on board the *Kirkpool* who said it was the curse of the Ancient Mariner; those who had been here before smiled knowingly and pointed to the galley boy emptying the slop bucket over the side. Like all God's creatures, the albatross followed the food.

While all attention was focused on the planing albatross, no one noticed the other stalker. Far out on the starboard quarter, hulldown on the horizon, the German commerce raider *Thor* was also following in the wake of the unsuspecting merchantman.

The 4,842-ton British tramp *Kirkpool,* one of Sir Robert Ropner's out of West Hartlepool, was on the second leg of what was promising to be a very long voyage. It had begun nearly three months earlier in late January 1942, when the *Kirkpool* sailed from the River Tyne in ballast. She was bound around the Cape for Lourenço Marques in Portuguese East Africa, chartered to bring home a cargo of iron ore. For 32-year-old Captain Albert Kennington and his crew the voyage would make a pleasant change from their usual routine, which involved crossing the U-boat-infested North Atlantic to the Americas.

Sailing from the Tyne on a miserable January morning, the *Kirkpool* rounded the north of Scotland and joined the queue of ships anchored in the sheltered harbour of Oban to await orders. Her stay in the port was not enjoyable, for the winter of 1941/1942 in Scotland was one of the worst on record, with freezing temperatures and heavy snowfalls. It was therefore with no regrets that on 12 February 1942 the *Kirkpool* weighed anchor and left Oban astern. Some eight hours later, off a mist-shrouded coast of Ireland, she made a rendezvous with Convoy OS 19, which had left Liverpool twenty-four hours earlier.

When fully assembled, OS 19 consisted of thirty-six merchant-men, most of whom were bound around the Cape to the Far or Middle East. The presence of the convoy's escorts, the armed board-ing vessels HMS *Hilary* and HMS *Marsdale*, was far from reassuring. These two ex-passenger ships, each armed with a brace of 6-inch guns, put on a brave face as they fussed around the vulnerable merchantmen, but as neither was capable of speeds in excess of 14 knots, they were unlikely to be of much help in the face of an attack by a U-boat pack – or for that matter, a German commerce raider. In either event, it would be very much every ship to her own defence. To this end, the *Kirkpool* carried a 4-inch gun on her poop and several machine-guns on the bridge, with three depth charges mounted on a rack aft. However, the wisdom of launching the latter from a ship with a top speed of around 10 knots was questionable.

As might be expected at the time of the year, the weather in the North Atlantic ranged from indifferent to downright hostile, and the 3,000-mile passage to Freetown dragged out into a third week. Finally, on 3 March, when abreast of the West African port, the *Kirkpool* was free to break away and continue unescorted to the Cape. No one was more relieved than Captain Kennington, who like all merchant ships' captains found sailing in convoy irksome and unnecessary. Furthermore, the sky was now blue, the sun was pleasantly warm and the likelihood of meeting the enemy was receding in to the distance

All went well for much of the passage southward. Then, a few days north of Cape Town, the war suddenly caught up with the *Kirkpool* again. Late in the afternoon, the lookout at the masthead, idly scanning the empty horizon, was brought wide awake by a periscope breaking the surface on the bow. The periscope was followed by a conning tower streaming water as a submarine emerged like some monster from the deep.

Captain Kennington, called to the bridge, ordered the 4-inch to be manned, but by the time the gunners had loaded and trained the gun, the U-boat had dived, leaving only a patch of disturbed water behind her. Kennington decided that this was the ideal time to put his three depth charges to good use, and rang for more speed. Not being equipped with Asdic, he used his echo sounder to try to seek out the submerged submarine, but being primarily designed to record only the depth of the sea bottom, the instrument was of no assistance. The *Kirkpool*'s depth charges remained in their rack.

Darkness was already setting in, and to confuse the U-boat, Kennington turned under full helm and steamed north for a couple of hours, before resuming course again. Either his ruse worked, or the unidentified U-boat commander had been as surprised by his chance meeting with the merchantman as Kennington was. The *Kirkpool* carried on unmolested, the question of whether the depth charges might blow her stern off still unanswered.

Cape Town was reached on 16 March, the *Kirkpool* anchoring in Table Bay, where to everyone's surprise a change of orders was received. The ore cargo in Lourenço Marques had been cancelled, and she was instructed to proceed to Durban and load a full cargo of coal for Montevideo. The news was not well received on board, for it meant that the relatively short voyage they had all been looking forward to, returning home for the summer, was no longer an option. Also, the prospect of loading coal, with all the filth it involved, was hardly welcome news. However, it was agreed that a run to South America, land of the non-stop fiesta, might be well worth the inconvenience.

Arriving in Durban on 24 March, the *Kirkpool* berthed under the coal hoists at the Bluff, which were suitably isolated from the main port, and there endured the indignity of having coal by the wagonload tipped into her holds from a great height. For much of the following week she was hidden from view by a cloud of black dust, which lay thick on her decks and penetrated every nook and cranny of the tightly sealed accommodation. Even the food served in the saloon and messrooms tasted gritty.

It was with no regrets that, on 31 March, the *Kirkpool* finally left Durban, sagging under the weight of some 10,000 tons of South African coal. Covered in a thick layer of black dust, she was a ship without pride. Even her ensign at the stern hung limp and ashamed, but once clear of the breakwaters, powerful jets of water soon washed away her shame. By the time the sun went down, the *Kirkpool*'s paintwork was once again pristine, and her accommodation, thrown open to the cleansing breeze, was habitable. Captain Kennington set his course close to the land to take advantage of the west-flowing Agulhas Current, and the heavily laden ship was soon reaching speeds she had not seen since her trials fourteen years earlier. It was autumn in these southern waters, and the blue skies and gentle breeze complemented the *Kirkpool*'s mood of emancipation as she sped west to the Cape and into the South Atlantic. Many years later, Able Seaman Alfred Round wrote:

Some were worried as these waters were notorious for German surface raiders. But the days passed and our fears were unfounded, and no one could have wished for a more beautiful style of life. The hours passed and everything went like clockwork, as shipboard life usually does. We performed our watches and other duties, ate, slept and played cards. During the day we splashed around in our homemade swim pool, whilst tanned bodies lay spread-eagled on the hatch tops soaking up the sun and flying fish flew off and away from the bows. Indeed, this voyage was nothing less than a millionaire's cruise and we joked with each other, 'To think that we were being paid for it!' Here we were six thousand miles from England a little speck on the bluest ocean, and it looked as though we would make it safely as we were already half way across sailing in calm seas, and we sat with our mugs and talked about the River Plate which was now only a thousand miles away.

While Round and his shipmates yarned on the hatch tops, they were completely unaware that their friendly albatross was not their only follower. From a discreet distance, the *Kirkpool* was being observed through binoculars by Kapitän zur See Günther Gumprich from the bridge of the German auxiliary cruiser *Thor*.

The 3,862-ton *Thor* had started life in the Hamburg shipyard of Deutsche Werft as the cargo/passenger liner *Santa Cruz* of the Oldenburg Portuguese Line, built to trade between European ports and Spain and Portugal, with occasional calls at Madeira and the Canaries. She was still in her fitting-out berth when war broke out in the autumn of 1939 and was summarily requisitioned by the German Navy, then converted for service as a commerce raider. Armed with six 5.9-inch guns, a variety of smaller calibre guns, four torpedo tubes and an Arado Ar 196 seaplane, she was manned by a naval crew of 349. The spotter plane was hidden in a hangar on deck, and all the guns were concealed behind shutters that could be raised at the touch of a switch. To all outwards appearances the *Thor* was an innocent merchantman sailing under whatever neutral flag and colours Gumprich might choose. Her real role was to wreak havoc amongst Allied shipping, preying primarily on merchant ships sailing alone, and at this she was an immediate success. Under the command of Kapitän zur See Otto Kähler, on her first war patrol, which lasted eleven months, she disposed of twelve Allied merchantmen totalling 96,547 tons gross. She also challenged and sank the British armed merchant cruiser *Voltaire.*

Thor's success continued when, commanded by Günther Gumprich, she set out on her second patrol in November 1941. On her way south she was twice stopped by British cruisers, but each time Gumprich succeeded in passing his ship off as a harmless cargo carrier. On 23 March she found and sank her first victim, the Greek-flag *Pagasitikos* of 3,490 tons gross. A week later, when 500 miles south of St Helena, Gumprich used his Arado to intercept the British ship *Wellpark*, which he then sank. Twenty-four hours later, the Arado found another British ship, the 4,565-ton *Willesden*. *Thor* opened fire with her 5.9s as soon as she came in sight of the *Willesden*, setting fire to drums of oil she carried on deck. Some of her crew abandoned ship right away, others stayed and attempted to fight back with their 4-inch, but the gun duel was one-sided. *Thor* pumped 128 shells into the *Willesden*, then finished her off with a torpedo. On 3 April the 5,630-ton Norwegian *Aust* was sunk in a similar manner in the same area. Of these three ships, none had been able to broadcast the QQQQ message indicating they were under attack by an enemy merchant raider, and Gumprich decided it would be safe to continue his mission in these profitable waters. So it was, a week later, that he came across the *Kirkpool.*

The weather had been deteriorating all night as a South Atlantic depression tracked from west to east across the area, and by the time *Thor* first sighted the *Kirkpool* it seemed that Alfred Round's 'millionaire's cruise' was coming to an abrupt end. He wrote:

> On 10 April the weather changed. It got rougher, followed by a very black night with neither moon nor stars to be seen. There was now a stiff southerly and steadily rising seas that seemed to mark the end of our fantastic run of good weather. The inside of the wheelhouse where I was on the helm was dark and quiet, except for the usual creaks and groans of a riveted ship labouring against the Atlantic swell.

As the day wore on, it got worse, the wind keening in the rigging and the long Atlantic rollers assuming mountainous proportions, their crests beginning to break in the crosswind, filling the air with flying spray and spume. The *Kirkpool*, then passing about 240 miles north of the lonely island of Tristan da Cunha, was straining every

rivet as she pitched and rolled with an agonising corkscrew movement, and in order to avoid damage to his ship Captain Kennington
was forced to reduce speed. When the sun reached its zenith behind
the heavy overcast, the *Kirkpool* was barely making steerage way.
And to add to the sheer misery of it all, as the relatively warm air
of the depression passed over the colder water it condensed out to
form a blanket of fog. Very soon, the *Kirkpool* was steaming blind.

The weather, the low cloud and the fog should have been the
Kirkpool's saviours, hiding her from the searching eyes on the
Thor's bridge and allowing her to escape, but the German raider
had an ace up her sleeve: she was equipped with an early form of
radar. Primitive though it might have been, with a 6-inch cathode
ray tube giving no more than vertical blips to indicate a target, the
radar enabled Gumprich to keep track of his intended victim as
he closed in.

It was dark by the time *Thor* came within easy range of the
Kirkpool, but by now the fog had lifted, allowing Gumprich to see
his victim clearly. At 2007 he fired a single torpedo at the British
ship as she wallowed in the heaving swell. Given the weather conditions, it was perhaps not surprising that the torpedo missed its
mark. However, the *Kirkpool* being now in plain sight, Gumprich
was able to bring his guns to bear. The first salvo from the 5.9s
also missed, but three shells of the second salvo scored direct hits
on the *Kirkpool*'s bridge, creating bloody carnage. On fire, and
with her steering knocked out, the doomed ship veered off course
and quite inadvertently lurched towards her attacker. Gumprich,
assuming that the *Kirkpool* was attempting to ram his ship, opened
fire with every gun he could bring to bear. Shell after shell rained
down on the helpless tramp, smashing, burning and killing.
Unable to offer any resistance, Captain Kennington gave the order
to abandon ship.

Alfred Round described the chaos:

> The ship was now burning fiercely out of control and
> lighting up the surrounding sea. We could see the car-
> nage and the deck strewn with wounded and dying ship-
> mates. Powerful searchlights shone from nowhere and
> swept over the ship. I got caught in their glare and stood
> momentarily paralysed. They struck more fear into me
> than anything else, knowing that these eyes of the enemy

exposed us to yet more destruction. They were suddenly switched to the lifeboats which some crew were working frantically to launch. Another salvo burst, demolishing the stokehold ventilators and part of the funnel, but the most sickening sight was to see the blasting away of the lifeboats and the brave men who, in the face of such withering fire, had been trying to launch them.

The *Kirkpool*, on fire from end to end and sinking lower and lower in the water so that her main deck was soon awash, was a tragic sight as she lay stopped and at the mercy of the pounding waves. Her lifeboats had been reduced to smouldering matchwood and her life-rafts were on fire or jammed fast in their cradles, while seventeen of her crew lay dead or dying on her ravaged decks.

Round's report continued:

> During a lull in the action 17 survivors, some seriously wounded, took shelter in the forward well deck. The Chief Engineer took command as our Captain was missing, presumed dead. What a sorry sight we were, with one engineer wounded in his right kidney, his insides exposed, and his right arm shattered at the elbow. The Bosun, with head wounds, was now just regaining consciousness. An Indian clutched a broken arm, and nearby two young ratings lay dead. A radio officer had shrapnel in his lung and the galley boy was shell-shocked and out of his mind. I passed a first aid box to Sid Powell, the steward, who quietly set to work bandaging his mates. To cap it all, over a dozen crew were missing, either killed or drowned. Several Indian firemen were standing in a group and wailing and calling, 'Allah! Allah!' They were giving themselves up to their fate and mourning their own funeral.
>
> The ship meanwhile was only just managing to keep her nose above the waves, but an occasional roller would come over, and so we all began to grab at anything that would float, hatch boards, a long ladder, anything. These we now lashed together with an ample supply of rope from No. 2 derrick. What a splendid team we made as we grasped this last chance of survival offered to us . . . Meanwhile our attacker was getting impatient at the time

the ship took to sink, because they started to open fire once again, which was a signal for us to take to our crude rafts, and so along with the wounded we jumped in to the sea.

Robert Denmark, one of the *Kirkpool's* DEMS gunners, wrote in later life:

All hell was let loose as salvo after salvo of very heavy gun-fire rained down on us, smashing parts of the superstructure to pieces and causing fires to start everywhere. The gunfire continued for a long time without respite and at a very short range. It seemed that the raider was intent on sinking us by surface fire as the torpedoing was taking longer than expected to achieve its aim. Under such intense bombardment and heavily under-armed in comparison to our enemy, it was impossible to retaliate and survival became essential. Most escape rafts were either released or smashed in the action. The starboard lifeboat was blown from the davits with several Indian firemen attempting to escape by lowering it. The whole episode seemed a shambles, but mercifully the firing stopped . . . Several of us gathered in the after welldeck searching for something to evacuate safely on. Captain Kennington then arrived and advised us to abandon ship as she was sinking fast. Seeing we had no escape material, he suggested a cargo net with buoyant material attached on the forecastle head was possible escape material. Several hands went with him to release it and the remainder of us waited patiently with hope of its arrival. Heaven sent, the net duly came floating down the port side and we all jumped in union.

Myself a very moderate swimmer, I was very relieved to grasp the net which proved to be a life-saver to several of the crew. We drifted slowly away from the *Kirkpool*, now well alight and providing a firework display as small arms bullets began exploding. The illuminations kept us abreast of happenings with the *Kirkpool*.

Denmark added:

Most of us were scantily clad, myself only in a singlet and kapok lifejacket. Gathering thoughts of possible sharks in the area were not comforting. Possibly in the water for over an hour, time did not seem to register while clinging onto life. The weather conditions became darker and our thoughts of survival likewise.

Chief Engineer Burley, who saved his own life by clinging to a wooden hatch board, also remembered:

> I felt so tired, real tired, and cramp was getting into my legs, and the thought came to me all I had to do was to let go and end it. It seemed so easy, but somehow, someone, somewhere seemed to always want attention, especially two wounded men . . . we were a sorry lot of fourteen of us on hatch boards, a rough sea, a burning ship astern of us, nothing else in sight, and possibly a thousand miles from anywhere on a black night.

Having subjected the *Kirkpool* to a prolonged and unnecessary shelling while it was quite obvious that her crew were abandoning ship, Günther Gumprich appeared to have a change of heart. Despite being aware that his victim had broadcast a call for help, he spent the next three hours cruising around looking for survivors. This late compassionate gesture resulted in thirty men who would otherwise have died being plucked from the icy waters. Among them were Captain Albert Kennington and Chief Engineer C. Burley. That these men were found and saved was largely due to an innovation in British merchant ships: small red lights attached to lifejackets that ignited on contact with the water. Furthermore, to the credit of Gumprich, his officers and men, when the survivors were taken on board the *Thor* they were well treated. DEMS gunner Robert Denmark put this on record:

> The wounded were attended to straight away and the rest of us were made comfortable; the German officers and men plied us liberally with cognac and rye bread sausage sandwiches. I remember going to bed quite tipsy. A moderate interrogation took place mainly to get records for kith and kin notification . . . Now warm and nourished we settled into our temporary accommodation for the remainder of the night. Next day we were roused early and taken to our more permanent prison quarters. These were in the central position in the bowels of the ship

below the waterline. Access and egress were by a companionway with a heavy steel sheet lockable lid. Exercise on deck was allowed one hour in the forenoon and one hour in the afternoon daily.

The *Kirkpool* survivors found they were sharing their prison accommodation with those rescued from the three other vessels sunk by the *Thor*, namely the British ships *Wellpark* and *Willesden* and the Norwegian-flag *Aust*. However austere and restricted their quarters might be, they were air-conditioned and provided with a number of flushing toilets.

During the first three days of their captivity Captain Kennington and his men enjoyed the freedom of the deck, which helped to speed their recovery from the ordeal they had suffered. On the fourth day there was a complete change of mood aboard the raider, and all prisoners were locked in their quarters below decks under armed guard. This regime prevailed for a number of days, presumably while the *Thor* was stalking another victim. This proved to be the British cargo/passenger vessel *Nanking*, which was stopped and captured on 10 May, resulting in another influx of prisoners, this time including some women and children.

The *Thor* now moved into the Indian Ocean, where her prisoners, some 200 in all, were transferred to the German blockade runner *Dresden*, then on her way to Japan. She reached Yokohama a month later, when all prisoners were handed over to the Japanese authorities. Captain Kennington and the twenty-nine others who survived the sinking of the *Kirkpool* were sent to a prisoner of war camp near Fukushima, called Kawasaki No. 1, some 125 miles north of Tokyo. The conditions they suffered there were appalling. Robert Denmark described them:

> The two-storey structure we were housed in proved to be an unsanitary and bug-infested dwelling with cold water only external washing facilities and external primitive toilets. The toilets were narrow wooden huts with earthenware pots sunk into the ground, with a 12" x 5" hole cut in the floor. Within days of use the pots became a seething mass of maggots. Consequently, the inevitable happened – vast amounts of sickness and dysentery . . . Work schedules were prepared and, in Japan, to not work

meant you would not eat despite how unwell you might be . . . a typical Japanese diet for prisoners of war: breakfast consisted of a small bowl of rice and some hot liquid called soup, containing very little solid food and some added *misau*, a curd material to cloud the absence of vegetables. This menu was repeated at midday on site and on our return to camp in the evening with no variation for the whole of our stay in Japan. Later, the rice became short and was substituted by Korean rice, which was reddish in colour, and coarse rolled barley. The midday meal, carried from camp to camp in wooden rice buckets, often turned sour, especially in the summer months, but this had to be eaten or we starved. Some meals often arrived with rat droppings cooked in it. Prisoners would extract the faeces and as little as possible of the discoloured area. Such a revolting situation was necessary for such hungry men performing such manual tasks. To be expected to live without bread, butter, meat, cheese and all other forms of the European diet was a total contravention of the Geneva Convention for prisoners of war, but our captors were a sadistic bunch of animals.

The *Kirkpool* survivors remained incarcerated in the hell hole of Kawasaki No. 1 until 10 September 1945, when they were finally released by an Anglo/American naval task force. For Captain Albert Kennington it was too late. He died of malnutrition on 14 March l944.

CHAPTER TEN

A Meeting by Moonlight – *Athelknight* 27.05.42

In the early summer of 1942 Britain's oil and petroleum reserves were at a dangerously low ebb. Historically, the bulk of her fuel had come from the Middle East via the Suez Canal and the Mediterranean, but with that route now virtually closed to the tankers, they faced the long haul around the Cape of Good Hope. This almost doubled the time the oil was at sea, and running the gauntlet of Japanese submarines roaming the Indian Ocean was a hazard too far. The only alternative supply lay to the west, in the warm waters of the Caribbean. The Royal Dutch Shell refinery on the island of Curaçao alone was said to be producing 11m barrels a month, and it was there that in May 1942 the motor tanker *Athelknight* found herself heading.

The 8,940-ton *Athelknight*, built on the Clyde in 1930, was owned by the United Molasses Company of London, better known as the Athel Line. She was powered by two 12-cylinder Kincaid diesel engines, which gave her a service speed of 11 knots, and was armed with the usual 4-inch anti-submarine gun mounted aft, plus a handful of machine guns for defence against air attack. She carried an all-British crew of fifty-two, which included seven DEMS gunners. In command was Captain Hugh Roberts, who hailed from the Lynn Peninsula on the Atlantic coast of Wales, where master mariners were as thick on the ground as the wild flowers of the fields than ran down to the sea. Forty-seven-year-old Roberts was a seaman of considerable experience, having 'come up through the hawse pipe', first going to sea as a mess-boy in a tramp steamer at the tender age of fifteen.

The *Athelknight* had been in dry dock in Barry, South Wales when orders came through for her to sail in ballast to Curaçao to load a cargo of fuel oil for the Admiralty. The May blossom was in bloom, but winter was reluctant to relax its icy hold, and the prospect of a voyage to the warm and relatively safe waters of the West Indies had immediate appeal to all on board.

Once clear of the Bristol Channel, the newly scrubbed and painted tanker joined Convoy OS 28, bound for Freetown. In line with routine practice at the time, the *Athelknight* was scheduled to leave the convoy when abeam of the Straits of Gibraltar and then proceed alone to the Caribbean.

OS 28 consisted of thirty-nine merchant ships sailing in nine columns abreast, escorted by three sloops and a corvette of the Royal Navy. The merchantmen were bound for various destinations in West Africa, the Indian Ocean and beyond, while four other tankers, also in ballast, would be taking the same route as the *Athelknight*.

The voyage south under blue skies and with light winds was without incident. It seemed that the enemy had taken time off for the summer, for not one U-boat came within Asdic distance of the convoy, and not one menacing Focke-Wulf darkened the sky. Averaging 8½ knots, OS 28 was abreast of Gibraltar in the early hours of 21 May. Here the Caribbean-bound tankers prepared to go their separate ways, but before they went, the enemy, quite by chance, was given the opportunity to show his teeth.

Shortly before sunset on the 20th, U-159, a long-range Type IXC sailing alone to join others of her kind already in American waters, had sighted the masts and funnels of the convoy on the horizon ahead. Her commander, Helmut-Friedrich Witte, unable to resist the temptation to strike a blow against the Allies, increased to full speed and pulled ahead of the convoy under the cover of darkness. By midnight he was well placed to attack.

Undetected by OS 28's escorts, Witte moved in closer and emptied his four bow tubes into the close-packed ships. He then turned U-159 short-round and fired his two stern tubes in the same direction. The effect of six torpedoes ploughing into the massed ranks of slowly moving ships was spectacular. What had once been a warm, untroubled sub-tropical night suddenly erupted into a blazing Dante's Inferno. Witte's torpedoes exploded in a rolling peal of thunder, smashing, burning and killing. Distress rockets went soaring into the sky, bursting overhead in showers of brilliant white stars; snowflakes and starshell followed, until night was turned into day and the scene of death and destruction was shown up in stark relief. The convoy's escorts, galvanized into action, added to the chaos with a frenzy of random depth charging.

When the uproar had died down, it was discovered that only two ships had been hit, Elder Dempster's *New Brunswick*, deep-loaded with military stores and aircraft, and the small fleet oiler *Montenol*, which was in ballast. The *New Brunswick* went down almost immediately, but the *Montenol* stayed afloat, although she was so badly damaged that she had to be sunk by gunfire by the escorts later in the day. Despite the ferocity of the unexpected attack, only six lives were lost in the torpedoed ships.

When the last depth charge had gone down and the brilliant display of pyrotechnics overhead had faded, all went quiet again. Helmut-Friedrich Witte, satisfied he had caused serious damage, was content to slip away and continue on his voyage.

By this time, OS 28 was nearing the departure point for the tankers, but Captain Hugh Roberts was so appalled by the apparent impotence of the escorts in the face of the enemy, that he decided to take the *Athelknight* out of the convoy there and then. He opened his sealed orders and set course for Trinidad, where he was instructed to await a convoy to Curaçao. Unknown to Roberts as he made his decision, just 500 miles ahead of the *Athelknight*, U-172 was also on course for the Caribbean, although proceeding at a more leisurely pace.

U-172, another Type IXC, had left the yard of AG Weser in Bremen just six months earlier, an example of the best in German marine engineering. Displacing nearly 1,200 tons, she was 250ft long and 22ft in the beam, and her two supercharged MAN diesels gave her a top speed of 18.3 knots on the surface. Underwater, two Siemens double-acting electric motors produced 7.3 knots, and at 10 knots she had a maximum operating range of 13,450 miles without refuelling. Her armament consisted of six torpedo tubes with twenty-two torpedoes, a 105mm deck gun with 180 rounds and two AA guns, one 37mm and one twin 20mm. She was on her maiden war patrol, and had yet to cross swords with the enemy.

In command of U-172 was Kapitänleutnant Carl Emmermann. A native of Hamburg, he had joined the *Reichsmarine* in 1934, graduating to the U-boat arm in November 1940. After a brief spell as First Watch Officer in U-A with Hans Eckermann, he had taken command of U-172 in November 1941. What he lacked in experience he was determined to make up for in enemy ships sunk.

Alone at last, at sunrise on the 21st the *Athelknight* was bowling along under an azure-blue sky dotted with clumps of fair-weather cumulus of the purest white. It was typical North-East Trades weather, with the wind fresh from astern and embryo white horses flecking the tops of the waves. The convoy was long out of sight, and the horizon all round was unsullied by even a wisp of funnel smoke. Thanks to the efforts of Chief Engineer Will MacDonald, the tanker was making a steady 11 knots to the southwest, with the promise of arrival in Trinidad by the end of the month. Meanwhile, away from the threat of war, the ship was able to settle down to her normal sea-going routine. Captain Roberts, master of his own command again, was content. Had he been able to see far over the horizon ahead, however, to where U-172 was on an identical course and running at economical speed, he would have been looking at a more uncertain future. The *Athelknight* was overtaking the U-boat at the rate of seventy miles a day.

The idyll continued for another five days. It was warming up, a taste of things to come; the trades had fallen away but the ship was making her own breeze, just enough to keep the accommodation cool. The tropical twilight was short, darkness coming swiftly soon after the sun dropped below the horizon. The nights that followed were full of magic, the sky black velvet, speckled by a myriad of twinkling stars. This was what the crew had signed on for; not a man amongst them yearned for the land again.

On the evening of Tuesday, 26 May the *Athelknight* was 1,400 miles north-east of Trinidad, the slap of her bow wave and the muffled thump of her diesels indicating that the voyage was still going well. At about 2200 Captain Hugh Roberts wrote up his night orders in the chartroom and left the bridge. Back in his cabin, he made himself tea from the supper tray and tried to relax.

Relaxation did not come easy, and Roberts found his thoughts straying to what he might find when they reached the Caribbean. Before sailing from Barry he had been warned that the U-boats had begun a new offensive in the West Indies, the low point of which had come in February, when U-67 entered Curaçao's Willemstad harbour and sank three tankers. A similar attack had been carried out in San Nicolas harbour on Aruba, where three more tankers were torpedoed while they lay at anchor. Italian submarines had also been reported operating in the eastern approaches to the Caribbean, one having sunk the *Athelqueen*, commanded by Hugh

Roberts' boyhood friend, Captain John Roberts. The U-boats were running rings around the unprepared Americans.

Earlier that evening, enjoying the last rays of the dying sun in the conning tower of U-172, Carl Emmermann had been brought back to reality by a report that the masts of a ship were visible on the horizon astern. Using his binoculars, he identified the stranger as an oil tanker – and she was overtaking the U-boat at a smart pace. Emmermann immediately cleared the conning tower, submerged to periscope depth, and waited.

At 2215, Captain Roberts, no longer able to be alone with his thoughts, decided to take a turn on deck. He was just leaving his cabin when Emmerman's torpedo struck the *Athelknight* on her starboard side, directly below the bridge.

The resulting explosion was muted, but when the tanker shuddered and lurched to starboard, Roberts, who was no stranger to the U-boat war, knew exactly what had happened. Stopping only to scoop up his lifejacket, he made his way up to the bridge.

By the time Roberts reached the wheelhouse, the *Athelknight* had taken a dangerous list to starboard, and Third Officer Bill Cook, who had the watch on the bridge, was already making preparations for abandoning ship. Roberts took over, his first move being to stop the engines. As the crippled ship slowed to a halt, he gave the order for the crew to assemble at their boat stations. He later wrote:

> I then ordered the boats to be lowered at approximately 2240 hrs. My own boat, No. 1, on the starboard side of the bridge, caught on a bulge on the ship's side just above the water and was later cleared, but as I feared it would be further damaged if left there, I ordered it to be hauled forward clear of the jagged plating. The remainder of the boat's crew and myself slid down the painter with the boat. As the boat was being lowered the submarine started shelling from ahead and as I went over the ship's rail a shell passed through my accommodation and also through the wheelhouse and wireless cabin.

The shelling was remorseless and unceasing. Shells pounded the *Athelknight*'s bridge, demolishing the wheelhouse and chartroom and completely wrecking the wireless room, where Radio Officer Leonard Hill was making desperate efforts to get away an SOS.

Everywhere aboard the dying ship there was confusion, but no outright panic. Third Officer Cook described the scene:

> Sparks and I went on the lower bridge and shells were falling near the port boat, which three or four men were attempting to lower. I told them to leave off and come with us to my (port after) boat, but they took no notice and Sparks and I went aft to my boat. The Second Mate's boat was clear of the ship. The Chief Officer had already started lowering my boat away, and we cast off with 12 men aboard, mostly my boat's crew, but some of them had gone in the Captain's boat . . .
>
> We pulled away and the sub was firing QF tracer shells over the boat. The port amidships boat was now in the water and the men were calling out to us that they were making water and needed help. We pulled over to them, thus putting ourselves in the line of fire from sub to ship. We were quite close to them when a shell struck the *Athelknight* port side amidships, and also the port midships boats. Shells were now falling thick and fast, and as there seemed to be great danger of our boat being shelled too, we pulled away from the ship. Two of our boat's crew were injured by either shell splinters or m.g. [machine gun] bullets, McAlinden in the face and Sheenan in the finger, and I got some in my left hand.
>
> In pulling away we lost Dewar, fireman. He jumped or fell overboard, but Chief Officer and I managed to haul him back on board again. The boat was making water fast and we had to keep bailing continuously. Rowing was difficult for we had to keep ducking down below the gunwale to miss the m.g. bullets, which were passing over the boat. We had some difficulty in steering because we had a broken rudder pintle.

When Captain Roberts boarded his lifeboat he found it was completely waterlogged and floating on its buoyancy tanks. Putting his men to the oars, he succeeded in pulling clear of the ship, and when about 100yds off, hove to and attempted to bail the boat dry. With the U-boat's shells still whistling overhead, and bullets ricocheting off the water, this was not an easy task, but after half an hour's frantic bailing the water level in the boat was low enough to enable the leak to be plugged. The boat was still making water, but at a rate that could be contained by bailing.

Later, when the shelling had died down, Roberts closed on the only other boat visible, which was in the charge of Second Officer Douglas Crook. He was discussing the situation with Crook when the U-boat was seen approaching, her machine-guns firing over their heads as she came. It was too late to escape, and when Carl Emmermann demanded that the ship's master show himself, Roberts, who was in uniform, was obliged to comply, even though he knew he would almost certainly be taken prisoner and end up in a camp in Germany. He described what followed:

> He asked for me, and told me to come on board. He asked where we were from and where bound, and the name of the ship. He apparently did not believe me when I said we were British, but kept repeating, 'You are American.' I insisted we were British, and apparently satisfied he asked if we had provisions. I said yes, but could do with more, whereupon he gave some orders, and a bag containing half a dozen loaves was passed into the boat. During the interview on the submarine's deck I was fully aware that a man stood behind me with a Tommy gun. When he ordered me back to the boat, he also remarked that he was sorry for us, and I replied that he could not possibly be sorrier for me than I was for myself and all ahead of us. The nearest land was Barbuda in the West Indies, and this was nearly 1200 miles away. The Azores were also about the same distance away, but the prevailing wind would favour the West Indies.

U-172 backed away, and went off at full speed. Later, she resumed shelling the *Athelknight*, which was still stubbornly afloat. Hugh Roberts, forced to witness the wilful destruction of his command, wrote in his report:

> When he left us he circled out of our sight at a fast speed and later resumed the shelling of our ship, causing the starboard side bunkers to catch fire which later enveloped the whole after end. This fire continued all night, we lost count of all the number of shells fired, but the number was considerable. We remained stationary after the submarine

left us and later saw lights flashing. We closed this and found it to be the port bridge boat with five men in it, of whom two, Gainsford and McGrath, were dead from shrapnel wounds. Two seriously wounded, Paulson and Moore, and AA Gunner Oliver with shrapnel wounds in the right forearm. These three were transferred to our boat as their boat appeared to be badly damaged by shrapnel.

Paulson, a fireman, was found to have a badly shattered left shoulder and severe injuries to the left jaw. Moore, O.S. had a shrapnel wound in the abdomen. These men were attended to by the Chief Steward Boniface, who did all that was possible for them with the first aid kit in the boat. Their injuries were so severe that I doubt if any treatment could have saved them. Moore died during the forenoon of the 27th May and Paulson at about 8 pm. At dawn we thought we could see the other boat close astern of our vessel but we soon found this to be the submarine, as he again resumed shelling the vessel. Later we saw a huge column of water on the starboard side abreast of the engine room and sound resembling a torpedo explosion. In about 3 minutes after this the vessel had gone under, stern foremost, the bow from the foremast forward being completely out of the water for a few seconds before it finally disappeared.

There seems to have been no logical reason for Carl Emmerman to open fire on the *Athelknight* while her boats were being lowered. It must have been quite obvious to him that the tanker was stopped and being abandoned. Furthermore, these were very remote waters, and there was little likelihood of anyone coming to her help, even if the tanker's radio officers had managed to get away an SOS. This can only be seen as a wanton act of destruction, and the deaths of the four men who died as a result of the shelling as murder. Emmermann's generosity in allowing Captain Roberts to return to his boat, and the gift of loaves of bread, even if they were mouldy, was in stark contrast to his earlier actions.

Although the leak in the hull of the lifeboat had been plugged, despite continuous bailing the water level rose during the night. When daylight came the gunwales were again awash, and it was obvious to Captain Roberts that the boat would not stay afloat for much longer. Salvation came later in the morning, when Second Officer Douglas Crook's boat hove in sight. The two boats came together, and Roberts and his crew were taken off. The transfer had only just been completed when the waterlogged boat sank.

Crook's boat now had a total of thirty-nine men on board, and to say that the survivors were packed like sardines in a can would have been an understatement. It was fortunate that during the day they met up with the other lifeboat to survive the sinking of the *Athelknight*, which was under the command of Chief Officer David Davies. Third Officer Bill Cook, who was with Davies, wrote in his log:

> We took 13 men on board our boat making us 25 in all and leaving them 26, two of whom were severely injured. The Captain told us the sub had promised to radio our position when he was clear of the area. The sub had given No. 3 boat a bucket to bail with and several loaves of hard German black bread. The Captain passed two loaves over to us.

The two boats then set sail for the nearest land, which Captain Roberts estimated to be the islands in the vicinity of Antigua, some 1,200 miles to the south-west. They had no navigation aids other than the boat compasses, and the food and water on board was limited, each boat carrying twenty-four tins of ship's biscuits, forty-eight tins of condensed milk, twenty-four tins of Pemmican, a quantity of Horlicks milk tablets, a few tins of chocolate and forty gallons of fresh water. All now depended on the wind and current.

For the first three days the wind was fair from the east, and the two boats remained in sight of each other, but on the fourth day there was a complete change in the weather. The wind went round ahead and was accompanied by driving rain squalls, which persisted for the next five days. Ships' lifeboats are not designed to sail close to the wind, so little progress was made during those days. Eventually, the two boats became separated and would not meet up again.

Anticipating a long voyage, Captain Roberts began rationing food at once, allowing each man one biscuit, two spoonfuls of condensed milk and two ounces of water in the early morning, one biscuit, one spoonful of Pemmican and one ounce of water at noon, and one biscuit, one spoonful of Pemmican and two ounces of water at sunset. The Horlicks tablets and chocolate were issued sparingly at odd times during the day. It was barely enough to sustain life, but Roberts could not afford to be profligate. Subsequent events would prove him right. He wrote:

> This procedure lasted until the 24th day, when all the biscuits and Pemmican were exhausted. We kept on sailing the whole distance and were fortunate to land on St Bartholomew, a Vichy French island 60 miles from our intended destination on our 28th day in the boat, when we landed in a small cove.
>
> What bothered me most was the heat of the sun, and when we sighted the island at dawn on 23rd June 1942 my strength was fast ebbing. I now realize that following a major operation for the removal of the gall bladder I was not in a fit state to do such a journey as this. At times it became necessary to warn all the men against drinking sea water. Some pretended to wash their mouths out only, but this had to be prohibited. The youngest on board was only sixteen, and the eldest, an old Kinsale seaman, was well over sixty-five. When we touched the beach at Bartholomew, the islanders did not come near until we were actually ashore. The boat's crew, with the exception of myself and the Kinsale man, managed to get over the side of the boat and crawl ashore. We had to be carried and were laid down inside some boat shelters where we were given coffee.
>
> It was about noon when we landed and two hours later a police boat arrived and we had to re-enter our lifeboat to be towed to the harbour about four miles away. We stayed there for two days, some, like myself, in hospital under the tender care of a very old Breton nursing sister, others in hotels. A small Dutch West Indian schooner then took us all aboard for the sixty miles trip to St Kitts. On our arrival the Port Medical Officer came aboard and examined us all. Most of us were prevented from moving hand or foot, and the ambulance had a busy time bringing us up the hill into the hospital at Basseterre under the care of Dr Steddefer, the Hospital Superintendent, who had fled from Hitler's Germany before the summer of 1939.

On 9 July the survivors were taken by a Cuban ship to San Juan, Puerto Rico, and from there a US navy vessel took them to New York. There followed a train journey to Halifax, Nova Scotia, where they boarded the troopship *Strathmore* for Glasgow. They reached Glasgow at the end of September, four months after their meeting with U-172.

Whilst in New York, Captain Roberts learned that Chief Officer David Davies and his crew had also reached land. The final entries in Third Officer Bill Cook's log read:

Wednesday 17 June – Day 22

Everyone feeling weak and thirsty now. Some of the men are drinking salt water, but if one stops them during the day, they drink twice as much at night time.

Sunday 21 June – Day 26

Opens cloudy, calm and smooth sea.

Breakfast: ½ bisc; 1 choc; 2 milk tablets; 1 tsp brandy; 1 oz water; 1/6 oz pemmican.

Dinner noon: ½ bisc; 1 choc; 2 milk tablets; 1/6 oz pemmican; 1 oz water.

1400 approx. Sighted ship. Picked up by s.s. *Empire Austin*, bound for Capetown. All hands aboard by 3.45 and lifeboat sunk.

Davies and his men were landed in Cape Town, and sailed for Glasgow on the troopship *Warwick Castle*.

Thanks largely to the leadership of Captain Hugh Roberts and his officers, forty-three of the *Athelknight*'s crew of fifty-two survived. The nine men who lost their lives probably died when U-172 shelled and machine-gunned their lifeboats.

CHAPTER ELEVEN

The Winston Special –
Clan Ferguson 12.08.42

The sun was setting over Ailsa Craig when, on the evening of 2 August 1942, Convoy WS 21S cleared the Firth of Clyde and altered to starboard to enter the North Channel. In the lead was Port Line's 8,535-ton *Port Chalmers* with the convoy commodore, Commodore A.G. Venables RNR, on board. In her wake came eleven other fast cargo liners and two deep-loaded oil tankers. This impressive array of the cream of the day's merchant shipping included the *Almeria Lykes* and the tanker *Santa Elisa*, both flying the Stars and Stripes, while the others were all under the British flag.

By the standards of the day, WS 21S, comprising just fourteen merchantmen, was a small convoy, but the cargo the ships carried, 150,000 tons of military equipment, ammunition and food, and 25,000 tons of high octane aviation fuel, was of vital importance. On the success or failure of this convoy depended the fate of the beleaguered island of Malta, Britain's last remaining outpost in the central Mediterranean.

The importance of this 'Winston Special' was evident in the size and strength of the convoy's escort: two cruisers and eighteen destroyers, now preparing to draw a ring of steel around the vulnerable merchantmen which no enemy U-boat or aircraft could hope to penetrate.

The island of Malta is just 17 miles long by 9 miles wide and lies 50 miles south of Sicily, roughly halfway between Gibraltar and Egypt. Said to have been first settled in 5,200 BC, it was used by the Phoenicians as a stopping off point on their trading voyages to Cornwall, and over the years came to be of huge strategic importance to anyone wishing to exercise control over the Mediterranean. Malta became a British colony in 1814, its main harbour Valletta being chosen by the Royal Navy as one of its major bases.

When Italy entered the war in 1940 and the struggle for supremacy in North Africa began, 'Fortress Malta' became vital to the Allied cause. Aircraft and ships based on the island were ideally placed to attack Italian, and later German, supply ships, and this they did to good effect. As might be expected, Malta soon became a primary target for the Luftwaffe and Mussolini's *Regia Aeronautica*, who were determined to bomb it into submission. Over a period of two years the Axis powers flew a total of 3,000 bombing raids against military and civilian targets. The island fortress came very near to being reduced to a pile of smoking rubble, and it was only the indomitable spirit of its people and the gallant efforts of a small band of RAF fighter pilots and the men who manned the anti-aircraft guns that held the enemy at bay.

Convoys from Gibraltar and Alexandria fought their way through to Malta with food, ammunition and fuel, but the cost in ships and men was very heavy. By the early summer of 1942 the sheer mass of German and Italian bombers, torpedo bombers, submarines and motor torpedo boats ranged against the relief convoys was proving too much. Few ships were getting through, and it seemed likely that Malta's days of freedom were numbered.

In mid-June the situation had become critical, leading to a last desperate attempt to maintain supplies to the island. It was decided to run two convoys simultaneously, one from Gibraltar and one from Alexandria. Operation Harpoon, consisting of six fast merchant ships carrying 43,000 tons of supplies and fuel, sailed from Gibraltar on 12 June. The ships had a close escort consisting of an anti-aircraft cruiser, nine destroyers, a minesweeper and six MTBs. In support, but keeping their distance, were a battleship, two aircraft carriers, three cruisers, and eight destroyers.

With such an unprecedented escort force it seemed that Harpoon could not fail to reach Malta. Then, when the convoy was just twenty-four hours from the island, hundreds of German and Italian aircraft swooped on the ships. The enemy bombers, based on Sardinia, less than 100 miles to the north, were able to fly multiple sorties and subjected the convoy to unrelenting attack throughout the daylight hours. At the height of the battle, Harpoon's covering force was recalled to Gibraltar. The remaining escorts put up a spirited defence, but when the enemy bombers were joined by two Italian cruisers and five destroyers, it was completely overwhelmed. Four merchantmen, with their precious cargoes, were lost, and one destroyer was sunk, while the anti-aircraft cruiser and a minesweeper sustained severe damage.

Abukir. The last ship out of Ostend. (www.oostendsenostalgie.be)

Athenia. Torpedoed a few hours after the declaration of war.

A convoy to Russia.
(UK Government poster)

A convoy to Malta. (*Courier Mail*)

Fort Bellingham. Torpedoed in the Barents Sea. (MoWT)

Clan Macphee. Torpedoed and sunk in the Atlantic on 16 August 1940.

A German E-boat in the North Sea. (Hans Schaller)

A Japanese long-range submarine. (Daily Lazy)

Khedive Ismail. An unlucky recipient. (Painting by Robert Blackwell)

Royal Sceptre with a full timber deck cargo.

The *Otaio*, carrying cargo and passing under the Sydney Harbour Bridge before the war.

Rose Castle in 1942. One of Churchill's Thin Grey Line. (*Unknown*)

Wooden liferaft. (*Unknown*)

The *Athelknight*.

The *Adlington Court*.

A show of force. German U-boats are put on display for
Admiral Miklos Horthy, the regent of Hungary.

And there was worse to come. That evening, when approaching Valletta, the surviving ships ran into an unmarked minefield. One destroyer was sunk, two others were damaged and one of the only two remaining merchantman was also damaged.

Coincident with Harpoon, Operation Vigorous was launched from the other end of the Mediterranean. A convoy of eleven similarly loaded merchantmen sailed from Alexandria with an escort of eight cruisers, twenty-six destroyers, four corvettes and two minesweepers. In support was a decommissioned battleship which had been converted to mount batteries of anti-aircraft guns.

Vigorous came under heavy attack by surface ships and torpedo bombers soon after leaving Alexandria. One merchantman was damaged and had to return to port, another dropped out with engine trouble.

The attacks went on, with German E-boats joining in what had begun to resemble a turkey shoot. Two merchantmen fell to the torpedo bombers, and the E-boats sank a destroyer and damaged a cruiser. German Stukas based on Crete joined in as the convoy fought its way past the island, and by the afternoon of the 15th another destroyer had gone and only six merchant ships were still afloat. That evening, when news was received that the remnants of Operation Harpoon had reached Malta, the Admiralty decided that no more could be achieved by Vigorous, and the operation was abandoned. The tattered remains of the convoy returned to Alexandria.

The two merchantmen of Operation Harpoon that broke through to Malta, one a tanker and the other a cargo ship, were gratefully welcomed by the island, but they were not enough. Malta had only a few weeks supply of aviation fuel for its defending fighters, and its population was on the brink of starvation. An idea of the gravity of the situation in the island may be gained from a statement made by the official in charge of food distribution in Malta at the time:

> The present island-wide soup kitchen arrangements are fully organized and working well. The tinned and dehydrated ingredients are issued daily to the organizers, prepared on field kitchens and distributed from fixed points. These ingredients are the ideal for control and orderly administration but the last issue – the absolute last issue

from island reserves – occurs in five days, on 15 August. After that we are down to the slaughter of horses and goats, once considered adequate for six months . . . The present census of animals in the island is estimated to last from five to ten days.

If in fact I chop and change between tinned supplies and slaughter without causing panic we might last until 25 August.

As the summer of 1942 drew to a close, the outlook for the island of Malta had never been so bleak.

On the morning of 3 August, Malta's last hope of relief, Convoy WS 21S, was off the north coast of Ireland and heading out into the open Atlantic. The fourteen merchant ships had formed up in four columns abreast, with the Commodore's ship *Port Chalmers* leading Column 2. The weather was fair, the often turbulent ocean putting on its summer face. During the day, the convoy's already powerful escort force was joined by the battleships HMS *Nelson* and HMS *Rodney*, 34,000-tonners armed with an array of 16-inch, 6-inch and 4.7-inch guns, plus the aircraft carriers *Eagle*, *Indomitable* and *Victorious*. Then, on the morning of the 4th, the escort was even further reinforced by the arrival of the aircraft carrier HMS *Furious*, accompanied by the heavy cruiser *Manchester* and another five destroyers. The fourteen merchantmen, themselves well armed, were now protected by an unprecedented force of two battleships, four aircraft carriers, four cruisers and twenty-three destroyers. To many in those merchant ships WS 21S now seemed unassailable. Others who had travelled this dangerous road before were not convinced. One such was Captain A.N. Cossar, commanding the *Clan Ferguson*.

Sailing as second ship of the port outside column, the 7,347-ton *Clan Ferguson* was typical of the British cargo liners dedicated to keeping open Malta's lifeline. Owned by Clan Line Steamers of Glasgow, she was four years old, a 17-knot twin-screw steamer with a raked bow and cruiser stern. For much of her life she had been employed on voyages to and from Australia and New Zealand, general cargo out, wool and frozen lamb home, but for the past twelve months she had been a regular on the Malta run. Taken under Admiralty control, her Indian ratings had been replaced by British volunteers and she bristled with guns.

In addition to her 4-inch anti-submarine gun she mounted two 40mm Bofors quick-firing AA guns, eight 20mm Oerlikons, a battery of light machine guns and an assortment of FAMS and PAC rockets. These weapons were manned by a highly trained force of twenty DEMS gunners.

The *Clan Ferguson* was a ship to be reckoned with, but she was also highly vulnerable in that her cargo included 2,000 tons of aviation spirit in drums and 1,500 tons of high explosives. Thomas Kay, a DEMS gunner in the ship, described the situation in a blunt seaman's manner:

> The *Clan Ferguson*'s cargo was explosives. There were 800 tons of block TNT in the forward holds plus gunnery shells, ammunition and explosives (including, it was rumoured, poison gas shells). We also had petrol tanks on the decks. All in all the ship was a floating bomb! Just before we left Greenock a Commodore came on board and gave us a lecture warning us that if we got hit it would be every man for himself as there would not be much time for a proper abandon ship routine.

In times of peace, for the fast, well-found ships that formed the core of Convoy WS21S, the run south to Gibraltar would had been considered a pleasant three-day passage, the grim overcast of northern waters giving way to cloudless skies and warm sunshine as the miles went by. It was usually a time to prepare for the long voyage ahead, be it South America, the Far East or beyond.

Those balmy days were now just fond memories. Under strict Admiralty routing the convoy headed some 500 miles out into the Atlantic before turning south. In this way it was hoped to keep well clear of the U-boats based in the Biscay ports and the long-range Focke-Wulfs operating out of Bordeaux. And so what had once been an easy-going three-day passage became eight days of constant alert, with bridges double-manned and nervous gunners never straying far from their guns.

Whether it was the utmost secrecy surrounding the movements of WS 21S, or the reluctance of the enemy to tangle with the convoy's massive escort force, is a matter of conjecture, but the run south proved completely uneventful. At no time did the constantly probing Asdics of the escorts detect a threat under water, no hostile aircraft sullied the untroubled skies.

When on the morning of 9 August the ships reached a position due west of the Straits of Gibraltar and altered course to enter the Mediterranean, it was assumed that the enemy was unaware of their approach. Unfortunately, this was not so. It later transpired that German Intelligence had been tracking the convoy from the time it left the North Channel. Berlin was aware that the fate of Malta rested on the safe arrival of WS 21S and the supplies it was carrying, and German and Italian forces in the Mediterranean were being mustered to provide a hot reception. Some 700 German and Italian bombers, dive bombers and torpedo bombers were standing by on the airfields of Sardinia and Sicily, eighteen Italian and three German U-boats were patrolling the anticipated route and a large force of motor torpedo boats, German and Italian, was also poised to attack.

Approaching the Straits of Gibraltar under the cover of darkness on the night of the 9th, with every ship completely blacked out, the convoy hoped to pass through the 8-mile-wide channel hidden from the prying eyes of the numerous German intelligence agents known to be keeping a watchful vigil from Algeciras on the Spanish side and Ceuta in Morocco. Luck was with WS 21S that night, for as the ships approached the narrows a blanket of dense fog descended on them. This was a mixed blessing, however, for although the fog shielded them from the shore, it also presented an unwelcome hazard to the fifty-eight ships, naval and merchant, steaming in close proximity to each other. None of the merchantmen and only a few of the naval ships were equipped with radar, and a game of 'Blind Man's Bluff' ensued. Ships were forced to switch on their navigation lights, and in some cases their deck lighting, to avoid running into each other.

The fog lasted into the early hours of the 10th, a nerve-racking experience for all concerned. Speed was reduced to a crawl, but even so there were a number of near-misses. Multiple collisions, any one of which could have caused a disastrous pile-up of ships in the opaque darkness, were avoided only by extra careful ship handling and alert lookouts.

Fortunately, when the sun lifted over the horizon the fog was quickly dispersed, allowing the now hopelessly scattered convoy to resume some semblance of order. During the course of the day, the heavy units of the escort left to return to Gibraltar, leaving WS 21S, now officially Operation Pedestal, with its close escort. This consisted of the four carriers *Eagle*, *Furious*, *Indomitable* and *Victorious*, the heavy cruisers *Kenya*, *Manchester* and *Nigeria*, the anti-aircraft cruisers *Cairo, Charybdis, Phoebe* and *Sirius*, plus twenty-five destroyers. That evening, the RFA fleet oilers *Brown Ranger* and *Dingledale* arrived, and some of the thirstier escorts had their bunker tanks topped up.

The night that followed was quiet, and when dawn broke on the 11th the convoy, then passing 70 miles south of the Balearic Islands, was moving east at a good pace and still unmolested, a state of affairs that was shortly to change. The Italian submarine *Uarsciek*, under the command of Arezzo de la Targia, had been cruising on the surface at night and was just about to submerge when the leading ships of Pedestal came in sight. Astonished by the size of the convoy, Targia went to periscope depth and waited for the ships to approach.

When the convoy was within range, Targia chose one of the most vulnerable targets, the 23,000-ton aircraft carrier HMS *Furious.* The *Furious*, built in 1916 as a battlecruiser and converted to an aircraft carrier between the wars, was fulfilling a dual role, having on board thirty-two Spitfires to be flown off to Malta as well as being part of Pedestal's escort.

Luckily for *Furious*, the Italian submarine's brace of torpedoes went wide, and the carrier sailed on unscathed. Targia, meanwhile, confident that he had sunk *Furious*, was slipping away to safer waters, leaving Pedestal completely unaware that it had been attacked. But Targia's botched effort was not completely in vain. As soon as *Uarsciek* was over the horizon, she radioed the German/Italian submarine base at La Spezia alerting it to the presence of a huge eastbound convoy.

However, Spezia was already aware that a large British operation was under way. An entry in their war diary for the night of 10 August reads:

> According to an agent, a strong formation passed eastwards through the Straits of Gibraltar during the night of 9/10. According to an air report this formation was in CH 8178 at 1900, and consisted of two battleships, 2 aircraft carriers, 14 destroyers and 15 steamers. The boats were given permission to attack any targets of the formation.

On the morning of the 11th, other reports began to come in:

> A large enemy convoy escorted by several aircraft carriers and battleships, as well as a large number of light units,

was spotted by our air reconnaissance after 0800 and shadowed constantly.

Our air forces contacted a convoy eastbound from Gibraltar. Shadowers' reports, composition and formation of the convoy were passed on to the boats. Convoy consists of about 65 vessels as follows: First group: 1 carrier, 4 cruisers, 7 destroyers, 1 merchant ship; second group: 3 battleships (the *Rodney* and the *Nelson* among them), 20 escort vessels including cruisers and destroyers, about 20 merchant ships; third group: 6 destroyers.

At 1827 the following radio signal with time of origin 1145 was received from U 73 (Rosenbaum): 'Enemy convoy sighted in 9118. Enemy is proceeding at 12 knots, course 090°.'

Immediately after the transmission of this radio signal a radio message was transmitted by a boat, containing 1) Composition of one of the convoy groups 2) Success report and 3) Report on depth charge hunt. This radio message was probably also transmitted by U 73.

U-73, commanded by 29-year-old Kapitänleutnant Helmut Rosenbaum, had been operating in the Mediterranean since mid-January of that year, but had yet to sink an enemy ship. When the great armada that was Operation Pedestal came in sight, Rosenbaum wasted no time in attacking. Closing in at periscope depth, he turned his sights on the largest target in range, which happened to be the aircraft carrier HMS *Eagle*.

The 22,600-ton *Eagle*, whose keel had been laid down as the dreadnought battleship *Almirante Cochrane* for the Chilean Navy but had never been delivered, had finally been commissioned in 1924 as one of the Royal Navy's first aircraft carriers, complete with 1918-vintage Sopwith Camels on her flight deck. She had narrowly missed being sunk while escorting Operation Harpoon two months earlier, and now her luck had finally run out. When within 550yds of the carrier, Rosenbaum fired a four-torpedo spread from his bow tubes, all of which hit the *Eagle*. Nineteen-year-old Fleet Air Arm air mechanic A.W. Rowell described her end:

We had shortly stood down from action stations from a threatened air attack, which at least on our side of the convoy had not developed, and I and a shipmate (Alistair

Rintoul) had not gone down below, we had remained at our action station on the starboard side of the 'Island' (the superstructure on the starboard side of the flight deck). At about 1.15pm, 4 torpedoes struck HMS *Eagle*'s port side. She immediately listed to port, and although we did not hear any instruction to abandon ship, it became very apparent that she was sinking, so my shipmate and I blew up our lifebelts, tied a rope to a stanchion, went down it as far as the anti-torpedo blister (a second hull designed to absorb torpedoes), now about 15 feet out of the water, and jumped into the sea. We swam to get away from the possible suction, and saw *Eagle*'s last moments no more than 7 or 8 minutes after she was struck.

The ageing British carrier went down without a struggle, taking her aircraft and 160 of her total complement of 1,087 men down with her. Operation Pedestal was only 400 miles east of Gibraltar, and had already lost one of its most valuable escorts. Her executioner, Helmut Rosenbaum, in recognition of his audacious and successful attack, received an immediate award of the Knight's Cross.

The air attacks began on the afternoon of the 12th, when the convoy was passing south of Sardinia. A lone German bomber appeared out of the clouds and swooped on the leading mer-chantmen. The 7,740-ton Blue Funnel cargo liner *Deucalion* was first in the line of fire, straddled by a stick of four bombs. Three of the four were near-misses, but the fourth scored a direct hit in her No. 5 hold. Listing heavily to port as the sea poured into her breached hull, the *Deucalion* slewed out of line, and dropped astern. The *Clan Ferguson* moved up to take her place as lead ship of Column 1.

Some three hours later, shortly after the sunset, the battle for Operation Pedestal began in earnest. A large force of German air-craft, consisting of thirty Ju88 bombers and seven He111 torpedo bombers, accompanied by six Me110 fighter bombers, came roar-ing in from their Sardinian airfields. The *Brisbane Star* in Column 3 was first to be hit, followed by the *Clan Ferguson*. David Royale, manning a gun in the escorting cruiser *Charybdis*, remembers:

The *Clan Ferguson* was steaming along – a fine-looking ship of around 12,000 tons, at approximately fourteen knots – following in our wake. I saw three Junkers Ju88s diving from astern but could not bring my gun down to bear because of the training stops. In any case our after guns had opened up. They hit the leading aeroplane but not before he had let go his bombs, scoring direct hits. It was a sight I shall never forget . . . one minute there was this fine vessel, the next a huge atomic-like explosion and she had gone, disappeared with just a blueish ring of flame on the water and a mushroom of smoke and flame thousands of feet into the sky. The other two Ju88s were caught in the blast and never reappeared, but that was a poor price to pay. Huge chunks of blasted ship splashed into the sea close to me, I thought some of the stern of the *Charybdis* must have been struck. Actually, only one of our crew was wounded by this rain of debris.

Second Officer Arthur Black, who was on watch on the bridge of the *Clan Ferguson*, gave a more detailed account in his report:

A signalman on watch saw the torpedo approaching from our starboard beam. He shouted, 'Hard to starboard' but the ship did not swing quickly enough. The torpedo hit between the engine room and No. 4 hold. Both flooded immediately and the ship caught fire; I could see flames coming up from the engine room skylight and through the ship's side. The hatch covers were blown off No. 4 hold and 2 landing craft stowed on top of this hatch were blown off. I could not see any other damage to the ship as the flames were so intense.

We had high explosives stowed in No. 5 and No. 2 holds, and as the fire was spreading rapidly the order to abandon ship was given. We had 4 life boats and 1 jolly boat. No. 3 boat was destroyed by the explosion, and the remainder of the boats, with the exception of No. 1 which we got away, caught fire. We managed to release 3 rafts immediately while the ship still had way on and before the water caught fire round the ship, but the fourth one jammed in the rigging and was eventually cut adrift. The remainder of us who were still on board just got over the side as the ship sank, and I was so close that the paravanes caught against my steel helmet. Luckily the paravanes did not foul this raft so we were all able to get on to it. The ship sank at 2110, about 7 minutes after being struck by the torpedo. A little before the ship finally sank there was a violent explosion which appeared to be from No. 5 hold.

The oil on the water around the position in which my ship had sunk blazed furiously for about 48 hours. Cans of petrol kept floating to the surface and catching fire, and at one time there was dense black smoke rising which I think must have been caused by the fuel oil which was ignited on coming to the surface.

The convoy carried on, leaving in its wake the flotsam of the sunken *Clan Ferguson* and the crippled *Deucalion* drifting and abandoned. It seemed a small price to pay, but there was much worse in store.

The next day was Friday 13th, and for Operational Pedestal the day certainly lived up to its mythical reputation. In a prolonged and fierce running battle in the restricted waters between Sicily and the Tunisian coast, German and Italian aircraft, MTBs and submarines wreaked havoc amongst the Allied ships. The British escorts and the merchantmen in their charge fought a gallant action, but they were completely overwhelmed by the sheer numbers of their aggressors. When the final reckoning was made, it showed that Operation Pedestal had been an extremely costly undertaking, resulting in the loss of the aircraft carrier HMS *Eagle*, the cruisers *Manchester* and *Cairo*, the destroyer *Foresight* and nine merchant ships out of a convoy of fourteen. With those ships had gone 100,000 tons of cargo desperately needed in the besieged island of Malta. The total loss of lives in the ships, both naval and merchant, was put at 350, with an equal number ending up in Italian prisoner of war camps.

Four cargo liners, the *Brisbane Star*, *Melbourne Star*, *Port Chalmers* and *Rochester Castle*, survived to enter Malta's Grand Harbour on the night of the 13/14th. They were battle-scarred but triumphant. Forty-eight hours later, they were joined by the British-manned American tanker *Ohio*. She was blackened by fire, her engines damaged beyond repair, and she was kept afloat by two destroyers lashed alongside her, but she still had most of her 12,000 tons of aviation spirit still on board. Only the courage and determination of her crew, who in the most perilous of circumstances had refused to abandon ship, had saved her.

The fog of war still surrounds Operation Pedestal, but of the *Clan Ferguson*'s crew it is known that nine men, including Chief Engineer John Wilde, were killed in her engine room when the torpedo struck. Above deck, First Radio Officer William McCory, Surgeon Hugh Bruce and DEMS Petty Officer Bill Goodban also lost their lives. The remainder of the Glasgow ship's complement survived, thirty-two being rescued by a German flying boat and seven by an Italian Red Cross plane, while the rest, led by Second Officer Arthur Black, landed on Zembra Island, which was Vichy French territory.

Second Officer Black reported on their welcome, which was the stuff of comic opera:

> We eventually landed in a little cove about 1200 and 2 Europeans came down to take us ashore. They took us to a fishing station where we were treated very kindly by the Italians living there who gave us food, wine and cigarettes.
>
> They reported our presence to the Military Authorities who came from the next village to take us away. Two of the men who were unable to walk were taken by donkeys. As we arrived in the next village the French population came out to welcome us. They treated us very well, all the women of the village joined together to give us a good meal from their rations.
>
> We left the village about 2000 and were taken by the Military Authorities to a camp at Bonficha where we arrived on 17th August. When I arrived at the camp I was surprised to see our 3rd Officer, he had been one of the 50 people who got away from the ship in the lifeboat.
>
> From Bonficha we were taken to Le Kef. At this camp Lieutenant Morelle of the Spahi Regiment did everything he could for us. He was very pro-British and made himself very unpopular with the French Military Authorities.
>
> We were never officially released and when we were trying to escape from the camp Monsieur Chastelle, the Civil Controller, and his assistant Monsieur Gantes remained behind in Sfax to cover our retreat, and had it not been for their assistance I do not think we should have been able to escape.

CHAPTER TWELVE

Voyage Not Completed –
Viking Star 25.08.42

The *Viking Star*, with her tall funnel, straight stem and cutaway counter stern, was distinctively a ship of the 1920s. Built in the aftermath of the First World War, a replacement for one of the many ships lost, she was a 6,213-ton refrigerated meat carrier flying the house flag of Lord Vestey's Blue Star Line. Sadly, in the depression-plagued days of the late 1920s she had fallen on hard times. Captain E. Ashton-Irvine, who joined her as a first-trip cadet in 1927, in later years recorded his first impressions:

> My first sight of the ship was really a sickener. She had been laid up for nearly a year at the buoys and had just been taken off them to bunker. She was a ship of about 8,000 [*sic*] tons, flush decked, with a three-tier bridge-house; number 3 hatch, or the bunkers, amidships, and the afterhouse and fidley [grating] around the funnel, which was large, had a dome top, and looked awful. Coupled with the fact that she was rusty from end to end and covered in coal dust.
>
> I found my way up the ladder and after stumbling through feet-deep coal (and coal dust that was more like mud), I found myself in the officers' alleyway and managed to locate the cadets' room. My two mates were lying in all their glory – dungarees, coal dust, et al. – in the lower of the four bunks. The room was thick with smoke, both ports were open, and it looked as though they had been open for the past year, because everything was so dirty and it was impossible to tell what colour the bulkheads were. I found they were both 3-year cadets and well experienced. They both suggested I should beat it home forthwith and, frankly, I think I would have done well to have done so. I was taken to see the Mate, a hard case 'Geordy' who hated two things – the sea and 'silly ass cadets'. I got

small change from him. I went to meet the Captain, a very old gentleman of 71, who had shares in the company, had been an ex-sailing ship owner, and was in his dotage. He promptly forbade me to go ashore because the Tyne was full of pubs and loose women. Needless to say, I stayed on board that night, and earned the derision of my mates, who came back stoned and said they had had a fine time. I still wonder if they did. I was sent to bed after a very poor dinner, but it was all new to me and I think I put up with it and made as if I liked it, but doubted if I really did.

The next day was up at 5.00 am, got tea for the other two, shaving water and a bucket of water to bathe, scrubbed out the room and bathroom – that was really a misnomer as it was about the size of a wardrobe, 3 feet by 3 feet and 6 feet high, and there was nothing in it but cold air, of which there was plenty, so we bathed in the room which, as I said, had four bunks in it, one settee like a shelf, and nothing else. All our gear went into the spare bunk. I then went out on deck to try to clean up the mess, shovelled coal all day, had meals off the table in the pantry – and what meals! Ugh – they weren't fit for pigs. We left the coal berth, went to get water and on the 4th April we sailed for the River Plate. What a trip! We shovelled coal all day and after it was out of one deck, we shovelled it into another deck and into the stoke hold.

Fifteen years had now gone by since that dreary episode, and the *Viking Star* had regained much of her self-respect. Painted over- all in wartime grey, with only the merest wisp of smoke trailing from her tall funnel, she left Montevideo on 9 August 1942 bound for the UK with 4,500 tons of frozen beef and 200 tons of fertil- izer. While in the River Plate her boilers had been converted to oil-burning, and she was a much cleaner and happier ship for it. In command was 43-year-old Captain James Mills, and she had a total complement of sixty, including five DEMS gunners. The latter, with the assistance of several of the ship's crew who held gunnery certificates, manned her armament, which consisted of a 4-inch, a 12-pounder and five .303 machine guns. Both galley and pantry matched the ship's new image, and she was known as a 'good feeder' by those who had sailed in her.

The *Viking Star*'s voyage had begun nearly two months earlier in Liverpool, where she had loaded a general cargo for Buenos Aires. Now she was to retrace her steps, taking a long dogleg across the Atlantic to Freetown, where she would join a convoy for the passage north. Meanwhile, she was to sail unescorted, the powers that be in the Admiralty considering it highly unlikely that she would meet up with the enemy on the way across to Africa.

The ocean crossing was indeed without incident; fine, warm weather, and the horizon day after day unsullied by hostile strangers. It was not until the morning of 25 August, when the *Viking Star* was some 250 miles south-west of Freetown, that she experienced her first contact with reality. A Sunderland flying boat displaying the reassuring red, white and blue roundels of the RAF appeared out of the clouds and began to circle the ship. The ensign and signal letter flags were hoisted and an attempt was made to contact the plane by Aldis lamp, but there was no reply. The Sunderland then flew off again, and it was assumed that all was well.

In fact, it was anything but: the flying boat had been under false colours, having been captured by the Vichy French in Dakar earlier in the war, and was acting as a spotter plane for the Germans. She regularly patrolled the approaches to Freetown on the lookout for Allied ships, radioing their position to waiting U-boats when spotted.

On this occasion her report was received by U-130, a Type IXC under the command of the experienced Korvettenkapitän Ernst Kals which had sailed from Lorient on 4 July. Kals, who had served sixteen years in surface ships of the German Navy before joining the U-boat arm in 1940, was on his fourth war patrol in U-130, with orders to create as much havoc as possible on the Freetown–UK convoy route. Already, cruising in the vicinity of the Cape Verde Islands, he had sunk five Allied ships totalling over 40,000 tons gross, after which he had moved south to explore the approaches to the convoy assembly port of Freetown. The move proved justified when at about 1600 on 25 August, with another two hours of daylight left, the *Viking Star* came in view. Kals dived, and waited at periscope depth for the unsuspecting ship to cross his sights.

It was not surprising that with the crossing from South America having been so untroubled, and the safety of Freetown being less than twenty-four hours away, morale was riding high aboard the

Viking Star. Sixteen-year-old deck boy Clifford Maw in later life recollected:

> We had left Buenos Aires with a full cargo of frozen beef, and some of us were sunning ourselves on deck in the first dog watch and talking about 'fish' – torpedoes – their construction and method of firing them. Two or three were in bathing costumes; there was Kelly the donkey-man in overalls and a beret, and myself wearing only a pair of rope-soled shoes and grey shorts hitched up by a sixpenny belt. The lamp trimmer in his birthday suit was splashing happily in a canvas bath on the after well deck.
>
> I had just opened my mouth to say something when there came the muffled sound of an explosion. A couple of seconds later a louder explosion came from somewhere deep under the galley, near to where some of us were sitting. It was a real case of 'talk of the devil'.

Chief Officer Frederick MacQuiston explained what happened next in his report to the Admiralty:

> At 1645 local time on 25th August in position 6.00 N 14.00 W we were struck by a torpedo in the engine room on the port side, followed almost immediately by another torpedo which struck almost in the same position. The explosions were very loud, there was a strong smell of cordite and a tremendous column of water was thrown up over the bridge.
>
> I was on watch at the time, the 4th Officer was on watch with me and was on the monkey island, also a lookout man was stationed in the starboard gun nest.
>
> Immediately after the torpedoes struck, the ship listed 10–12 degrees to port. After a few moments she righted herself and remained upright. Both boats on the port side were blown to pieces by the explosion, the derricks were smashed, the hatch covers were blown off the bunker hatch, the stoke hold and the engine room and bunker hatch immediately filled with water. The W/T transmitter and aerials were destroyed by the explosion and no W/T message was sent. As we could not see the submarine and there was no point in keeping the guns manned,

it was decided to abandon ship. The engines had stopped of their own accord but the ship carried her way for about 10 minutes.

Able Seaman Stan Mayes added:

> I was off watch and in my cabin below deck – all lights went out and with much shouting we groped our way in the darkness to the companionway up to the boat deck and as we ran along the deck to our boat stations we were showered by debris thrown up by the explosion.

This was the nightmare they all dreaded and had rehearsed for so often, at the same time hoping it would never happen. There was no time to waste. With her engine spaces flooded, the *Viking Star* was settling fast. Captain Mills gave the order to abandon ship, the last order he would ever give, for he would go down with his ship.

It soon became apparent that leaving the sinking vessel would not be a straightforward operation. The *Viking Star* carried four 28-man lifeboats and eight large life-rafts, more than ample to accommodate her entire crew of sixty. However, both lifeboats on the port side had gone, destroyed by the exploding torpedoes, and one of the starboard boats was damaged. Darkness had descended, and in the ensuing rush to get away an element of panic crept in. Chief Officer MacQuiston explains:

> We started to get the starboard boats away, but one of the sailors let go the forward fall of No. 1 boat, which was the motor boat. Fortunately, it was held by the gripes and the after fall, but when it was finally lowered the boat filled with water immediately. I think it must have been damaged by flying debris from the explosion. We attempted to bale this boat out, but the water gained too rapidly, so the occupants abandoned it and swam to No. 3 boat, where they were taken on board. We transferred the food, wireless and water breakers from this boat into No. 3. Eight life-rafts were released before the ship was abandoned.

All those on watch in the *Viking Star*'s engine room, Third Engineer William Clark, Donkeyman Michael Gibbons and firemen Thomas

Anderson, Leonard Hartley, Francis Meehan and James Spencer, were missing, probably killed when the torpedoes struck. Captain Mills was also missing, being last seen launching a life-raft on the after deck. This left Chief Officer MacQuiston in command of what remained of the *Viking Star*, which was one crowded life-boat containing thirty-six men, and two life-rafts with seventeen men clinging to them. The ship herself was still afloat, but she had not long to go. Ernst Kals had brought U-130 to the surface and closed in to deliver the *coup de grâce*. A third torpedo completed his night's work, breaking the *Viking Star's* back, and with her bows and stern reaching for the sky and forming a grotesque V-sign, she slid under, leaving in her wake only a spreading oil slick in which bobbed a few pieces of charred wreckage.

U-130 now approached the only remaining lifeboat, and Kals questioned its occupants regarding the ship and her cargo. The answers he received were vague and grudgingly given, and when he asked if the Master or any officers were on board, he was greeted with a stony silence. Anticipating this request, all the officers in the boat had discarded their badges of rank and had merged with the crew. The boat being so crowded, there was little point in pursuing the matter further. The U-boat backed away and disappeared into the twilight.

Kals did not leave the area, and next morning torpedoed and sank the British steamer *Beechwood* on her way north from the Cape with a cargo of potash. Only one crew member was lost, but her master Captain Samuel Dring was taken on board U-130 as a prisoner of war. The others were picked up by the RFA fleet oiler *Fortol* and landed at Freetown.

U-130 had now been fifty-three days at sea and was running low on fuel and provisions. Ernst Kals, having sunk a total of 51,528 tons of Allied shipping since leaving Lorient in July, considered it was time to set course for home.

As soon as the U-boat was out of sight, Chief Officer MacQuiston, in the *Viking Star's* sole surviving lifeboat, ordered the emergency W/T transmitter to be rigged. At 1815 Second Radio Officer Sloan tapped out an SOS, but this being the height of the rainy season, the atmospherics were so bad that in Sloan's opinion it was most unlikely the message would be readable by any station, ashore or afloat. It was decided to wait until daylight before trying again.

AB Stan Mayes takes up the story again:

At dawn we hoisted sail and attempted to tow the rafts but it proved futile, so Chief Officer MacQuiston suggested we try to make land in the boat and have help sent to the rafts. This idea was not accepted by the men on the rafts and they pointed out that we had been seen by the Sunderland flying boat and our non-arrival at Freetown would prompt a search for us. We began rationing food and water. For each man – two pieces of chocolate a.m., two biscuits and Pemmican and a spoonful of condensed milk at midday, and in the evening it was two pieces of chocolate and a malted milk tablet. Water was issued three times daily – half a cupful each time.

The lifeboat was of wooden construction and was leaking badly. Having 36 men in it, we had only 14 inches of freeboard so it was being bailed out constantly. During the second night a strong wind caused a choppy sea and there was frantic bailing out as water came over the gunwales. During daytime the heat of the sun was unbearable, but during the night-time it became very cold and, as most of us were wearing very little clothing, we suffered from both extremes. Our position was a few miles north of the Equator.

At dawn on 27th August the Chief Officer decided to leave the rafts and try to sail to the land, so we took G. Patterson, Cadet from a raft onto the boat, and then I witnessed a very heroic act by AB Daintith of Liverpool. He gave up his relatively safe place in the lifeboat to an injured DEMS gunner, A. Hancock, from a semi-submerged raft, knowing he had far less chance of survival, or none at all, in the shark-infested seas. After passing water, provisions, blankets and a large yellow flag to the men on the rafts we set sail and departed. The Bosun and myself steered the boat as we both had experience, mine being four and a half years in coastal sailing barges. We had four hours on and four hours off at the tiller while others were on a rota in bailing out the leaking boat. A metal bailer and empty biscuit tins were used. We steered by the sun and stars as our lifeboat compass had been stolen in a recent port of call. We were constantly accompanied by sharks and often saw many barracudas, dugongs, large rays and myriads of small fish. With so many men in the boat there was much discomfort from lack of space.

The *Viking Star* had been torpedoed roughly 165 miles south-west of Freetown, not an insurmountable distance to cover even in a ship's lifeboat, a notoriously difficult craft to handle under sail. Fortunately, the wind was from the south-west – a following wind – and with the prevailing current also setting in towards the land, MacQuiston's boat, although substantially overloaded, was making progress at around 2 knots.

In later life, Clifford Maw recalled the conclusion of the perilous boat journey:

Short commons, seasickness, work, dangerous moments, spells of boredom, hopes raised, only to be shattered – such formed our lot over four days and nights on the ocean. Time and time again someone jumped up to point out 'a sail' that proved to be no more than a wisp of cloud on the horizon or a shadow on the sea. So when Kelly yelled out one drizzly night, 'Look! There's land, fellows!' he was told brusquely to 'Pipe down and stop rocking the boat!' But he was right, and we raised a hoarse cheer when doubts were dispelled. None of us was feeling too strong and I had taken my belt in to the last notch. But we kept rowing against the ebb tide until caught by the heel in a breaking crest of sea. The First Mate ordered, 'Ship the oars!' and the boat rushed forward amid surf with foam creaming over the stern and gunwales.

Another giant roller struck us and our boat was hurled up and over, flinging us all into the sea. It looked like 'curtains' for me. My kapok life-jacket had been soaked frequently and had lost its buoyancy. Instead of keeping me afloat it dragged me down and I was lucky to find myself lying on the beach and Chippy, the carpenter, who had rescued me, bending over and applying first aid with ham-fisted vigour. The other chaps were ashore and had hitched the sea anchor to a thorny bush to hold the overturned lifeboat fast, then rigged a sail for a windbreak, and we all waited in this rough shelter for the dawn.

The lifeboat had been thrown ashore on a remote sandy beach at the entrance to the Sherbro River, close to the border between Sierra Leone and Liberia. Shortly before dawn, the survivors were found by a local fisherman, who took them to a nearby village where, largely through the efforts of a young Creole girl who had trained as a missionary in Freetown and spoke passable English, they were made welcome and given a meal. Their hunger assuaged, they lay down in one of the huts, and slept the sleep of the just.

Stan Mayes later wrote:

> Emerging from the huts later on we found every piece of our boat had been carried from the shore and was in the village. We were asked if we wanted any part of it but of course we did not. Later, we left the village and began walking through the jungle in single file with natives escorting us, and they were making sure the way was clear of snakes and animals. After a few hours we stopped at another village and stayed overnight. Our escort returned to their own village but the missionary stayed with us. Here we were given a meal and again slept in mud huts. Next morning we left and again we were escorted and accompanied by the missionary and later that day we arrived at a creek and stayed overnight in a village. A native was sent ahead to Bonthe to inform the District Commissioner of our presence, and next morning we were taken through swamps in canoes to deeper waters where a large launch was waiting for us. After thanking the missionary and the escorts we left, and three hours later we arrived at Bonthe Shebar – nowadays known as Sherbro. We were all accommodated in the homes of Swiss and French traders.

While in Bonthe Shebar, where there was a Government radio station, Chief Officer MacQuiston sent a message to the Admiralty in Freetown informing them of the loss of the *Viking Star* and the approximate position of the two life-rafts. Freetown despatched a Sunderland, an armed trawler and an MTB to search for the rafts, but they had no success.

In charge of the survivors on the two missing life-rafts was Third Officer John Rigiani. The rafts were of substantial wooden construction, 8ft by 8ft, buoyancy being provided by empty 40-gallon drums, around which the frame was built. They were designed to float either way up and had food, water and distress flares on board. Unfortunately, one of the two rafts had been damaged on launching, had lost most of its buoyancy and was completely waterlogged. The seven men on board this raft had little comfort, for they were virtually sitting in the sea. It was only due to the superb seamanship and leadership shown by John Rigiani that they survived the stormy seas to reach land. After ten days at sea they were cast ashore on a Liberian beach some 150 miles south-east of Freetown. They eventually arrived in Freetown, where they were reunited with the rest of the *Viking Star*'s survivors. There they learned that telegrams had already been sent to their next of kin informing them that the *Viking Star* was missing and all her crew lost. They were written off with their ship as 'Voyage Not Completed'.

Stan Mayes has the last word:

> I was an Able Seaman on *Viking Star* and my pay was £22.12s 6d per month. £10.12s 6d paid by the shipowner and £12 War Risk Money paid by the Ministry of Shipping. From the day your ship was sunk all wages for the crew were stopped, as in my case, and were only paid again on my arrival in the UK, when I reported myself alive at Tilbury Shipping Office (shipowners regarded us as unemployed – without a ship). My wages from Blue Star were backdated to the date of sinking and to the day of arrival in Liverpool. The War Risk Money paid by the Government ceased with the loss of the ship. The next of kin of seamen who lost their lives received no payments.

CHAPTER THIRTEEN

Voices from the Past – *Peterton* 17.09.42

As dusk falls I think a lot of home. I always do on a Sunday. That little Welsh village in North Pembrokeshire. The evening service is now about to begin in the chapel of which my father is Pastor. I close my eyes and dream that I am there in the old family pew with my dear mother and sisters. The singing is wonderful, rendered as only a Welsh choir can . . . I fall asleep only to wake in a little while to find myself still in an open boat adrift somewhere out on the vast Atlantic Ocean.

Jonathan Islwyn Davies, First Radio Officer, late of the Newcastle tramp *Peterton*, and his twenty-one fellow survivors crammed into a 24ft lifeboat had already endured thirty-one days afloat on the great ocean. Thirty-one days at the mercy of the boiling sun and lifeless air of the Doldrums, ever searching for a landfall that seemingly would never come. Now, with food and water running low and exhaustion beginning to take its toll, all they had left were dreams of home.

The voyage had begun on the last day of August 1942 in the port of Hull on England's north-east coast when the *Peterton*, down to her summer marks with a full cargo of best Durham coal, had set sail for Buenos Aires.

She was not a ship to turn heads. Built in 1919 for R. Chapman & Son, also known as the Carlton & Cambay Steamship Company, she was the archetypal British tramp steamer. Weighing in at just over 5,000 tons gross, she had a conveniently box-shaped hull and a tall 'Woodbine' funnel that provided natural draught for her three Scotch boilers. Her 3-cylinder, triple-expansion engine, driving a single screw, gave her – in theory, at least – a service speed of 9½ knots. Commanded by 33-year-old Captain Thomas Marrie, she carried a total complement of forty-three and was armed with the usual vintage 4-inch and a brace of machine guns.

After a trouble-free passage around the north of Scotland, the *Peterton* joined up with the Gibraltar-bound convoy OG 89 off the Firth of Clyde. When complete, this convoy consisted of twenty-one merchantmen, all British-flag, most of them small short-sea traders carrying coal or coke to Spanish and Portuguese ports. The *Peterton*, being bound for the South Atlantic, was the odd ship out. Escorting OG 89 were the sloop HMS *Fowey* and four Flower-class corvettes.

The convoy first steamed due west into the open Atlantic until clear of the U-boats' hunting grounds, before turning south to pass 300 miles west of Cape Finisterre. This irksome diversion paid dividends, for although the U-boats were sinking up to 100 ships a month in the North Atlantic at the time, OG 89 cleared the danger area unmolested.

When 250 miles due west of Lisbon the *Peterton* said her goodbyes and slipped away from the other ships to begin her long, lonely trek to South America. Captain Marrie had been advised that the only U-boat activity reported to the south was off the coast of Liberia, in the Gulf of Guinea. Accordingly, he set course to pass midway between Madeira and the Azores, confident that his passage would continue uninterrupted.

The 'U-boat activity' reported was the work of one man, the much-decorated Kapitänleutnant Heinrich Bleichrodt, who commanded the Type IXB long-range boat U-109. After just two years in command, Bleichrodt had already joined the growing list of Admiral Dönitz's 'aces' by sending 140,000 tons of Allied shipping to the bottom. He had taken U-109 out of Lorient on her sixth war patrol some seven weeks earlier and while hunting in the Gulf of Guinea had added another three ships to his score, culminating with the destruction of Blue Star Line's 11,449-ton *Tuscan Star*.

The *Tuscan Star*, sunk with two torpedoes on the night of 6 September, provided a most satisfactory conclusion to U-109's sixth war patrol. Loaded with 7,300 tons of frozen beef and 5,000 tons of general, she was a prime target, and her loss was a serious blow to the British cause. Bleichrodt later regretted the lives lost – forty-eight of the *Tuscan Star*'s crew and three passengers had been killed by his torpedoes – but war was war. Now, with the U-boat's fuel and provisions at a low ebb, he considered he was justified in requesting permission to bring the patrol to an end. Lorient agreed, so soon after the *Tuscan Star* had sunk beneath the waves and her survivors had been interrogated, Bleichtrodt set course for Biscay, aiming to pass outside the Cape Verde Islands and then north between Madeira and the Azores. In doing so, he unwittingly put U-109 on a collision course with the southbound *Peterton*.

Thursday, 17 September 1942 dawned fine and warm, with a flat calm sea, a cloudless blue sky and the lightest of north-easterly breezes that barely stirred the tropical air. The *Peterton* was then 240 miles north-west of the Cape Verde Islands and making a steady 9 knots on a south-south-westerly course. Since leaving Convoy OG 89 eleven days earlier she had passed within sight of the odd northbound ship; otherwise, her only company had been a few inquisitive porpoises and the occasional wandering sea bird.

After a restless night in his airless box of a cabin, First Radio Officer Jonathan Davies was enjoying the comparative cool of the *Peterton*'s lower bridge deck before taking over the watch in the wireless room at 0800. Because of a shortage of radio officers, since sailing from Hull Davies had been keeping watch-and-watch, four hours on and four hours off, with Second Radio Officer Thomas White. It was a punishing routine. Davies had kept the midnight-to-four watch during the night and had slept little since. This happened every second night, and after nearly three weeks at sea he was beginning to feel the strain. Not that radio watch-keeping in wartime was arduous work; with strict radio silence being kept, the watch entailed nothing more strenuous than four hours sat in front of the receiver reading a good book. Incoming messages were few and far between, and for most of the time the ether was eerily quiet, the silence only occasionally broken by a plaintive cry for help from a ship torpedoed far to the north. It was a lonely existence, almost boring.

At precisely 0800 Davies relieved his junior in the wireless room and settled down with his book. He was relieved for breakfast at 0830 but was back on watch by 0900. With so little to occupy his mind for the next three hours, boredom soon began to set in, boredom that would have been very quickly dispelled had he been aware that his ship was being watched by a hidden enemy.

The thin spiral of smoke on the horizon heralding the approach of the *Peterton* had been spotted by a lookout in U-109's conning tower at first light. Bleichrodt waited until the British ship was hull-up and recognizable as a southbound merchant ship, then he submerged to periscope depth to wait for her to come within range.

Jonathan Davies takes up the narrative:

> At 9.30 terrific explosion amidships followed by another two within thirty seconds of each other; knew these to be three torpedoes, and the ship took a list to port immediately and began to sink. Sent out the necessary distress signals giving ship's position, four times and then found the wireless room door jammed due to force of explosion and could not get out that way. Crawled through communicating window into living cabin, grabbed life jacket, and ran out on to lower bridge. Noticed there were no lifeboats on the davits, and realized that the ship had been abandoned. Hurried up to the navigating bridge to ascertain what direction the boats had taken. Saw lifeboat full of men pulling away astern, so ran down to main deck and along aft and got up on to the poop. Noticed port rails of ship now under water and likely to roll over any second, so jumped over the stern and swam out for the lifeboat. Suction from ship making progress difficult and eventually when not very far from reaching boat was exhausted, but two men swam out with a line and we were hauled aboard to safety. On looking round found ship had disappeared and only wreckage floating about. The port lifeboat had been blown to pieces by explosions and the starboard bridge boat was floating upside down. The port bridge boat luckily had floated off; this was retrieved and eleven men with the Chief Officer in charge were transferred into it. A raft was floating nearby so the fresh water tank and stores were taken off. We are twenty-three men in this lifeboat with the Captain in charge.

U-109 had now surfaced and could be seen heading towards the drifting boats. The survivors were aware of what was about to happen. For some time now, following an edict issued by Admiral Dönitz, U-boat commanders were under orders, whenever possible, to take prisoner the Captain and Chief Engineer of any ship sunk. Experienced senior officers, particularly those in command, were irreplaceable in the short term, and taking them out of circulation would have a serious effect on the manning of Allied merchant shipping.

Both Captain Thomas Marrie and Chief Engineer Thomas Gorman were in the *Peterton*'s crowded lifeboat, and there was nowhere to hide. The usual procedure adopted in a case like this was for the senior men to remove all badges of rank, while other survivors claimed they had gone down with the ship. Short of conducting a long interrogation of the survivors, which they could ill afford to do, U-boat commanders often had little option but to leave empty-handed. However, although Gorman, an older man, agreed to the deception, Captain Marrie refused.

He said to the others, 'I was captain of her when she was afloat, and I am still her captain. If you tell them that I went down with the ship and they find that I am in the boat, they might turn the guns on us, and that would be the end of us all, so for the safety of my crew I shall go aboard if asked for.'

Radio Officer Jonathan Davies, who had begun keeping a log on scraps of paper, wrote:

> By now the submarine is close to us and the Commander gives orders to come alongside. He wants to know the name of our ship and asks for the Captain and Chief Engineer. Our Captain makes himself known and adds that the Chief has gone down with the ship. This is believed and orders are given for him to come aboard. An officer takes him on to the conning tower where the Commander shakes hands, and some conversation follows between them. Our Captain then informs us that he has been taken prisoner, and has tried to get us some extra fresh water; unfortunately there are no tins available to hold it. He wishes us the best of luck, gives the correct course for the nearest land, which is the Cape Verde Islands. We wave our farewells to him as he is taken from view inside – as fine and brave a man as ever sailed the seven seas.

When the U-boat had disappeared out of sight, the lifeboat and jolly boat came together and a head count was made. It then became clear that eight men, three engineer officers and four engine room ratings, along with Second Radio Officer Thomas White, were missing. It was known that the missing engine room personnel were below when the torpedoes struck, and it was assumed they had died in the explosions. Radio Officer White was last seen standing on the poop deck of the *Peterton* as she went down. Those in the boats had called to him to jump, but he refused and so lost his life.

The *Peterton* had been sunk some 250 miles north-west of the Cape Verde Islands, not a great distance to sail, even in a ship's lifeboat, given favourable winds and currents. Unfortunately, wind and current were anything but favourable: the wind was light and variable, barely enough to fill a sail, and the prevailing current was flowing in the wrong direction. Against such odds, the voyage promised to be long and arduous.

In the absence of Captain Marrie, Second Officer George Howes was in charge of the lifeboat, while Chief Officer Francis Fairweather was in the jolly boat. The two officers discussed their situation at length and decided there was no alternative but to set course for the Cape Verdes, hoping to be picked up by a passing ship on the way. There was an emergency radio in the lifeboat, already being set up by Jonathan Davies, who would send out periodic distress signals. Furthermore, both boats were well stocked with food and water, and although they were crowded, with twenty-three in the lifeboat and eleven in the jolly boat, a prolonged voyage, up to thirty days perhaps, was possible. Optimistically, Davies wrote in his log, 'We shall not be in the boat for long, and even if we are not picked up, should make the Cape Verde Islands in about six days.'

It was decided that the boats would lie to sea anchors for the night in case help was already on the way. This proved to be a forlorn hope, for when first light came on the 18th, the horizon was disappointingly empty. However, as the sun rose, so the wind rose with it, and soon a fresh north-easterly was blowing. After the inactivity of the night the survivors were quick to hoist their sails and set course to the east with confidence Their destination, the Cape Verde Islands, lying 300 miles off the African mainland, are an archipelago of fourteen islands with peaks of up to 4,500ft, theoretically visible at over 70 miles. This was a target they surely could not fail to hit, even taking into account their unreliable magnetic compasses and the vagaries of wind and current.

Such optimism proved to be sadly misplaced. Jonathan Davies' prediction of six days stretched into six weeks, and then beyond, and throughout this long ordeal, using a stump of pencil and any scraps of paper he could lay his hands on, he kept a day-to-day journal of the progress of the lifeboat and its occupants. On the journal's opening page Davies wrote, 'Everybody is quite happy and contented.' And this was after a breakfast which consisted of biscuits spread with Pemmican, surely the vilest tasting meat extract ever conceived by man.

The two boats kept within sight of each other throughout the day, coming together at night to discuss progress. The heavy wooden craft were difficult to steer in the prevailing wind, so it was decided to tack to the north-east during the night, altering on to south-east at daylight. In this way they hoped to make a mean course to the east. As soon as it was dark, when radio reception would be at its best, Davies rigged the wireless aerial and broadcast an SOS to all ships, giving the position of the boats. Except for the crackle of atmospherics, nothing was heard in reply; but as all ships would be keeping strict radio silence in accordance with Admiralty orders, the survivors consoled themselves with the thought that help must surely be on the way. Davies wrote in his log:

> Now we spread out as best we can for the night, taking turns at the tiller and lookout. Four officers take over watches at the tiller, and the men one hour each at the lookout. This goes on night and day. I stretch out as best I can on my lifejacket and try to get a little sleep after first saying my prayers and asking God to keep me and my shipmates safe, and guide us soon to land. It is very hard and uncomfortable on the seat. It is getting very cold and all I have on is a pair of shorts and an open shirt. I wish I had some more clothes: I did have a patrol jacket but I gave it to the young apprentice.

As the *Peterton* had been torpedoed in tropical waters and had gone down in a matter of minutes, none of the survivors had been wearing much in the way of clothes. Most had just thin cotton shirts and shorts, and some who had been sleeping after a night watch were near naked. They all suffered in the fierce sunlight during the day and the bitter cold at night.

The first few days went well. The myth of early rescue or landfall prevailed, and everyone was in good spirits. Other than a magnetic compass of uncertain accuracy and a small scale chart, the boats had no other means of finding their way to land, in which case Second Officer George Howes' navigation was largely a matter of guesswork. Chief Engineer Tom Gorman had devised a make-shift log from a length of sail twine and an empty Pemmican tin, which was a great help. With this he calculated that the lifeboat was making good about 2 knots. This put them roughly 180 miles from the Cape Verde Islands at noon on the 21st. The weather was holding fair, with a steady north-easterly breeze, and although the days were unbearably hot and the nights cold, and the diet of Pemmican, hard ship's biscuits and Horlicks tablets was monotonous and unappetizing, morale was high in both boats.

And so they sailed on, the two boats keeping in sight of each other, sometimes neck and neck, each striving to take the lead and be the first to sight land. In the crowded lifeboat, although conditions were far from easy, the certain knowledge that the tall peaks of the Cape Verdes would soon be visible on the horizon made the discomfort easier to bear.

At sunset on the 21st, Jonathan Davies wrote in his log:

> Just before dark the other boat is seen to be about half a mile away on our starboard beam, and seems to be making a more southerly course than we. She makes a pretty picture in the setting sun, with her red sails and yellow distress flag flying at her mast head. We sail on through another night.

First light on the 22nd brought a complete change of fortune. The jolly boat, a familiar and comforting sight ever since they had lost the *Peterton*, had disappeared completely from view, and with it had gone the friendly breeze that had urged them on their way. At sunrise the air was still, and they were alone on a lifeless sea. Davies' daily log, which had until then had been so full of optimism, was suddenly devoid of hope:

> The afternoon is as much as I can bear; the sun is blazing down on us from a cloudless sky. I can hardly get my breath, and am terribly thirsty. Oh, for a gallon of cool, clear water! I am not hungry although I have eaten practically nothing since the start – I can't, my mouth is too dry. I have now five biscuits in my possession which I have not been able to eat. I try bathing my lips with sea water.

It looks cool and inviting to drink, but I understand it would drive me mad if I drank it. In truth, I now quote the words from 'The Ancient Mariner' – 'Water, water everywhere and not a drop [*sic*] to drink!' What a pity that the sea is salty. I am glad when the sun goes down and I look forward eagerly to my ration of water.

Although the *Peterton*'s lifeboat was well stocked with food and water and it had been anticipated that the voyage to safety would be brief, Second Officer Howe had wisely instituted rationing from the beginning. Each man was given two biscuits spread with Pemmican and a small measure of water at daybreak, one biscuit and a similar amount of water at noon, and two biscuits with Pemmican washed down with water at night. It was a desperately inadequate and unappetizing diet, barely enough to ensure subsistence. However, it was the merciless heat of the sun beating down all day, coupled with the lack of proper sleep at night, that did the most to sap the spirit of the survivors. The boat was so crowded that it was impossible for a man to find shelter or stretch out on the bare boards. There were no blankets, and the thin tropical gear most of them wore did nothing to keep out the bitterly cold night air. Whereas in the beginning they had whiled away the dark hours with tales of life at home, of past voyages and ports visited, they had now lapsed into a silence broken only by the slap of the waves and the creaking of the boat's timbers as it rolled in the long Atlantic swell.

Hope returned on the 24th when the breeze picked up enough to fill the drooping sails. The boat began to move again, albeit at no more than one knot, as measured by Chief Engineer Gorman's patent log. The wind, gentle though it was, brought some relief from the burning sun, and life began to have some meaning again for the flagging survivors. In the late afternoon an excited cry from the lookout in the bow brought them fully alert. A ship was in sight.

Davies described the reaction:

There is great excitement, we shall soon be having plenty of food and drink. She is getting nearer to us all the time and we can now see her derricks and ventilators quite plainly. She is an Allied merchant ship, because we can make out the guns on her stern. We burn smoke floats and flares, and wave yellow flags to attract attention . . . Only a shipwrecked sailor can understand our disappointment when she passed about a mile ahead and never saw us . . . However, it is tea-time now and we cheer up after our biscuit and water, and there is always tomorrow and another ship, and anyway we shall hit one of the islands within the next few days – we can't miss them.

It beggars belief that those twenty-three men, after more than a week enduring the cramped conditions in the boat, the unrelenting sun, the cold at night and a starvation diet, could face disappointment so bravely. Yet they did, and it was this dogged determination not to give in to despair that would sustain them through the coming days.

In the early hours of the morning of the 25th they ran into a violent thunderstorm, with gale force winds and torrential rain. The boat became uncontrollable, and they were forced to lie to a sea anchor. But what at first had seemed like another setback proved to be a blessing. The rain was warm and they stripped naked to let it wash the caked salt from their wasted bodies. When the sun rose, they greeted it refreshed in mind and body. Their joy was unrestrained when, later in the morning, the mast of what appeared to be a small ship – a fishing vessel, perhaps – was seen on the horizon. The wind had fallen away again, so they shipped their oars and pulled towards the mast. It was early afternoon before they realized they were in for a disappointment. Jonathan Davies wrote in his log:

> When we get nearer we find that it is an empty ship's lifeboat, and as we come alongside we recognise it to be the Chief Officer's boat. The sail has been neatly furled and there are two or three lifejackets left. We assume that they must have been picked up by the ship that had passed and which failed to see us last night.

The assumption was correct. The *Peterton*'s jolly boat and its eleven occupants had been rescued by the British ship *Empire Whimbrel*, which was almost certainly the ship they themselves had sighted. The *Empire Whimbrel* was on her way to Buenos Aires, where she landed Chief Officer Fairweather and his boat's crew.

On the fourteenth day of their long ordeal, still with no land in sight, Jonathan Davies and his fellow survivors were obliged to accept that they had missed the Cape Verde Islands and had no alternative but to carry on until they reached the African mainland. Davies, now reduced to writing his log between the lines of an old letter from home, commented:

There is a small chart aboard, so this is consulted to ascertain the nearest point of land ahead. We find that it is Bathurst on the West Coast of Africa, and the distance is about 520 miles. We must, therefore, keep on the same course and make the mainland. It is a long way. Will we ever make it?

Another thirty-four days were to drag by before Radio Officer Jonathan Davies' question was answered. The final entry in his log was made on 5 November, forty-nine days after the *Peterton* was sunk. It reads:

Very hot day, sun blazing down on us from a cloudless sky, and sea calm. Making no progress, and drifting south all the time. Lapsing into lengthy silences again, and everybody is lying down. Another lad has joined the ones that are ill today, and is delirious. Wally is bathing his forehead with cool salt water. When this is finished, he leans over the side to refill the tin, but suddenly drops it, and shouts – 'Don't move anybody, there's a ship coming towards us.' I think that he too is delirious, but on looking in the direction he is pointing, I find to my great joy that his words are true. It is actually a real ship, or am I seeing things?

It was not an hallucination. Steaming towards them with her bow-wave frothing and black smoke rolling back from her funnel was the armed trawler HMS *Canna*, which had been sent out from Freetown to look for them. Within half an hour all twenty-two survivors, who with no food for six days had been very near to death, were enjoying their first real meal for seven long weeks. It was hot soup, and it tasted like the nectar of the gods.

On a sad concluding note, 15-year-old Apprentice Edward Briggs Hyde, after surviving the long ordeal, died in hospital in Freetown a few days after landing. He had been on his first trip to sea.

Jonathan Islwyn Davies returned to sea after a brief spell of survivor's leave and remained a sea-going radio officer until he died aboard the Liberian-flag vessel *Cavalier* in November 1964. His early death, at the age of 52, was most probably hastened by the conditions he endured during the long voyage in the *Peterton*'s lifeboat in 1942.

CHAPTER FOURTEEN

Pastures New –
Aldington Court 31.10.42

The 4,891-ton motor vessel *Aldington Court* was a product of Pickersgill's yard at Sunderland, built in 1929 for the British United Steamship Company, later to become Court Line of London. Her maiden voyage had been to Vladivostok, and thereafter she had been employed in the cross-trades, rarely returning to her country of origin. When war came in 1939, life carried on much as normal for Captain Alfred Stuart and his British crew of thirty-three, the *Aldington Court* continuing to roam the world's oceans in search of lucrative cargoes. Outwardly, the only change war had brought was the addition of a team of ten DEMS gunners and a selection of near-antique guns.

In September 1942, having been eight months away from British waters, the *Aldington Court* came under Admiralty control and was sent to Philadelphia to pick up a cargo of military stores for Alexandria, supplies urgently needed by Montgomery's advancing army in North Africa. Fully loaded, she sailed from Philadelphia on the 16th, calling first at New York for a convoy to Guantanamo Bay, where she then joined another convoy for Trinidad. She arrived in Port of Spain on 3 October, and after taking on bunkers sailed again on the 8th. Once clear of the islands, she was on her own, embarked on an 11,000-mile voyage which would take her to Cape Town, around the Cape of Good Hope into the Indian Ocean and then north to Suez. With summer approaching in southern waters the weather promised to be fair, and for the most part the *Aldington Court* would be in waters reputedly free of enemy submarines. Captain Stuart looked forward with some confidence to a quiet voyage. He was then unaware that far away, off the Cape of Good Hope, the lights were going out.

When it had become evident in early 1942 that it was too dangerous for Allied merchant shipping to transit the Mediterranean, all ships bound to and from the Middle East were routed via the

Cape of Good Hope. This long diversion added as much as three weeks to the passage, but the time lost and extra fuel burned were considered to be well justified. Before long, the Cape was witnessing a flow of traffic not seen since before the Suez Canal opened in 1869, and Table Bay was habitually a mass of ships anchored awaiting bunkers and stores. This offered a previously undreamed of opportunity for Admiral Dönitz's U-boat arm, and as soon as he had enough long-range boats to spare he acted.

After sinking the British tanker *Athelknight* off Bermuda on 27 May, U-172 went on to dispose of another 31,679 tons of Allied shipping before returning in triumph to Lorient, where she arrived on 21 July 1942. In just ten weeks at sea Carl Emmermann had proved his ability to command by sinking in excess of 40,000 tons of enemy shipping, this leading to U-172 being chosen to join other Type IXCs in a new and challenging enterprise.

On 19 August, after a month in port, U-172 sailed out of Lorient in company with three other long-range boats. They were U-68 (Karl-Friedrich Merten), U-156 (Werner Hartenstein) and U-504 (Hans-Georg Friedrich Poske). The newly-formed Eisbär ('Polar Bear') Group, unofficially known as the 'Capetown Patrol', was bound for waters as yet unfamiliar to the U-boats. The sailing of the four boats was surrounded by the utmost secrecy. The Admiralty Tracking Room in London was aware that they were at sea, but it was not known where they planned to operate.

In order to mask their real intentions, the Eisbär boats were forbidden to attack shipping on the passage south to the Cape. The order was strictly adhered to until, when 120 miles northeast of Ascension Island, Werner Hartenstein in U-156 sighted a target he could not pass by. She was the 19,695-ton *Laconia*, an ex-Cunard passenger liner in service with the Admiralty as a troopship.

The *Laconia*, sailing without escort, was on her way from Suez to Canada with a special 'cargo', namely 1,809 Italian prisoners of war captured in the Western Desert. Blissfully unaware of the presence on board the liner of so many of his country's allies, Hartenstein sank the *Laconia* with three torpedoes. When he brought U-156 to the surface to interrogate survivors he was horrified to see over 2,000 people struggling in the water. It was only then that he learned the majority of them were Italians. He notified Lorient, and Admiral Dönitz ordered the Eisbär boats to abandon their South African venture and mount a rescue operation. When Hitler heard of this he was furious and countermanded Dönitz's order. Other U-boats were called in, but by the time they arrived, 98 crew members, 133 passengers, including a number of women and children, and 1,394 Italian prisoners, along with 33 of their Polish Army guards, had perished in the shark-infested waters.

Retribution was swift. Twenty-four hours after the *Laconia* went down, U-156 was caught on the surface by an American B-24 Liberator operating out of Ascension and so damaged that she had to withdraw from the Eisbär Group. Her place was taken by U-159 (Helmut Witte), then on her way to take up a patrol off the Congo Delta.

After refuelling from U-459 when 600 miles south of St Helena, the four boats, U-68, U-159, U-172 and U-504, continued on to the Cape. Their orders were to mount a surprise attack on the anchorage at Table Bay, where German agents were reporting as many as fifty ships. The approaches to Cape Town were said to be totally unprotected, and no attempt had been made to black out the port at night. Two boats were to make the first attack, followed by the other two twenty-four hours later. It was anticipated that Eisbär would inflict such heavy casualties in the attack that the flow of Allied ships around the Cape would be seriously interrupted. This could spell disaster to British forces fighting in North Africa, then being supplied via the Cape and Suez.

The U-boats arrived off Cape Town in the early hours of 5 October, U-68 being the first to sight the light on Robben Island, which lies 7 miles from Cape Town itself. That night, Carl Emmermann took U-172 in at periscope depth to reconnoitre the port. Contrary to the information supplied, with the exception of a few fishing boats he found Table Bay anchorage to be completely empty of shipping. Furthermore, the bay was being swept by the beams of several powerful searchlights. It was later learned that this was the result of a recent attack on the naval base at Diego Suarez by Japanese midget submarines, which had brought home to the South African authorities the vulnerability of the Cape Town anchorage. All shipping had been diverted to other ports. However, although Cape Town appeared to be on full alert, nothing had been done to even dim the lights of the town. Emmermann reported:

The picture which the town and harbour presented was so beautiful and peaceful that we stayed a few hours on the surface and called the crew up one by one to the bridge to enjoy the sight of the brilliantly illuminated city.

It was now all too clear that the four U-boats had come nearly 6,000 miles on a wild goose chase, and as soon as Dönitz was informed, he abandoned the mission. U-159 and U-504 were ordered to carry on around the Cape to try their luck off Durban, while U-68 and U-172 were left to attack shipping in the approaches to Cape Town.

Emmermann moved back out to sea and began patrolling some 65 miles off Green Point with the object of intercepting shipping rounding the Cape of Good Hope. He did not have to wait long for his first victim. Shortly before dawn on the 7th, the American steamer *Chickasaw City* hove into sight, bound from East Africa to Trinidad with a cargo of chrome ore, coffee and hides. Up until that morning the dead hand of war had not reached out to South African waters, and ships were proceeding much as they had in peacetime. The *Chickasaw City* was no exception; she was not zig-zagging, and her navigation lights were burning brightly – easy meat for Emmermann, who sank her with two torpedoes. The same could be said for the Suez-bound Panamanian-flag *Firethorn*, sighted three hours later. Deep-loaded with military equipment, including tanks on deck, she was also quickly despatched. Late that night, the Greek steamer *Pantelis*, sailing from Beirut to Buenos Aires in ballast, followed the others down. In the space of twenty-four hours U-172 had opened the war off the Cape of Good Hope by sinking 14,741 tons of Allied shipping. However, her voyage almost came to an abrupt end on 8 October, when she was attacked by patrol craft of the South African Defence Force. She narrowly escaped serious damage by crash-diving and going deep.

Accepting that his presence was unwelcome, Emmermann withdrew to a position 150 miles further out to sea, and there, at first light on the 10th, the 23,456-ton troopship *Orcades* came over the horizon, bound north. The ex-Cunard liner was on her way from Suez to Liverpool with 741 military personnel, 3,000 tons of general cargo and 2,000 bags of mail.

By the time U-172 had manoeuvred into position to attack, the weather was deteriorating as a Table Bay south-easter moved across, bringing gale force winds and blinding rain squalls. Luckily for Emmermann, the *Orcades* was running at reduced speed to conserve fuel, and it was comparatively easy to put a brace of torpedoes into her hull. The liner, built by Vickers Armstrong at Barrow-in-Furness, was not easily stopped, however, and for the next three hours she limped on, fighting a running gun battle with the U-boat. The arrival overhead of aircraft of the South African Air Force brought the fight to an end, but by then it was too late for the *Orcades*. Hit by seven torpedoes, she finally sank with the loss of forty-five lives. U-172 again escaped with only minor damage and later in the day received orders from Lorient to proceed to the coast of Brazil, where ill-prepared American merchantmen were going down like ninepins.

Eisbär's 'Capetown Patrol' had not been a resounding success, but neither was it a complete failure. U-172 alone had sunk 38,000 tons of Allied shipping, while the other boats of the group brought the total score to over 100,000 tons. However, their efforts did bring home to the hitherto complacent South African authorities the need to look to their defences. From then on, any U-boat operating off the South African coast did so at its peril.

Having escaped the wrath of the South African Air Force, after arranging a rendezvous with U-459 to refuel and re-arm, U-172 set course for Brazil. In doing so, she also put herself in the way of another encounter, this time with the Cape-bound *Aldington Court*, which was then with Convoy TRIN 16 off the coast of Guyana. The convoy, consisting of seventeen merchantmen all bound for the Cape and escorted by a US Navy destroyer, a Dutch minelayer and four submarine chasers, was designed purely to see the ships safely clear of the South American mainland. This was considered done late on the 11th, at which point the convoy dispersed and the merchantmen went their separate ways.

Once clear of the convoy, Captain Stuart increased speed to 10 knots and set a south-easterly course direct for Cape Town. Although wind and current would be against them, it was anticipated that fine weather would prevail for much of the way, with blue skies and a fresh, cooling breeze. For Captain Stuart and his 43 British crew it would be a welcome break, a time to relax into the normal sea-going routine not possible further north.

On the 21st, when the *Aldington Court* was in mid-ocean and about 850 miles north-west of St Helena, a radio message was received from Cape Town diverting her to Saldanha Bay, 90 miles north of the Cape. Twenty-four hours later, for no apparent reason, this order was countermanded. The long tentacles of officialdom were reaching out for the *Aldington Court*.

For the next eight days the southward passage was uninterrupted. Then, on the morning of the 30th, Chief Engineer Harry Goodfellow paid a rare visit to the bridge to inform Captain Stuart that one of the cylinders of the main engine had developed a crack and he would have to stop to carry out repairs. The *Aldington Court* lay stopped for the following twelve hours, during which a further message came through from Cape Town instructing her to close the coast in the vicinity of Walvis Bay and then continue south to Saldanha Bay.

Third Officer Joseph Mitchell had the 8–12 watch on the bridge on the night of the 31st. It was a fine night, with a gentle southerly breeze and a calm sea. The sky was cloudless, there was no moon, and the darkness was complete except for the faint glow cast by the stars. Lost in his thoughts, Mitchell was pacing up and down in the starboard wing of the bridge when, at about 2045, he saw two streaks of phosphorescence racing towards the ship from the beam. At first he took them to be the wakes of playful porpoises and expected them to shear away and run with the ship, a sight he had become familiar with on the passage south. It was only when he heard the rushing sound of propellers that he realized the imminent danger.

There was no time to take evasive action, and as Mitchell moved to sound the alarm the first torpedo struck directly under the bridge with devastating force. The ship staggered, and debris was thrown high in the air. Mitchell, who had been thrown to the deck, got to his feet just as the second torpedo slammed home in the *Aldington Court*'s engine spaces. The second explosion was even more violent, the stricken ship taking on a list of 30° to starboard, from which she did not recover. In a report written later, Third Officer Mitchell described the visible damage:

> Both starboard boats were destroyed and the davits buckled by the explosions. The gun nest on the starboard side of the bridge was wrecked, the Marlin gun was knocked off, and the bridge ladders collapsed. I did not see any hatches blown off, but there was cargo on top of them which probably kept them in place.

By the time Captain Stuart reached the bridge, the ship had heeled over so far that her starboard bulwarks were almost under water, and he knew he must act quickly to save his crew. Ordering Mitchell to sound the abandon ship signal, Stuart clawed his way aft to the wireless room, where he instructed the radio officer on watch to send out a distress.

The *Aldington Court* carried four lifeboats, a 34-capacity boat each side of the boat deck and two jolly boats on the bridge deck able to carry twelve men each. Both starboard boats had been completely wrecked by the explosions, and owing to the heavy list the survivors had great difficulty in lowering the port boats. The port jolly boat had been previously damaged in bad weather, and after inspection in Philadelphia its carrying capacity had been downgraded to seven. But this was no time for splitting hairs, and when this boat pulled away from the ship with Third Officer Mitchell at the tiller it had thirteen men on board. Chief Officer John O'Hagan was in charge of the port lifeboat, which with only fifteen aboard was half empty.

Both boats lay 100yds off the sinking ship, and at 2055 they watched her roll over and go down. As she was going, four men appeared on deck, Captain Stuart, Second Officer James Hepburn, Second Radio Officer Donald Savage and Able Seaman Ronald Jones, one of the DEMS gunners. Third Officer Mitchell wrote in his report:

> The Captain, 2nd Officer, 2nd Radio Officer, and Gunner who were left on board jumped into the water as the ship rolled over. Their red lifejacket lights were plainly visible, so both boats pulled towards them. I picked up the 2nd Radio Officer and Gunner Jones, making a total of 15 in my boat; the Chief Officer took the Captain and 2nd Officer into his boat, making a total of 17 men in his boat.
>
> I had not previously seen the submarine, but it now approached the boats from astern, and ordered us alongside. I pulled alongside, whereupon he asked for the Captain. I replied that he had gone down with the ship, he then ordered the Chief Officer to go on board. The Chief Officer afterwards told me that he took him down inside the submarine, saying, 'I am sorry, I will have to blindfold you.' He enquired the name of the ship, cargo and destination, gave him 20 cigarettes, and ordered him

back to the boat. When he had returned to his boat, the
Commander shouted, 'Are you all right in the boats?' then
submerged quickly.

Satisfied that by sinking five ships totalling 43,000 tons he had in part
made up for the failure of the 'Capetown Patrol', Carl Emmermann
set course for the coast of Brazil, confident that there he would
make another substantial contribution to Germany's cause. He was
to be bitterly disappointed, for his new hunting ground proved to
be anything but fertile, adding just three more ships to his score.

When U-172 was out of sight, the *Aldington Court*'s boats came
together. Captain Stuart counted heads, which revealed that ten
men were missing. Six of them were found next morning clinging
to a life-raft and were taken on board Stuart's boat. A search was
made for the others, but without success. It was assumed that First
Radio Officer Reginald Newbold, last seen in the wireless room
sending out distress signals, and the three DEMS gunners who
had been standing by the 4-inch gun on the poop when the torpedoes struck, had all gone down with the ship.

It was reported that Newbold's signals had been acknowledged,
but the two boats were adrift 1,000 miles from the nearest land and
in an area through which few ships passed. Their chances of survival were not good, yet the survivors, full of optimism, hoisted
sail and set course for the South African coast, their goal being
Port Nolloth, a small mining town 280 miles north of Cape Town.
The voyage ahead of them was long and full of the unknown.

Before setting off, numbers were evened up by transferring five
men from the jolly boat, which was grossly overcrowded, into
the lifeboat. The lifeboat then had twenty-eight on board, while
the jolly boat had ten. Captain Stuart's boat had the advantage of
two sails, a lug and a jib, and soon drew ahead, leaving Mitchell's
boat with its single sail struggling astern. By the morning of 3
November the smaller boat was alone.

Resigned to being many days, even weeks, at sea, Third Officer
Mitchell commenced strict rationing of food and water from the
start. He wrote in his report:

> I allowed 3oz of water per day, 2 biscuits, with a tin of
> Pemmican (divided into ten), 4 milk tablets in the morn-
> ing, and 4 at sunset. Every third day I allowed an extra
> biscuit with 2 pieces of chocolate.

This was hardly a diet men would grow fat on, but it was just enough to keep them alive, and as the days went by with the horizon empty of ships, Mitchell's prudence became increasingly justified.

On the morning of the 5th they ran into head winds which quickly increased to gale force, and they were forced to heave to and lie to a sea anchor. The gale was accompanied by heavy rain squalls from which the survivors hoped to top up their dwindling supply of fresh water, but nature was against them. The squalls passed ahead and astern on both sides, but none dropped its life-saving nectar on the tossing boat. Then, late in the afternoon, as suddenly as it had risen the wind dropped and then veered round to the west. The sail was hoisted again, and running before the wind, the boat surged forward, according to Mitchell's estimate at a good 4 knots. The morale of the survivors, which had plunged to its lowest depth, picked up again. However, it was a false dawn; late that night the wind faltered and then dropped right away. Once again, the jolly boat lay becalmed.

And so it remained for the next eight days. The sail hung limp and useless at the mast, and the small boat drifted aimlessly on a flat calm sea. In desperation, Mitchell persuaded his crew to ship the oars, but the boat was so crowded that only two could be used at a time. The ten survivors took watches to man the oars, but progress was so slow as to be hardly worth the effort. In fact, the boat was then in the grip of the Benguela Current, which was pushing them to the north.

Conditions in the small boat began to deteriorate quickly. Although Mitchell had brought in strict rationing, their water supply was almost exhausted and thirst was becoming a problem. Food was also running low, and the Pemmican, not appetizing at the best of times, had become almost inedible. Ironically, shoals of small fish swam around the boat, but without fishing lines or hooks none could be caught. To add further to their discomfort, the bottom of the boat was constantly awash, and nobody had the strength, or the will, to bail out. Mitchell insisted that they all massage their feet with whale oil. but inevitably trench foot set in, brought about by the persistent damp and lack of movement. Worst of all, the survivors, none of whom wore much in the way of clothing, were tortured by the merciless sun beating down through the day and the bitter cold at night. Conversation was limited to a minimum as they huddled in the boat awaiting their fate.

By the afternoon of 13 November, their fourteenth day adrift, all hope of rescue had been abandoned. Then Able Seaman John Aldred, who had been keeping a lookout at the mast, let out a hoarse shout and pointed ahead. A ship was in sight, and heading towards them. The boat came alive again.

Third Officer Mitchell described the moment in his report:

> We threw over a smoke float, after carefully following the instructions in detail, but it failed to function. Another one was tried which, after about 4 seconds, commenced spluttering before any smoke started. This smoke only lay on top of the water to a depth of about three feet.
>
> We saw the ship alter course 90° to the southward away from the boat, so I assume that she had seen us but was unable to identify us.

Mitchell was correct in his assumptions. The ship sighted was the 4,940-ton Ellerman-Hall passenger/cargo liner *City of Christiania*, bound from the East to the River Plate. To those on the British ship's bridge, the *Aldington Court*'s jolly boat at first looked suspiciously like the conning tower of a U-boat, with the smoke of the distress float rolling astern as if from her exhausts. The liner immediately took evasive action, turning stern-on to run away from the perceived danger. It was then that Joseph Mitchell, in desperation, stripped off his shirt and climbed the mast waving it frantically. Someone aboard the *City of Christiania* then grasped the situation, and she turned back to investigate.

When picked up by the *City of Christiania*, the ten survivors were emaciated and suffering from exposure, but only one, Bo'sun Alphonse Peviskis, whose feet were badly swollen, had to be hoisted aboard. When the survivors were landed in Montevideo thirteen days later, Peviskis was hospitalized, but too late to save his foot. Gangrene had set in, and the foot was amputated.

When the *Aldington Court*'s jolly boat was found by the *City of Christiania* on 13 November, it had covered just 260 miles and had made good a course of N 60° E. The *Aldington Court*'s lifeboat, with Captain Stuart and twenty-seven others on board, was never heard of again. Whether it sank in bad weather or was dashed ashore on the fog-bound, uninhabited coast of Namaqualand, may never be known.

CHAPTER FIFTEEN

The Fleet Oiler –
Scottish Heather 27.12.42

The 7,087-ton oil tanker *Scottish Heather*, built on the Tyne in 1928 for Tankers Limited of London, later to become Athel Line, was, to quote her builders Armstrong Whitworth, 'designed for economy and reliability'. Economical she may have been, but her claim to reliability was open to question. In fact, over the years, she had proved to be severely accident-prone.

It began early in her career, in 1934, when she was involved in a collision with another tanker in the Gulf of Mexico and sustained significant damage. In July of the same year she was reported laid up in Port Said with steering engine trouble, and five months later she was again under repair, this time in the Dutch port of Terneuzen, after one of her boilers failed. Two years on and she lost an anchor in South American waters, resulting in another delay, and when war came along in 1939, she was attacked and damaged by German bombers in the North Sea. Some would say, and perhaps with good reason, that the *Scottish Heather* was jinxed from birth.

When 30-year-old Douglas Crook joined the tanker in November 1942 as Second Officer, it is unlikely that he was aware of her reputation. This was just as well, for Crook had only recently returned to sea, having recovered from an epic 38-day voyage in an open lifeboat following the torpedoing of the tanker *Athelknight* (see Chapter 10). Showing exceptional leadership and seamanship, he had navigated the boat with its eighteen occupants 1,100 miles across the North Atlantic to reach the shores of a tiny island in the West Indies. For his achievement, a generous nation had awarded him an MBE.

For Britain and the few Allies she had left the war at sea was not going well. Through diligent and persistent lobbying of the German High Command, Admiral Karl Dönitz had increased his U-boat fleet to 365, of which some 200 were fully operational. This gave him a considerable advantage on the North Atlantic convoy routes. At the same time, and unknown to the Admiralty, B-Dienst, the German Intelligence Bureau, had penetrated the British naval code used by the convoys. The net result was that over 100 Allied merchantmen were being sunk every month, most of them in the North Atlantic. When the *Scottish Heather* sailed from Smith's Dock in North Shields on 16 December 1942, her past record was not the only reason she had a very uncertain future ahead of her.

The *Scottish Heather* had been temporarily commandeered by the Admiralty as a fleet oiler, and with 750 tons of oil on board was to join the westbound convoy ON 154, her assignment being to keep the convoy's escorts supplied with fuel on the crossing to America. She did not enjoy an auspicious start to the voyage, her three-day passage around the north of Scotland being marred by sleet, snow and perpetual semi-darkness. It was not a pleasant experience.

Convoy ON 154, when formed up off Malin Head, consisted of forty-five merchant ships, most of which were in ballast. They were escorted by a destroyer and five corvettes of the Royal Canadian Navy's Mid-Ocean Escort Force. Also with the convoy were the French-manned Special Service Vessel HMS *Fidelity* and the rescue ship *Toward*. A second destroyer should have joined, but she had been withdrawn owing to engine trouble. Lieutenant Commander G. S. Windeyer, Senior Officer Escort, in the destroyer HMCS *St Laurent*, was painfully aware that in the event of attack by a U-boat pack the defence of such a huge body of slow-moving merchant ships with so few escorts was more than likely to be a traumatic experience.

The convoy was in twelve columns abreast, with its commodore ship *Empire Shackleton* taking her place at the head of the middle column. Windeyer had arranged his corvettes around the merchantmen in a defensive screen with *Chilliwack* on the port bow, *Battleford* on the starboard bow, *Kenogami* on the port quarter, *Napanee* on the starboard quarter and *Shediac* bringing up the rear. HMS *Fidelity*, a seaplane carrier armed with four 4-inch guns and four torpedo tubes, and something of an unknown quantity, was positioned at the rear of the merchant ships, along with the rescue ship *Toward*. HMCS *St Laurent* would be scouting ahead of the convoy, which in all covered an area 5 miles across by 2 miles deep.

Convoy speed was set at 8 knots, but this proved wildly optimistic, for as soon as the ships left the shelter of the Irish coast, the North Atlantic showed its angry face. The wind began to howl in the rigging, the cloud lowered until it was brushing the mast-tops, and the oncoming swells were grey-green mountains streaked with flying spume. Soon the cumbersome merchantmen were burying their blunt bows in the rising seas, while their tiny escorting corvettes wallowed and struggled just to stay afloat. Windeyer's slender 1,500-ton destroyer *St Laurent*, her decks awash, resembled a half-tide rock as she gallantly led the way into what was later described as the North Atlantic's 'most ferocious winter in living memory'. Organized defence had become a minor consideration.

The departure of Convoy ON 154 had not gone unnoticed by German Intelligence. Word had been passed to Lorient, and Admiral Dönitz was preparing a reception committee deep in the Atlantic. A total of eighteen U-boats, then on various patrols, were called in and formed into two packs, code named Spitz ('Point') and Ungestüm ('Stormy'). These then set up a 400-mile-long patrol line across the projected track of the convoy, and waited. A major Atlantic battle was brewing.

There was some relief for Convoy ON 154 when, on the early morning of the 24th, the weather moderated, and the ships, which had become scattered in the storm, were able to re-form their ranks and increase speed. When the 25th dawned, apart from a heavy westerly swell, the weather was almost benign. A weak sun broke through the overcast, and an air of optimism prevailed. Christmas Dinner was served in the ships in relative comfort.

Despite attempts to enter into the festive spirit, the needs of the convoy had to be met, and during the afternoon the *Scottish Heather* was ordered to drop back to the rear of the convoy to refuel the *St Laurent*. With some difficulty, owing to the heavy swell still prevailing, the operation got under way, but had to be abandoned after the destroyer had taken only 100 tons on board. The convoy was then some 900 miles west of Land's End and rapidly approaching the ambush set up by the U-boats of Spitz and Ungestüm.

Unknown to either side, the convoy was actually steering a course that would take it to the south of Dönitz's net, and it would have passed unseen had it not been for the simple navigational error of a U-boat commander. U-664, a Type VIIC under Oberleutnant Adolf Graef, stationed at the southern end of the net, was some 50 miles south of her assigned position when her lookouts sighted the masts and funnels of ON 154 on the morning of the 26th. Graef closed in on the convoy and radioed its position, course and estimated speed to Lorient. Dönitz ordered Graef to shadow the Allied ships and transmit positional reports for the other boats to home in on.

First to arrive, just after midnight, was Günther Ruppelt in U-356. Ruppelt waded in without hesitation, taking the convoy's escorts by surprise. In quick succession, he sank the British ships *Empire Union*, *Melrose Abbey* and *King Edward*, and then damaged the Dutch steamer *Soekaboemi*. Fortunately, the rescue ship *Toward* acted equally quickly, scooping up a total of 113 men from the water, which on a dark night with a heavy swell running was no mean achievement.

This devastating and completely unexpected attack sent shock waves through the ranks of the convoy, with ships scattering in all directions. Lieutenant Commander Windeyer's escorts were at first confused, but recovered quickly and retaliated in force. U-356, attempting to escape under water, was caught in a spider's web of Asdic beams, promptly depth-charged and sunk with all her crew. Stunned by this swift reaction, the other U-boats withdrew, and the sun had set before they saw the opportunity to make another attack. This came at a bad time for the convoy, for the corvette *Chilliwack*, having run perilously short of fuel, had dropped astern to be refuelled by the *Scottish Heather*.

At about 1900 *Chilliwack* and the tanker were 15 miles astern of the convoy, steaming at very slow speed, when U-225, commanded by Wolfgang Leimkühler, approached on the surface. Anticipating an easy kill, Leimkühler watched and waited for the opportunity to strike. This was a mistake, for shortly after the refuelling was finished, *Chilliwack*'s lookouts sighted the surfaced U-boat and the corvette gave chase. U-225 was saved by her speed, being at least 2 knots faster on the surface than *Chilliwack*. She soon disappeared into the darkness.

Meanwhile, the *Scottish Heather*, zigzagging wildly, was chasing after the convoy at full speed. *Chilliwack* kept guard on her starboard quarter, while U-225 followed in their wake. After about an hour, Leimkühler lost sight of the two ships, and they probably would have got away if *Chilliwack* had not decided, rather foolishly, to signal the *Scottish Heather* with a dimmed lamp. This gave the U-boat a target to aim at. Still on the surface, Leimkühler closed in on the fleeing tanker and fired a single torpedo from his bow tubes.

U-225's torpedo slammed into the *Scottish Heather*'s starboard side directly below the bridge. It exploded with a brilliant flash, ripping a huge hole in her hull. The tanker rolled heavily to port, then came upright again as the sea poured into her ruptured tanks. Fortunately, the explosion was well away from tanks containing oil, so there was no erupting fireball as might have been feared; but the ship began to settle on an even keel and appeared to be in imminent danger of sinking. Captain Thomas Maxwell, who had been injured by the explosion, gave the order to abandon ship.

The *Scottish Heather* carried the usual two full-sized lifeboats on her after deck and two smaller jolly boats on the bridge deck. The starboard side jolly boat had disappeared, blown away by the exploding torpedo, so Captain Maxwell and those who had been on the bridge with him cleared away the port jolly boat and, despite the heavy sea running, lowered it and scrambled aboard. Once clear of the ship's side, they began picking up other survivors who, fearing a raging conflagration, had jumped over the side. The small boat was soon full.

On the after deck, Second Officer Douglas Crook, assisted by Third Officer Thomas Gorst, was supervising the lowering of the two lifeboats. This was no easy task. The darkness was complete, the doomed ship was rolling drunkenly in the troughs, and over everything was the awful cacophony of the howling wind accompanied by the screech of escaping steam as the boiler safety valves blew.

When the boats had been launched and boarded, Crook took a last look around the ship before leaving. To his surprise, he then realized that the *Scottish Heather* had steadied herself on an even keel and did not seem to be sinking any further. A firm believer in the old adage 'your ship is your best lifeboat', Crook returned to the boat deck and hailed the boats, which were still alongside, asking for volunteers to re-board. Nine men came clambering up the ship's side: Third Officer Thomas Gorst, Sixth Engineer Gerald Allen, 17-year-old Apprentice Donald Staddon, Cook Ernest Bainbridge, Greaser Denis Byrne, Cabin Boy Thomas Dillon and three able seamen, John Gilbert, Harold Rich and James Walker. The lifeboats then cast off and drifted away into the night.

Douglas Crook, who was now effectively in command of the *Scottish Heather*, discussed the situation with his volunteer crew, and it was agreed that they should try to save the ship. Sixth Engineer Allen and Greaser Byrne went below to see if it was possible to raise steam and start the main engine, and when it was established that there was no risk of fire, Ernest Bainbridge relit the galley stove. Hot food and drink was the first priority for the cold, wet and shocked survivors.

Daylight came reluctantly on the 28th, and with it came a complete change in the weather. The wind fell away to a light breeze and a blanket of dense fog descended, reducing visibility to a few yards. Only the still mountainous swells were left of the previous night's storm. But there was some good news: after working all night in a darkened engine room, Gerald Allen and Denis Byrne had restarted the main engine.

Before assessing the possibility of rejoining the convoy, Second Officer Crook decided to look for the two lifeboats, which he thought might still be somewhere in the area. Because of the poor visibility the search would be difficult, but he began painstakingly to grope around in the fog.

For the next six hours the *Scottish Heather* quartered the area, but the search seemed like a lost cause. Then, around noon, the fog lifted, and at 1400 Crook's perseverance was rewarded when Captain Maxwell's jolly boat was sighted. An hour later, Maxwell and his crew, all cold, wet and thoroughly exhausted after a very uncomfortable night, were back aboard their ship. Maxwell resumed his command, and the search continued.

Sunset came early, shortly after 1600, and at that point Maxwell was all but ready to abandon the search for the other lifeboat, when a lookout at the mast-head let out a shout and pointed ahead. It was the missing boat, under full sail and on course for the Irish coast, nearly 1,000 miles to the north-west. Having resigned themselves to a long haul, those on board now lost no time in re-boarding their ship. Remarkably, considering the weather and the circumstances under which the *Scottish Heather* was torpedoed and abandoned, all fifty-four of her crew had survived and were now back aboard their ship.

In consultation with his officers and crew Captain Maxwell decided not to attempt to rejoin the convoy but to take their chances alone and set course for British waters. This was undoubtedly a wise decision, for Convoy ON 154 was now surrounded by U-boats and in a fight to the death.

The convoy had already lost five ships, including the *Scottish Heather*, which was presumed sunk, and now a constant stream of signals was flooding in from the Admiralty warning that the enemy was closing in on the convoy in force. The situation was, in fact, far more serious than Lieutenant Commander Windeyer could possibly conceive. The wolf packs Spitz and Ungestüm, now said to be eighteen or nineteen strong, were in position and preparing for a major attack on the remaining merchantmen. Windeyer's ships were outnumbered by three to one, and on the surface under the cover of darkness the U-boats were easily able to outrun and outmanoeuvre his corvettes. The destroyers HMS *Milne* and HMS *Meteor* had been ordered to reinforce the Canadians, but both were still several hundred miles away; by the time they arrived it could all be over. ON 154 was in imminent danger of complete annihilation.

The battle began in earnest on the night of the 28th when, just before 2200, Hans-Jürgen Zetzsche in U-591 torpedoed the Norwegian steamer *Norse King*. U-591 was on her fifth war patrol and had only a few days before been involved in the attack on another westbound convoy, ON 152, during which she sank a straggler, the 3,066-ton *Montreal City*. Although badly hit, the *Norse King* remained afloat, and her crew did not abandon her as she drifted astern.

Having, as he thought, dispatched the *Scottish Heather*, Wolfgang Leimkuhler crammed on all speed to renew contact with the convoy. Unseen, he moved in quickly, torpedoing first the *Melmore Head* and the *Ville de Rouen*, both British ships of around 5,000 tons gross. The *Melmore Head* sank, while the *Ville de Rouen* remained afloat but crippled. Half an hour later, U-260, under the command of Hubertus Purkhold, added to the chaos when he waded in with a spread of four torpedoes from his bow tubes. Three of these missed, but the fourth went home in the hull of the *Empire Wagtail*, which promptly sank. At about the same time, U-406 (Horst Dieterichs) torpedoed and damaged the 5,029-ton *Lynton Grange* and then hit United Africa's *Zarian* with the same result. Both ships dropped back to join the growing group of casualties straggling astern of the convoy.

After reloading his tubes, Wolfgang Leimkuhler brought U-225 back into the fray at midnight. The convoy was now in complete disarray, with Windeyer's escorts chasing shadows and hurling depth charges around in desperation. Leimkuhler had no difficulty in infiltrating the ranks of merchantmen, picking his targets with care. He fired four single torpedoes, two of which hit the Belgian tanker *President Francqui* and the Commodore's ship *Empire Shackleton*. Again, neither ship sank. Either the German torpedoes were having a bad night, or ON 154's ships were of sounder construction than envisaged. Even so, the toll of the night had risen to astronomical proportions. In the space of less than three hours the U-boats had torpedoed nine merchantmen, sinking six of them and adding more to the pitiful array of derelicts trailing astern of the convoy. And in the midst of all this confusion HMS *Fidelity* signalled that she had an engine breakdown. Reluctantly, Windeyer ordered the corvette *Shediac* back to cover the vulnerable seaplane carrier. Shortly afterwards, thoroughly worn down by the gargantuan task he had been set, he collapsed from sheer exhaustion, leaving his First Lieutenant to take command of the group.

HMCS *Shediac*, meanwhile, found herself fighting a war of her own. The U-boats had temporarily suspended their assault on the convoy to concentrate on clearing the debris cluttering up the ocean in its wake. There was no opposition and, one by one, they picked off the stragglers, some already abandoned by their crews, others attempting to escape to safer waters. U-591 disposed of the *Zarian*, U-123 stalked and sank the *Baron Cochrane*, U-628 put the *Lynton Grange* out of her misery, U-662 ended the *Ville de Rouen*'s long career with a spread of two. U-123 and U-435 shared the demise of the *Empire Shackleton*, while U-225 and U-336 each put a torpedo into the *President Francqui*. The *Norse King* was last of the merchantmen to go, sunk by U-435. On the afternoon of the 30th, despite *Shediac*'s efforts to defend her, HMS *Fidelity* was finished off by Siegfried Stretlow in U-435.

The shattered remains of Convoy ON 154 was saved from the ignominy of complete annihilation by the arrival on the 30th of the British destroyers *Meteor* and *Milne*, and later the same day, HMS *Viceroy* and HMCS *St Francis*. Seeing the odds turning against him, Dönitz withdrew his U-boats.

The proverbial stable door was now firmly shut, but too late to save the fifteen ships and 512 men lost in that Atlantic bloodbath. In compensation, just one U-boat, Günther Ruppelt's U-356, had been sunk. ON 154 had put up a gallant fight, but in the end had been overwhelmed by a vastly superior enemy, and no one in the ships had cause to hang his head in shame. The subsequent treatment of the survivors by the authorities in Britain, however, was on a totally different plane.

The majority of those who survived the loss of their ships in ON 154 were landed at Ponta Delgarda in the Azores, where they were well cared for. From the Azores they were repatriated to Liverpool aboard the troopship *Llangibby Castle*, arriving on 12 January 1943. One anonymous survivor recorded his impressions of their reception:

> Here we felt unwanted and a nuisance to local officialdom, whose manner in dealing with most of the survivors was most condescending and ungracious. It felt degrading to be treated like criminals because we had no papers, money, decent clothing, etc. One would almost believe that the largesse they were distributing was from their own pockets rather than an entitlement.

Another survivor complained that most of his four weeks survivor's leave was spent in obtaining a new seaman's identity card, clothing coupons, compensation for his lost sextant, nautical tables and binoculars, etc. He spent over £100 and received just £60 in compensation, the maximum allowed. Nor did it help when, kitted out in his new uniform, he was grilled by two CID officers, who accused him of impersonating an officer in the Merchant Navy. He subsequently joined another of his company's vessels, which was torpedoed and lost off the Canary Islands on 28 March 1943. Again, he escaped with his life, but no doubt was made to go through the humiliating process of claiming for belongings lost for the second time in three months. For a man already on a pitifully small salary to be out of pocket to the tune of some £80 seems poor recompense for twice putting his life on the line for his country.

On 2 January 1943, after an epic 5-day voyage running before the worst storm experienced in the North Atlantic for fifty years, Captain Tom Maxwell eased the battered and bruised *Scottish Heather* into the sheltered waters of the Firth of Clyde. When the tanker dropped anchor in Rothesay Bay, the reception she received was worthy of the deed. After the dust had settled, Second Officer Douglas Crook and Sixth Engineer Gerald Allen were given due recognition for saving the ship. Crook was awarded the George

Medal and Lloyd's Medal, while Allen received an MBE. The remainder of Crook's volunteer crew were also suitably rewarded. Ironically, if Douglas Crook, instead of remaining on board, had abandoned ship and taken his place in the waiting lifeboat, the *Scottish Heather* would have been classed as a derelict; then, by re-boarding and saving her he and the others would have been in line for a substantial salvage award. As it was, no money came their way.

Douglas Crook, the principal player in the *Scottish Heather* saga, was modest about his own role but gave credit where it was due, writing in his report, 'Without the skill, ability, courage and cheerful conduct of Sixth Engineer Gerald Allen, the whole project must have ended in dismal failure.'

Gerald Allen was equally modest:

> We made it by the skin of our teeth. The real hero was our cook. He produced hot meals to schedule without turning a hair, and we only knew what that really meant when we saw the chaps who had been in the boats all night. They had gone without much in the way of comfort, and told us they could not have survived a second night of it.

As for the ship herself, after several months under repair she returned to sea and survived the rest of the war. It was not long, however, before the jinx that had dogged her early years came back to haunt her. In February 1947, in Trinidad, it was discovered that the blades of her propeller were badly bent. What caused this was never discovered, but it led to a lengthy repair when the vessel returned to the UK. In September of that same year, again in Trinidad, while the *Scottish Heather* was tied up alongside another of the company's vessels taking on a cargo of molasses, the mooring ropes parted, resulting in a serious collision between the two tankers. The *Scottish Heather* sustained considerable hull damage, but was able to complete the voyage.

Two months later, while off Cuba, the *Scottish Heather* ran aground. After several attempts using her own power she was able to refloat herself, but a survey revealed that the ship's bottom was extensively damaged and at least two cargo tanks were leaking. The bottom was set up, bulkheads and frames were buckled and suction valves broken. The tanker spent months in dry dock while repairs, including thirty-three renewed shell plates, were carried out.

In March 1948 several cracks were found in one of the cargo tanks and some of the longitudinal framing. The *Scottish Heather* was obliged to put into Santiago for repairs. In July of that year, the *Scottish Heather* again ran aground off Cuba, but there was no apparent damage to her hull. Five months later, while on passage from Denmark to New York, the tanker hit heavy weather and received extensive damage forward. The repair bill came to $15,000.

The *Scottish Heather*'s name disappeared from the books in 1951, when she was renamed *Athelcrest*. In July 1954 she returned to the coast of her birth and was broken up in Blyth.

CHAPTER SIXTEEN

The Exile – *Congella* 21.10.43

Bank Line's *Congella* had been so long in the India–East Africa trade that it was sometimes hard to think of her as a British ship, even though she flew the Red Ensign and the port of registry on her stern was London. And her past was as convoluted as her present. A twin-screw motor ship of 4,533 tons gross, she had begun her long life in the Hamburg yard of Blohm & Voss in 1914, when the storm clouds of the Great War were gathering over Europe. Built for the Hamburg America Line as the *Secundas*, she had spent much of that war laid up in port and was then surrendered as a prize in 1919, passing into French hands. Thereafter she served three different owners while under the French flag, before being sold in 1927 to Barber Lines of New York, who renamed her *Sagami*. Her service under the Stars and Stripes was brief, lasting only a few months before she was sold to the Phoenix Navigation Company of London and given the name *Mindoro*. Finally, six years later, she was bought by Andrew Weir & Company, otherwise known as Bank Line, also of London, and renamed *Congella*. Having sailed under four flags for eight shipping companies, the *Congella* might be truly described as a mongrel of the seven seas.

By the 1940s the *Congella* was no longer able to attain the 12 knots she had achieved on her sea trials thirty years earlier, and although she had swapped her Bank line colours for a drab wartime grey, she was still a smart ship, well crewed and well maintained. In command was 38-year-old Captain Arthur Folster, who carried with him a crew of sixty-five, including seven DEMS gunners. His officers were all British, his ratings Indian, a typical mix for ships in that trade.

With 8,700 tons of Indian produce on board, including tea and jute, the *Congella* sailed from Colombo at dawn on 21 October 1943, bound for Mombasa, 2,500 miles away on Africa's east coast. Her route lay through the One and a Half Degree Channel, a wide gap in the long chain of the Maldive Islands, thence passing 130 miles north of the Seychelles and on to Mombasa. It was a lonely way, more frequented by Arab dhows than ocean-going ships. The South-West Monsoon, with its rain-laden skies and angry seas, had not yet run its course, and the further south they progressed the worse the weather became.

In the autumn of 1943 the North Indian Ocean was temporarily at peace. The German commerce raiders, which had once created mayhem amongst Allied merchant shipping, had been sunk or forced to retire into the Atlantic, and Admiral Dönitz's Monsun ('Monsoon') Group of long-range U-boats had also been dealt with by the Royal Navy. There were, however, an unspecified number of Japanese submarines said to be operating north of the Equator. Admiral Somerville's Eastern Fleet, much depleted by Japanese sea and air attacks, was unable to supply escorts for convoys in mid-ocean, with the result that away from the coasts merchant ships were sailing unescorted. In the event of an enemy attack, the *Congella* would have to defend herself with her antiquated, ironically Japanese-made, 3-inch anti-submarine gun.

Once clear of Colombo's breakwaters, Captain Folster settled the *Congella* on a south-westerly course and rang for full speed. Below decks, in the stifling heat of the engine room, Chief Engineer Maclachlan coaxed his ageing six-cylinder diesels up a few revs at a time. The *Congella*'s bottom was foul with barnacles and weed through being too long out of dry dock in the warm, fecund waters of the East. The best she could hope to achieve was a modest 9 knots.

As it turned out, even 9 knots proved to be wishful thinking. Before she was out of sight of the land, the *Congella* was burying her bows into a rising sea backed by a strong head wind. Noon sights on the first day showed that the deeply-laden ship was making just a fraction over 7½ knots.

Prior to sailing from Colombo, Folster had been advised by the Admiralty that no German or Japanese submarines had been reported near his intended route; so with the exception of posting extra lookouts he was inclined to take no other precautions. The *Congella* was steering a straight course, and her guns were not manned.

At 2,966 tons displacement and 373ft length overall, the Japanese submarine I-10 was more than twice the size of the German Type IX long-range U-boat. She carried a crew of 100, had a surface speed of 23½ knots and a range of 16,000 miles. Her armament consisted of six bow torpedo tubes with eighteen torpedoes, a 5½-inch deck gun and two 25mm AA guns. Housed in a hangar forward of her conning tower was a Yokosuka E14Y seaplane which could be launched to seek out her victims. In all respects, I-10 was a very formidable warship.

With 50-year-old Commander Tonozuka Kinzo in command, I-10 sailed from Penang on 2 September 1943 charged with a special mission. Kinzo's orders were to cross the Indian Ocean, penetrate the Gulf of Aden and reconnoitre Perim Island, at the southern end of the Red Sea, where it was thought the Allies were constructing an air base.

On the passage across the Indian Ocean, when south-west of the Chagos Islands, I-10 came across the Norwegian tanker *Bramora*, bound from Bandar Abbas to Melbourne with a cargo of oil. Kinzo sank the unsuspecting tanker and then machine-gunned her crew in the lifeboats, killing them all. This was in line with the murderous policy that Japanese submarines in the Indian and Pacific oceans seemed to be adopting. It was rumoured – and not without justification – that the Japanese High Command had issued orders that all survivors from merchant ships should be executed on the spot. Witnesses had already testified that when Kinzo sank the Norwegian tanker *Alciden* the previous July he had gunned down and killed thirty-seven of her crew as they took to the boats. There were many more instances of this particularly nasty policy being carried out, and to this day they remain an evil stain that can never be wiped from the record of the Imperial Japanese Navy.

I-10 arrived off Perim Island at dawn on 20 September and launched her seaplane as she approached. The aircraft came back to report no visible evidence of an airfield being built on the island. This left Kinzo free to continue his patrol in search of Allied merchantmen. For the next fourteen days he haunted the Gulf of Aden, sinking three ships with a total tonnage of 21,527. He then retraced his steps, crossing the busy shipping lanes between India, East Africa and the Cape.

The *Congella* passed through the One and a Half Degree Channel in the early hours of 24 October and altered course for Mombasa, 2,000 miles to the south-west. In the absence of any warnings from the Admiralty, Captain Folster, who had been on the bridge for the alteration of course, assumed that he could now go back to his bunk and sleep easy. He was concerned at a marked deterioration in the weather, but having seen the ship settled on her new course he went below.

When dawn came on the 24th it brought with it a typical South-West Monsoon heavy overcast. The wind was blowing force 6, gusting to 7, the white horses were running, the swell had a menacing heave to it and rain squalls were sweeping across the horizon. Folster, who had returned to the bridge, mentally added another half day to his estimated arrival time in Mombasa. He was unaware that the weather was not the only danger he faced.

A few miles off the *Congella's* port quarter, hidden in the rain, I-10 was on the surface, trimmed down so that her casings were awash and silently stalking the British ship. Kinzo, who was in the conning tower, wiped the spray from his binoculars and studied his prey carefully. She was not zigzagging, and the long-barrelled gun visible on her poop deck was clearly unmanned, good indications that he had the element of surprise. Kinzo called for more speed, and I-10 slowly began to overtake on the *Congella's* starboard side.

Placing too much reliance on the passing squalls to cover his approach, Kinzo became overconfident; although the *Congella* appeared to be an unsuspecting victim, her lookouts were vigilant. At 0930 a lookout in her crow's nest, fifty feet above the deck, caught sight of the submarine as she lifted on the swell, just half a mile off on the starboard beam. He reported to the bridge, but by the time Captain Folster and his officers had lifted their binoculars, some sixth sense had warned Commander Kinzo that his submarine was too exposed, and I-10 had submerged.

Having no reason to disbelieve the lookout's warning, Folster immediately brought the ship to action stations. The stern gun was manned, more lookouts were posted and course was altered to put the suspected enemy astern. With all the speed that Chief Engineer Maclachlan could coax out of his already hard-pressed diesels, the *Congella* zigzagged away from the danger. Her position on the chart showed her to be only 180 miles to the north-west of the Allied air base on Addu Atoll, so Folster ordered the wireless room to break radio silence and send a call for help. The distress was acknowledged by Addu Atoll, and it was confidently expected that an anti-submarine aircraft would be overhead within the hour.

Noon came and went, and no avenging aircraft appeared. The day wore on, and it became obvious that there would be no help from Addu Atoll. At the same time, there had been no reappearance of the enemy submarine, and Folster judged it would be safe to resume his original course. He did not, however, relax his vigilance. The ship remained on full alert, with her stern gun manned and loaded. More speed was called for, and as the *Congella*'s engineers obliged, she began shouldering aside the heavy, breaking seas. It was hot and sultry, the air heavy with moisture borne on the monsoon wind. The white uniform shirts of those on the *Congella*'s bridge were stained with sweat, and there was not a man, from Captain Arthur Folster down to the lowly Indian deck *topass* (cleaner), who was not aware of the danger threatening.

When the blessed dark of night at last drew its cloak around them, Folster was still on the bridge, the strain of the long hours of tension showing in his face. More than eight hours had passed since the enemy had first showed his face, but Folster sensed that the submarine was still there, shadowing them at periscope depth and waiting for the opportunity to strike. His intuition was correct; in fact, during the course of the day Tonosuka Kinzo had already fired and missed with two torpedoes. Due to the threat posed by the British ship's stern gun, he had been reluctant to surface in daylight to use his own gun. Now that night had fallen, the opportunity was there.

The heavy overcast had lifted with the coming of darkness and a weak moon was casting an intermittent glow through breaks in the cloud, but there was little other improvement in the weather. The wind continued to blow hard, the seas were rough and hostile. On the bridge of the *Congella* Chief Officer John Green had taken over the watch and was conversing in hushed tones with Captain Folster as they both swept the horizon with their binoculars. In the wheelhouse, by the dimmed light of the compass binnacle, the Indian quartermaster struggled to hold the ship on course as she rode the head seas. In each wing of the bridge a steel-helmeted DEMS gunner hovered by his 20mm Oerlikon, alert and ready to open fire at the first sign of the enemy. The tension in the air was electric.

In his cabin two decks below the wheelhouse, Second Officer C. B. Skinner, due on watch on the bridge at midnight, debated whether to alter his normal routine in the face of the enemy. Skinner, who had joined the *Congella* in Calcutta only a week earlier, was, like most keepers of the hated middle watch, in the habit of turning in soon after dinner to catch a few hours sleep before taking over the bridge at midnight. He made an attempt to read a book, but his concentration kept wandering. After about half an hour he placed his lifejacket handy, stripped down to his underwear, for despite the whirring fan it was unbearably hot in the small cabin, and lay down on his bunk.

Nineteen-year-old Third Officer Tony Rose, in spite of his youth, was also feeling the tension of the past twelve hours and was on the bridge twenty minutes early to take over the watch from Chief Officer Green at 2000. Having consulted the chart and checked the compass course, Rose moved out into the starboard wing, where Captain Folster and Green were keeping their vigil. As he joined them, the first shell from I-10's deck gun whistled through the air and exploded on the *Congella*'s after deck.

The explosion brought Second Officer Skinner rudely out of his shallow sleep and tumbling from his bunk. Only half awake, he acted instinctively, throwing on a pair of shorts, scooping up his lifejacket and heading for the bridge at a run. As he stumbled out on to the open deck he was blinded by the flash of another exploding shell, and the stink of burning cordite was in his nostrils. He later wrote in his report:

> The submarine attacked first from the starboard side, and later from the port side, being within a mile range of the ship. The first three shells were fired in rapid succession and all hit the ship; the first destroyed the fore part of the bridge, the second hit directly below the Captain's cabin, and the third in the vicinity of the wireless cabin. The latter was eventually completely destroyed, but the Wireless Operators had already transmitted a message to the effect that the ship was being shelled, giving the position.
>
> By the time I had reached the deck, the midship section was already seriously on fire, the bridge, No. 2 hatch and the after end of the accommodation all being alight. I learned that the Chief Officer, Third Officer and an Apprentice had been killed when the bridge was hit, and the Master, S. W. Folster [*sic*], mortally wounded. The Master's arm and a leg were blown off and there was a large, gaping wound in his stomach. The Chief Engineer had also reached the bridge by this time, to whom the Master said, 'I'm finished Chief. Stop the engines and abandon ship.'

While Chief Engineer Maclachlan went below to stop the engines, Skinner gave the terribly wounded Captain Folster morphia tablets to ease his dying pains. And there, amid the blood and destruction, the leaping flames and the exploding shells, the mantle of command passed to Second Officer Skinner, the only surviving navigating officer.

The *Congella*, burning furiously, her steering gear smashed, circled aimlessly in the dark night, but she was not going down without a fight. On the poop the 3-inch gun's crew, led by Gunlayer Lewis, were hitting back, but their gun was no match for I-10's heavier calibre weapon and they were firing blind, aiming for the flash of the enemy's gun. It was a fight they could not hope to win.

Later it was estimated that the Japanese submarine fired a total of about fifty shells at the *Congella*, more than forty of which found their mark. With the bridge and midships accommodation reduced to a mass of twisted, smoking metal, and with the way almost off the ship, Skinner decided the time had come to put into effect Captain Folster's last order. He mustered the survivors on the boat deck, and a hurried roll call showing that twenty men were missing or known dead, leaving forty-six to be distributed amongst the lifeboats. The *Congella* carried four boats in all, two full-sized lifeboats and two jolly boats. Under normal circumstances these would have been more than adequate to evacuate the ship's full complement of sixty-six men, but the Japanese shells had taken their toll: one of the large boats was a burnt-out shell, while the other was extensively damaged, and both the jolly boats were barely seaworthy. Skinner considered staying aboard to fight the fires, but the *Congella* was sinking lower in the water and obviously would not stay afloat much longer. He decided to launch the boats while there was still time, but before doing so he returned to the bridge, where he found Captain Folster to be still alive, but unconscious and beyond all human help. Skinner said his farewells and left the Captain to go down with his ship.

The *Congella* had by now drifted to a complete halt and was lying beam-on to the sea and swell, rolling drunkenly. With considerable difficulty the two jolly boats and the remaining lifeboat were lowered to the water and boarded. Second Officer Skinner took charge of one of the smaller boats, and with him were the Seventh Engineer and eleven Indian ratings. In the confusion that reigned, the other jolly boat, with Apprentice Ian Clark at the helm, went away crowded with twenty men. Chief Engineer Maclachlan, three DEMS gunners and eight engine room ratings crewed the damaged lifeboat. It was not an ideal distribution, but the best that could be done in the stress of the moment.

At 2040, less than an hour after the first Japanese shell came whistling out of the night to explode on the *Congella*'s after deck, the boats pulled away from the sinking ship, leaving her to her fate. Second Officer Skinner's report reads:

> Whilst passing across the stern of the ship, I saw the Chief Engineer's boat, and he shouted that his boat was in a sinking condition. My boat was also leaking badly, so I shouted back that we were in the same condition and told him to keep on bailing and that we would help him as soon as possible. However, we drifted away and I think his boat must have sunk, as it was not seen again, thus accounting for 12 of the missing men; the remaining 21 were probably killed by shellfire.

As they pulled away into the storm-tossed darkness, Skinner caught sight of a long, sinister shadow on the water that could only be the enemy submarine. His fears were realized when a machine-gun opened fire, and a line of tracer scythed across the intervening gap towards them. Ordering his men to take cover below the gunwales, Skinner waited in trepidation for the thud of bullets slamming into the thin wooden planking of the boat. Miraculously, nothing happened, and when he put his head above the gunwale again, the submarine was no longer visible.

Contrary to expectations, the *Congella* was still afloat, although she was only a burning hulk, but the light of her flames was a comfort Skinner was loath to leave, and with the remote possibility that she could be re-boarded at daylight, he lay to within half a mile of her. His hopes were dashed when at 0130 on the 25th the glow cast by the burning ship was suddenly extinguished. The *Congella*, ex-*Secundas*, ex-*Sagami*, ex-*Mindoro*, had gone to her watery grave.

When, at long last, daylight came, the sea around the jolly boat was empty as far as the eye could see; only the grey, breaking waves greeted the morning. There was not even a scrap of charred wreckage to show where the *Congella* had gone down. Presumably, having watched her victim sink, I-10 had departed in search of her next conquest, while of the other lifeboats there was no trace. Skinner spent the next hour searching for survivors. In the end he was forced to assume that the other boats had foundered during the night. He was aware that the *Congella*'s wireless operators had got away a distress signal, but in view of the remoteness of their position he saw little point in waiting around for a rescue ship that might never come. Sail was hoisted, and they set off in the general direction of the Maldive Islands, some 250 miles to the east.

Running before a rough following sea, the tiny jolly boat was frequently pooped and flooded, so that sometimes she was only kept afloat by her buoyancy tanks, and to Skinner and his crew it seemed that every hour of the day and night was occupied in bailing. Fortunately, the boat was well stocked with food and water, but by time night fell on the 25th every man on board was cold, wet and on the point of exhaustion. At Skinner's urging they kept going, but by 0100 on the 26th most had reached the end of their tether. Then, half an hour later, the navigation lights of a ship were seen.

By the look of her lights the ship appeared to be very low in the water, and at first it was thought that the enemy submarine had returned. The majority Indian crew of the boat favoured creeping away into the night, but Skinner was having none of it. There were no distress flares in the boat, but Skinner had a torch, which he used to flash an SOS. This was immediately answered by the approaching ship, which turned out to be the armed trawler HMS *Okapi*, sent out from Addu Atoll to search for them after the *Congella*'s distress had been received. The trawler had in fact already sighted the flickering glow of the jolly boat's compass light and was steaming towards them. An hour later, they were all safely on board the *Okapi*.

Second Officer Skinner's first concern after being picked up was for the *Congella*'s other boats, and at his urging the *Okapi* spent the rest of the day searching for them, but without success. Later, in Addu Atoll, it was learnt that Apprentice Clark's boat had been sighted within 70 miles of the atoll by two Catalina flying boats, who were part of the search operation set in motion by *Congella*'s SOS. Although the sea was rough in the area, both aircraft landed on the water and rescued all twenty survivors. Chief Engineer Maclachlan's boat and its occupants were never found, and it was assumed the boat was so badly damaged that it had foundered.

After sinking the *Congella*, I-10 returned to the Pacific, where she joined the Japanese Sixth Fleet. She was involved in a number of attacks on US Navy units but she sank no more ships, naval or merchant. Her end came off Saipan in July 1944, when she attempted to challenge a heavily defended convoy of six American fleet tankers. Before she could inflict any damage she was detected by the destroyers USS *Riddle* and *David W. Taylor* and subjected to an intensive depth-charging. She did not surface again, and next day an oil slick 9 miles long, thick with debris, was sighted. I-10 would plunder no more. The *Congella*, her last victim, was avenged.

CHAPTER SEVENTEEN

OHMS –
Fort Buckingham 20.01.44

From the day she was handed over by her builders in Vancouver the *Fort Buckingham* had been at the beck and call of HM Government. Mass-produced to a standard design, she was one of the many replacement vessels then coming out of shipyards in the Americas to help fill the gaping holes left in British shipping by Dönitz's U-boats. As was required at the time, she was a box-shaped no-nonsense cargo carrier, adaptable to any trade and economical on fuel. It was said of these ships that if they succeeded in carrying just one cargo across the Atlantic to beleaguered Britain, then they had served their purpose. Crudely put, they were disposable.

Owned by the omnipotent Ministry of War Transport, the *Fort Buckingham* was under the management of the Middlesbrough ship owners Joseph Constantine & Sons, fifty-eight years in the business and struggling to keep afloat in the face of heavy losses among its original fleet of eighteen vessels.

In command of the *Fort Buckingham* was 59-year-old Captain Murdo MacLeod DSC, a veteran of the Russian convoys, who had with him a crew of sixty-seven, comprising eleven British officers and fifty-five Indian ratings. Armed with a 4-inch anti-submarine gun, a 12-pounder, a 40mm Bofors, six 20mm Oerlikons and F.A.M and P.A.C. rockets, the *Fort Buckingham* also carried twenty-one DEMS gunners.

The *Fort Buckingham* sailed from Vancouver on her maiden voyage on 13 March 1943, entering the Atlantic via the Panama Canal and sailing north to New York, where she loaded a cargo for Liverpool and fulfilled her primary role by carrying it safely across the North Atlantic, arriving in the Mersey on 9 May. With this cargo discharged, she then found herself thrown into the thick of the war, moving up to Glasgow to load military stores for the Middle East. She sailed from the Clyde on 18 June with Convoy

KMS 18B, full to her hatch-tops and above with tanks, guns, vehicles and ammunition.

KMS 18B, sailing in support of Operation Husky, the Allied invasion of Sicily, was a slow convoy of eighteen merchantmen under heavy escort. Word of the convoy's sailing had reached Berlin, and soon after passing through the Straits of Gibraltar the ships were ambushed by a waiting pack of U-boats. A week-long running fight ensued, during which the convoy lost six ships. Those remaining discharged their cargoes at various North African ports, completing in Malta. The *Fort Buckingham* was one of the lucky survivors, and still being under MoWT control, she was ordered to proceed to Bombay via the Suez Canal, calling at Aden to replenish bunkers. She reached Bombay on 3 November and after lying at anchor for a month, on 2 December, much to the delight of her owners, was released from Government control, free to return to normal commercial voyaging.

India was then in the grip of the benign North-East Monsoon, the annual season of blue skies, warm sun and light winds, so the *Fort Buckingham's* crew, not least her Lascar seamen, voiced no complaints when their ship lay idle for another six weeks while her managers in Middlesbrough looked around for a suitable cargo. Finally, Captain MacLeod received orders to proceed to Buenos Aires in ballast, calling at Durban for bunkers. The assumption was that this would mean a cargo for the United Kingdom. The ship was going home at last.

The *Fort Buckingham* left Bombay on 17 January 1944, embarking on a voyage of 8,400 miles involving between five and six weeks at sea. With both Germany and Japan on the defensive, it was clear that the war had almost run its course, and her route via the Cape of Good Hope was considered to be relatively safe. Beyond that, in the South Atlantic, was clear water. No convoys would be involved. The *Fort Buckingham* would sail alone and hopefully unmolested.

Early in June 1943, Admiral Dönitz had formed the Monsun Group with a view to operating against the busy Allied shipping lanes in the North Indian Ocean and Arabian Sea. The group consisted of eleven Type IX long-range U-boats, one of which was a supply boat. They set out from Biscay carrying equipment for the construction of a U-boat base at the Japanese-held port of Penang at the northern end of the Straits of Malacca, but the enterprise was dogged by ill fortune from the start. Four of their number were sunk by Allied aircraft on their way south to the Cape, and some were diverted to supply other boats in the Atlantic running short of fuel. After a voyage of nearly three months, the remnants of Monsun, just five boats, finally reached the Indian Ocean. One of these was the Type IXC/40 U-188, commanded by 27-year-old Kapitänleutnant Siegfried Lüdden.

U-188 escaped the attentions of the enemy on the outward passage, but when rounding the Cape of Good Hope ran into a violent storm in which she sustained severe damage on deck. This did not seriously affect the boat's performance, so Lüdden decided to continue the voyage. However, on arrival at her operational area in late September, he found the hot, humid climate caused the exhaust temperatures of his diesels to soar. This resulted in excessively high lubricating oil consumption, a major problem given there was little or no opportunity to replenish supplies. In addition, the heat haze that often hung over the horizon badly affected visibility, and when he did find suitable targets, the high air and water temperatures caused his torpedoes to run erratically. Perhaps more significantly, Lüdden found that the heat and humidity were sapping the morale of his crew. Weather conditions in the North Atlantic may have been difficult and unpleasant at times, but the Indian Ocean, for all its fabled charms, was turning out to be a difficult hunting ground.

U-188's success rate was certainly disappointing. Two weeks had passed since her arrival, and she had succeeded in sinking just one Allied merchantman and damaging another. On 8 October Lüdden received orders to proceed to Penang, where U-188's long overdue weather damage repairs would be carried out. After that, she was to take on cargo for the return voyage to Germany.

By mid-January 1943, with her ports securely blockaded by the Royal Navy, Germany was running out of a number of vital materials she was unable to produce at home. Tungsten, rubber, copper, quinine and essential oils were all in short supply. By September the situation had become so critical that the High Command appealed to Dönitz for help. Dönitz offered to use his long-range U-boats to ease the situation. U-188 was one of the chosen, and when she had completed her repairs in Penang she sailed to Singapore. There she loaded 100 tons of tin, eleven tons of rubber, 1,000lb of quinine, four chests of opium and 1,500 sacks of wolfram packed in rubber. She left Singapore on 9 January 1944 with orders to first attack shipping in the Gulf of Aden, before returning to Germany with her cargo. C-in-C U-boats was demanding his pound of flesh.

Eleven days later, U-188 passed through the Nine Degree Channel, which separates the Laccadive and Maldive archipelagos, and was on the surface steering a course for the Gulf of Aden. The sun had just risen with spectacular abruptness, turning the drab grey of the dying night into an enchanted Arabian morning. The sky was a rich blue, unmarred by the merest hint of cloud, and not even a puff of wind disturbed the glassy calm of the sea.

As the horizon hardened, a lookout in U-188's conning tower sighted a tiny cloud of smoke bearing right ahead. Lüdden, called to the bridge, scanned the horizon through his powerful Zeiss binoculars and within minutes was rewarded by the topmasts of a southbound ship coming into view. He called for full speed, and the U-boat surged forward like a hound scenting the fox.

At about 1000, with the upperworks of a distant ship, the *Fort Buckingham*, clearly visible, Lüdden took U-188 down to periscope depth and waited for the opportunity to strike. As the distance between the two vessels shortened, it became clear that the merchantman was unescorted and flying light in ballast. She also appeared to be very heavily armed. Keeping a close eye on her guns, then unmanned, Lüdden approached with caution. At about 2,800yds he fired a spread of three torpedoes. The distance was great, and not surprisingly all three torpedoes wandered off course, completely missing their target.

Aboard the *Fort Buckingham*, although Captain MacLeod had doubled his lookouts, no one had the slightest inkling that they were under attack. Three days out from Bombay, nothing had been seen of the enemy, no radio warnings had been received and the ship's routine continued as normal. The wooden decks had been scrubbed down, breakfast served, and now, under the influence of the warm sun, a lazy day was promised. Apart from the extra lookouts and a certain tension in the air, it was almost as if peace had broken out.

Still completely unaware of any danger threatening, the *Fort Buckingham* had crossed ahead of U-188 and was now stern-on to her. Frustrated at the failure of his torpedoes, Siegfried Lüdden gave chase, but as his maximum underwater speed was only 7½ knots he was unable to close the gap. In desperation, he surfaced and switched to his diesel motors, but after a while these again began to experience high exhaust temperatures and it became necessary to reduce speed. By nightfall, U-188 was still two miles astern of her quarry, and her diesels were running too hot for comfort.

Reluctantly, with his hopes of being able to overhaul the ship in the dark fading, Lüdden decided to abandon the chase. Then, as he was about to give up, the *Fort Buckingham* suddenly made a bold alteration of course to port, this being common practice in British merchantmen, designed to throw off any U-boat which may have been stalking them during the day. In this case, the move proved fatal for the *Fort Buckingham* for it put her beam-on to U-188, presenting a target that would be difficult to miss.

Lüdden had not yet reloaded his bow tubes, but he was able to reverse course quickly and fire a spread of two from his stern tubes. After a run of 177 seconds, both torpedoes went home in the *Fort Buckingham*'s No. 4 hold, immediately abaft her engine room. The sea poured in through the huge gash made in the ship's side.

Seventeen-year-old Apprentice Norman Gibson, after a punishing day's work testing the hold bilges in preparation for the *Fort Buckingham*'s next cargo, was sound asleep in his tiny cabin on the port side of the boat deck. In later years he wrote:

> I was shaken awake by an almighty explosion. As the noise subsided I could hear the tremendous rush of water filling up No. 4 hold, where I had been working on the previous day. All lights were extinguished so I fumbled around my cabin and found a torch. Putting on battledress, shoes and lifejacket, I made my way to the starboard boat deck, my allotted boat station.
>
> On arrival I met the 3rd Engineer, a man named Coverdale. Between us we cleared the lifeboat falls ready for lowering the boat. The 3rd Mate – Willoughby – was shouting across from the bridge in an attempt to prevent lifeboats being lowered until our Captain had decided on the best course of action. At that point we were not sinking and were able to defend ourselves. Coverdale then went back to his cabin to get a lifejacket – he was never seen again. Various members of the crew now began to collect on the boat deck.

I briefly returned to my cabin and on my return I found that the Lascar seamen had filled the lifeboat, causing it to tilt. The davit guy rope had become jammed under the rudder pintle. The solution was to cut the guy rope free, and as I had a knife I set off with haste to the main deck to do this. When I arrived, I found the main deck under water – how could a ship sink so quickly in the space of three to four minutes!

Taffy Jones, a cool-headed gunner, and I ran to the bows in order to let down a raft. On the way the bows began to rise up and when we reached the bridge the deck was so steep we could not go on. We climbed onto the bulwark and prepared to jump. As the ship slipped below the waves we made our leap into the water. She went down vertically with tremendous rending noises. To our surprise we were soon back on the surface, just in time to see the bow, with its 12 pounder gun disappearing a few feet away from us. It was all over in less than six minutes. Fortunately, apart from the two of us, some other crew members had been swept clear.

What went through my mind? – how warm the water was! Although I had not been sucked down with the ship I was swimming 500 miles away from the land with no lifeboat. Nevertheless I was alive, survived the explosion and was not alone – I felt a feeling of euphoria – and Taffy seemed to know just what to do all the time.

Having seen a light from a raft some way off, we set about reaching it. We swam via a floating door which offered rest, and I picked up a food container on the way which was later to be a valuable supplement to our rations. Taffy and I climbed onto the raft together, and were joined by two Lascar seamen. We extinguished the light in case we were seen and shot at by the submarine, which we assumed to be Japanese. During the night, other seamen were spotted and some swapping of survivors took place to even up the numbers between the rafts. At first light we counted five rafts in all, with a total of 51 survivors. There were 11 men on my raft. Only one officer had survived, all the others including the Captain having been lost

We doubted that a radio message had been sent before the sinking.

Gradually the sun rose, the sea was blue and coloured fish surrounded us. It all seemed unreal – a beautiful and peaceful world but no sign of search aircraft! However, we had plenty to do and busied ourselves making the rafts shipshape. Two rafts drifted away that day and we had no further contact with them. The remaining three were tied together and protective awnings were made from canvas. We even had a mast and a semblance of a sail, coloured red. We hoped it would attract attention.

It seems most probable that Lüdden's torpedoes brought down the *Fort Buckingham*'s main wireless aerial, and it was later established that all three of her radio officers had gone down with the ship, so it is extremely unlikely that an SOS was sent. Adrift on tiny wooden rafts in the middle of a vast and empty ocean, with very little in the way of propulsion and even less in the way of navigational equipment, the future of Norman Gibson and his fellow survivors was, to say the least, very uncertain. However, miracles do happen at sea, and now one came their way.

On 29 January, nine days after the survivors had been cast adrift, the 4,992-ton British motor vessel *Moorby*, southbound for Australia, came across one of the missing rafts carrying five of the *Fort Buckingham*'s DEMS gunners and two Lascar seamen. All seven men were picked up, but the weather had by now deteriorated, the visibility was poor and the Master of the *Moorby* was not inclined to dawdle in the area searching for other rafts. He also decided not to break radio silence to report the rescue, and in this was fully justified; Admiralty orders were to maintain radio silence at all times, unless under attack. The *Moorby* carried on to Australia, and another two weeks passed before she landed her survivors.

Meanwhile, the other rafts drifted aimlessly and unseen. Norman Gibson described the hopelessness of their situation:

The days that followed were ones of utter desolation and deprivation. The north-east monsoon was blowing almost continuously and we were never really comfortable – the sea often awash over the raft. We collected some rain water in the sail but it was barely enough to wash out the salt deposited there. Our plight was pretty desperate and there was little we could do to help ourselves. Our sail was inadequate for sailing towards the coast of Africa or the Seychelles and we had no charts, compass or sextant. Our raft measured approximately 10 feet by 6 feet with insufficient space on it for all of us to lie down at the same time.

It now became clear that no distress signal had been sent and as we were not due in Durban for a fortnight, it seemed likely that we would not be missed for some time.

Three days later, Gibson's raft was alone on an empty sea, the other rafts having drifted out of sight. As the sun went down on their eleventh day adrift, morale on the raft was at rock bottom, all hope of rescue being seen as a pipe dream. Then, in the last of the short twilight, a puff of smoke was seen on the horizon. A ship! Hope soared again. Distress rockets were fired, and their impending deliverance was celebrated with a double ration of water.

The celebrations were premature. All attempts to attract the attention of the distant ship were in vain. When darkness fell, any hope there may have been of rescue was abandoned, but unknown to Gibson and the others, the smoke they had seen was from the Norwegian ship *Kongsdal*, which had sighted one of the two missing rafts and had stopped to pick up the survivors. She then broke radio silence to report the rescue, which resulted in the following signal being sent out by Colombo:

> 1st February 1944. Survivors reported to have been picked up by the ss KONGSDAL 400 miles west of Kelai. Stated their ship was the FORT BUCKINGHAM torpedoed 20th January and four liferafts still missing. Three aircraft are to go to Kelai to carry out search for these rafts and, if found, supplies are to be dropped.

The three Catalina flying boats, J-205 and T-205 of 205 Squadron RAF and F-413 of 413 Squadron RCAF, based at Koggala on the south coast of Ceylon (Sri Lanka), were allocated for the search, and within a few hours of receipt of the Norwegian ship's message they were ready for take-off. They were to fly to the RAF base at Kelai in the Maldive Islands, where they would refuel before searching for the *Fort Buckingham*'s missing life-rafts.

The operation began disastrously, when one of the Catalinas, J-205, crashed into the sea on take-off and her depth charges exploded, killing all her crew. The remaining two aircraft took off without incident, landing at Kelai five hours later. Refuelling at this island base was a primitive and time-consuming exercise, involving aviation fuel in 40-gallon drums being floated out to the waiting planes and pumped aboard by hand.

Catalina F-413 was first to take off, leaving Kelai at midnight. Flying due west for 450 miles, she commenced a search, which by the time her fuel was running low had revealed nothing. She was then recalled, landing back at Kelai before dark. She was refuelled overnight, but when she was ready to continue the search next morning her radio was found to be defective and she was withdrawn from service.

Unaware that a search for them was in progress, Norman Gibson and his crew had exhausted their stock of food and were down to their last drops of water after fourteen days adrift on the raft. They now faced a lingering death by thirst and starvation, but on the initiative of DEMS gunner Richard (Taffy) Hughes-Jones they succeeded in catching a small shark. Gibson wrote:

> The fish flesh was pure white, but far too tough and unpleasant to eat raw. Among the raft's emergency equipment were storm matches. With dry wood chipped from the raft we lit a fire. An old water container was filled with sea water and shark steaks. After ten minutes the fish was cooked and ready to eat. We did our best to swallow it, but with limited enthusiasm, as our real and desperate need was for water. We had long ago lost any yearning for food.

The only Catalina remaining operational, T-205 piloted by Squadron Leader Melville Jackson, resumed the search at dawn on 3 February, sweeping the same area as F-413. In the late afternoon Melville's perseverance was rewarded when the missing rafts were sighted. Norman Gibson takes up the story again:

> Yet another day dawned bright with very little wind, but there was a considerable swell. We were all weak and listless – suddenly one of us claimed that he heard aero engines – sure enough, we all looked and spotted a distant aircraft – but had she seen us? It was 4.30 in the afternoon and we all tried to signal the aircraft using empty

ration tins to reflect the sun – we even shouted! We were reassured as the aircraft appeared to be losing height – and then it happened, a Catalina – W8406 – flew past at what seemed like only 50 feet. We saw a crew member in the port blister waving, and an Aldis lamp was flashed, but we were all too elated to read what it said. We discovered later that this aircraft on sighting us had sent the following signal to its base:

> MTB1 WQM – 15 DR 7° 26' North 66° 16' East. Circling two rafts with red sails approx. 3 miles apart. 10–15 people on each

We watched spellbound as the 'Cat' circled and took photographs and waved. Then we were awestruck – the aircraft flew away and we saw the detonation of six depth charges. Surely there was not a U-boat lurking nearby? Apparently not, as the aircraft lowered its floats and a landing was attempted. However, because of the swell the landing had to be abandoned – her engines were opened up, height was gained and she flew straight at us, dropping a Thornaby Bag within an arm's length of the raft. We lifted it aboard and found inside water bottles, a Very pistol and cartridges, cigarettes, chocolate, biscuits and barley sugar. The Catalina continued to fly around us until 1900 hours and then flew away (back to her base at Kelai). That night we ate extravagantly.

Squadron Leader Jackson radioed news of the sighting to RAF Kelai, who then contacted the Norwegian tanker *Ora*, reported to be some 400 miles north of the life-rafts. The *Ora*, bound from Bandar Abbas to Melbourne with aviation fuel, altered course for the position given and on 5 February found all three rafts and took the survivors on board. Next day, they were transferred to the destroyer HMS *Redoubt*, which landed them in Bombay on the 9th. Unfortunately, five of the Lascar seamen had been so affected by their ordeal that they died before reaching Bombay. This brought the numbers of those lost with the *Fort Buckingham* to forty-three. Captain Murdo MacLeod and all his officers, with the exception of Chief Engineer Edward Greenway, perished with their ship. To this grievous casualty list must be added the eight-man crew of

Catalina J-205, who died when their aircraft crashed on take-off at Koggala.

After her chance encounter with the *Fort Buckingham*, U-188 went on to sink another six ships in the Arabian Sea before embarking on her long passage home. She landed her desperately needed cargo in Bordeaux on 19 June 1944, after a voyage lasting twelve months and two days. For what must be considered a remarkable achievement Siegfried Lüdden was awarded the Knight's Cross and went on to serve on Admiral Dönitz's staff at Lorient, Plön and Kiel. He lost his life in Kiel on 15 January 1945, when the accommodation ship *Daressalam*, aboard which he was living, was consumed by fire. This was an ignominious death for a brave man who, rightly or wrongly, had served his country well.

CHAPTER EIGHTEEN

Convoy to Russia –
Fort Bellingham 26.01.44

When in the summer of 1941 Hitler launched Operation Barbarossa, the invasion of the Soviet Union, he made the same three fatal mistakes his infamous predecessor Napoleon Bonaparte had made in 1812. Firstly, he underestimated the tenacity of the Russia people; secondly, he failed to take into account the sheer size of the theatre he was entering; and thirdly, he failed to reckon with the harsh Russian winter.

At first, Barbarossa promised to be no more than a large scale training exercise for the Wehrmacht. Taken by surprise, the Russians fell back in confusion before the massed ranks of German armoured columns backed by the Luftwaffe's umbrella of fighters and bombers. By early October the invaders were within striking distance of Moscow. On paper, the defending Russians had an overwhelming superiority in resources: they had half a million more men on the ground, their aircraft outnumbered the Luftwaffe's by four to one and they could field eight times as many tanks. However, closer examination would reveal that the Soviet forces were hopelessly out of date. The Russians were still relying on more than a dozen cavalry divisions for mobile operations, and what tanks they had were slow and poorly armoured. The same applied to their aircraft, many being of First World War vintage and most without radio.

Reluctant as he was to engage with the western democracies, Stalin was eventually forced to turn to Britain and America for help, and on 12 August 1941 the first Arctic convoy sailed from Liverpool. Operation Dervish, as this convoy was codenamed, consisted of seven merchantmen, six British and one Dutch, all carrying guns, planes, tanks, ammunition and spares to Archangel. Thereafter, similar British convoys sailed to Russia by the northern route at the rate of one a month. When America joined the war in December 1941, the size and frequency of the convoys increased. The hazards these convoys faced, particularly in the long Arctic winter, were many and daunting. A report written by Able Seaman William Smith, who served in the sloop HMS *Magpie* escorting convoys to Russia, paints a vivid picture:

> The sea was violent with waves of 30ft plus. When we met a gale in the Atlantic we went into it bow on and ploughed through, but in the Arctic, east of Bear Island, the sea was very narrow and we had to go east with no deviation. This meant we were rolling as much as 30 degrees to port and starboard.
>
> With the deck covered in ice and snow we had to use lifelines when going aft to the guns and depth charges. These lifelines were fitted very firmly and anyone going aft on deck had to fix a rope around the body with a hook on to the lifeline and gradually move aft when the ship was steady. But when she rolled your feet left the deck and at 30 degrees you were hanging over the sea. At maximum roll the ship shuddered for a few seconds and then decided to come back or turn over – some did.
>
> The temperature in those seas got as low as 60 degrees below freezing. Your eyebrows and eyelashes froze and your eyes were very sore with the winds blowing into them. When you got down to the mess deck there was about three inches of water from condensation. The older men, who had hair in their noses, found that these froze solid and were like needles. Many men came off watch with faces covered in blood as they had rubbed their noses without thinking.
>
> The main thing at this time was to keep the upper deck clear of ice and snow by means of axes and steam hoses or the ship would become top heavy.

The merchant ships, being bigger and higher out of the water, suffered marginally less, but they too had their problems, as related by Radio Officer David B. Craig aboard the *Dover Hill* in Convoy JW 53:

> As we sailed north the gale developed into a hurricane and ships began to get damaged. Six of the merchant ships were damaged and had to return to Iceland. On our

ship the deck cargo began to break adrift and we were not sorry to see the oil drums going over the side but when the lorries in wooden cases were smashed up and eventually went overboard things were not so good. But we managed to save the tanks and kept on battering our way northwards. I remember trying to use an Aldis lamp from our bridge to signal to a corvette and found it very difficult since one minute she would be in sight, then she would go down the trough of the wave and all I could see would be her top masts; then she would come up and our ship would go down and all that could be seen was water, but eventually we got the message through.

The Arctic convoys had been operating for two and a half years when, on 12 January 1944, the *Fort Bellingham* left the sheltered waters of Loch Ewe on Scotland's western coast. Duffle-coated and muffled against the biting cold, Captain James Maley peered through the wheelhouse windows as he conned the ship out past the headlands. The sky was a thick grey overcast, the wind was keening in the rigging and the swell rising. Somewhere out in the Atlantic a monster of a storm was brewing. It was, Maley concluded, a rotten way in which to begin the first voyage of the new year.

Convoy JW56A, of which the *Fort Bellingham* was Commodore ship, consisted of twenty merchantmen, thirteen American, five British and one Dutch, all loaded to their marks with war materials destined for the steppes of northern Russia, where Stalin's armies were bloodily ousting the German invader. Waiting outside the loch was the convoy's local escort of two destroyers, four corvettes and two minesweepers, which would stand guard over JW56A as far as Iceland. With Captain Maley on the bridge of the *Fort Bellingham* was Commodore Ivan Whitehorn RN and his staff of six, a questionable honour for Maley, whose command would be subjugate to Whitehorn until they reached Murmansk.

The *Fort Bellingham* was a 7,153-ton, Canadian-built wartime replacement, only four months out of her Vancouver shipyard. She had been built on very similar lines to Henry Kaiser's Liberty ships, having a capacious box-shaped hull that gave her a cargo-carrying capacity of up to 10,000 tons. Powered by a 628 nominal h.p. steam engine, with oil-fired boilers, she had an economical service speed of 11 knots. Although owned by the Canadian Government, she was on bareboat charter to the Ministry of War Transport, who had appointed the Hain Steamship Company of London to manage her. She sailed under the Red Ensign and was manned by a British crew of forty-five, which included DEMS gunners. Like all merchantmen sailing to Russia by the northern route, she was very heavily armed, mounting a 4-inch anti-submarine gun, a 12-pounder HA/LA, a 40mm Bofors, six 20mm Oerlikons, two twin 0.5 Colt machine guns and an assortment of rockets for use against low-flying aircraft.

Predictably, as the convoy moved north towards the Arctic Circle, the weather grew steadily worse, the wind increasing to storm force 10, gusting 11 from the west, with mountainous seas exacerbated by a huge Atlantic swell. All efforts at keeping station were abandoned, each ship being heavily engaged in fighting her own personal battle with the storm. They were beam-on to sea and swell, rolling their gunwales under and shipping seas over-all. The smaller escorts, being built for speed and manoeuvrability rather than stability, suffered most, being literally thrown from crest to trough, their decks continually awash. At the same time, the thermometer was dropping like the proverbial stone. The rain turned to sleet, and then to blinding snow, while ice began to form on decks and superstructure.

Before long, many of the merchant ships were in trouble, the incessant rolling and buffeting causing their cargoes to break adrift on deck and below in the holds. Lifeboats and rafts were swept overboard and main deck accommodation flooded. After six days of this mounting chaos, the Admiralty ordered the convoy to take shelter in a fjord on the north coast of Iceland to re-secure cargo and repair damage. After three days at anchor in the fjord near the town of Akureyri, the storm finally blew itself out, but it was found that five of the American ships were so badly damaged that it was necessary for them to return to Loch Ewe. Even before meeting the real enemy, Convoy JW56A was down to fifteen ships.

The importance of JW56A, and the pressing need for its cargoes to get through to Russia, became evident when the convoy's ocean escort arrived at Akureyri. Led by the destroyer flotilla leader HMS *Hardy* were the British destroyers *Inconstant*, *Obdurate*, *Offa*, *Savage*, *Venus*, *Vigilant*, and *Virago*, and the Norwegian *Stord*, plus the corvettes HMS *Daniella* and HMS *Poppy*. In addition, a distant escort comprising the three light cruisers HMS *Bermuda, Berwick* and *Kent* would follow in the wake of the convoy, ready to close up if any German heavy units should venture out of their hide-outs in the Norwegian fjords. This was a formidable escort for just fifteen merchantmen, and when at 1000 on the morning of 21 January JW56A set out for Murmansk there was a justifiable mood of confidence in the convoy. They were fit to fight off any attack.

Unknown to the Admiralty, their radio signal sent on the 17th ordering JW56A to take shelter at Akureyri had been intercepted and deciphered by German Intelligence, who deduced that the convoy would sail for Russia on or about the 20th. However, for reasons unknown, U-boat Command in Norway was not informed until the 24th. Only then did it contact Group Isegrim, a pack of six U-boats on station to the east of Bear Island, and order them to set up an ambush.

Isegrim consisted of U-278 (Joachim Franze), U-360 (Klaus-Helmuth Becker), U-425 (Heinz Bentzien), U-601 (Otto Hansen), U-739 (Ernst Mangold) and U-965 (Klaus Ohling). Another boat, U-737 (Paul Brasack), was on its way to join Isegrim, while five others, U-312 (Kurt-Heinz Nicolay), U-314 (Georg-Wilhelm Basse), U-472 (Wolfgang-Friedrich Freiherr von Forstner), U-716 (Hans Dunkelberg) and U-956 (Hans-Dieter Mohs), were ordered to sail from various Norwegian bases and head towards the area. At the same time, long-range Focke-Wulf Kondor reconnaissance aircraft were scrambled and ordered to locate and shadow the convoy.

While U-boat Command gathered its resources for the reception of JW56A, the convoy was making its way through the polar twilight towards Murmansk in blissful ignorance of the approaching threat. The merchant ships were steaming in three columns abreast, two of six ships and one of three, with the escorts arranged in a tight defensive screen around them. Convoy speed was 10 knots and course was set to pass south of Bear Island. The weather was fine and clear, and so far no reports of enemy activity in the area had been received. It seemed safe to assume that the Germans were unaware of the convoy's existence.

This assumption was of course not true, but Isegrim had set up its patrol line too far to the south of Bear Island, and JW56A would have sailed past unseen had it not been for the vigilance of the lookouts in the conning tower of U-739. Under the command of Oberleutnant Ernst Mangold, U-739 had sailed from Bergen on her first war patrol just seventeen days earlier and was the northernmost boat of Isegrim's patrol line. Mangold immediately reported the sighting and settled down to shadow the convoy. The other boats homed in on U-739's signals, and at 1015 on the 25th U-965 signalled 'Enemy in sight'. JW56A was then passing some 150 miles south of Bear Island.

The ether was now alive with radio messages as the rest of the pack contacted each other and moved in on their prey. At 1122 U-425 reported sighting smoke on the horizon, followed an hour later by a similar report from U-601. At 1455 U-360 signalled that she had two destroyers in sight. By late afternoon, JW56A was surrounded by ten U-boats, all at periscope depth and keeping out of Asdic range. They were waiting until the polar twilight turned to night.

Despite all the radio activity, the convoy appeared to have no inkling of the danger it faced and sailed serenely on. Then, at 1635, Otto Hansen in U-601 lost patience and fired a torpedo at one of the escorts. The torpedo missed, but when it exploded at the end of its run, the game was up. Ten minutes later, Klaus Ohling in U-965 reported that he had been depth-charged by two destroyers. He also tried a snap shot at one of his attackers, but again the torpedo missed its target.

It was not until 1835, when complete darkness had descended, that Isegrim scored its first hit. U-360, with Klaus-Helmuth Becker in the conning tower, approached the convoy on the surface and fired an acoustic torpedo aimed at the destroyer HMS *Obdurate*. Fortunately for *Obdurate*, the torpedo detonated short, and the damage sustained by the destroyer was confined to her starboard propeller, which was knocked out and its shaft flooded. She was able to carry on with one engine.

The Arctic night had brought with it snow squalls, making it even more difficult for the U-boats to attack, but at 2012 Joachim Franze in U-278 broke through the escort screen on the starboard side and fired a spread of three torpedoes into the heart of the convoy. He heard two detonations as he withdrew and claimed two ships sunk. In fact, his torpedoes had passed through the columns of the convoy until they found a home in the hull of the US Liberty ship *Penelope Barker*, second ship of the outer port column.

The *Penelope Barker* was completely wrecked, one torpedo hitting in her after cargo hold, the other in her engine room. She sank within ten minutes, taking with her fifteen of her crew and one passenger. The passenger was Surgeon Lieutenant Maurice Hood RNVR, who earlier in the day had boarded from HMS *Obdurate* to treat one of the *Penelope Barker*'s crew suffering from an inflamed appendix.

With the torpedoing of the *Penelope Barker* the night sky was rent by a spectacular display of distress rockets and snowflakes, and the convoy escorts raced to the aid of the stricken ship. The destroyer HMS *Savage* began picking up survivors, while others tracked down the U-boat and attacked with depth charges. So intense was the bombardment received by U-278 that she dived deep and left the scene as fast as her electric motors would take her. It was not until the early hours of the following morning that Franze felt it safe to surface and report his success to U-boat Command.

All went quiet after Otto Franze's audacious strike, the Isegrim boats withdrawing in the face of the massive retaliation by JW56A's escorts. They did not return until midnight, by which time the merchantmen, after much badgering by Commodore Whitehorn, had found those extra few engine revolutions, and the escort ring had tightened. The safety of the Kola Inlet was now only seventy-two hours away. Could they outrun their enemy? The answer was not long in coming.

Hans Dunkelberg in U-716 was first to return to the fight. At 0010 on the 26th Dunkelberg approached the starboard wing of the convoy undetected and fired a spread of three torpedoes into the massed ranks of ships. Two of the three ran through the columns without finding a target, the third slammed into another American Liberty, the *Andrew G. Curtin*. She was carrying 9,000 tons of general cargo in her holds, much of it steel, while on deck she had two locomotives and two PT boats, a cargo certainly worth its weight in gold to the Russians. Hit squarely amidships, the all-welded ship broke her back and began to sink. Three of her crew of seventy-one died, the others were rescued by the destroyer HMS *Inconstant*.

Captain James Maley had been in the chartroom of the *Fort Bellingham* when he heard the unmistakeable muffled thump as the *Andrew G. Curtin* was hit. He returned to the darkened wheelhouse, but before his eyes had adjusted to the night, the *Fort*

Bellingham staggered as U-360 put a torpedo into her. Captain Maley described events in his report to the Admiralty:

> No one saw the track of the torpedo, which struck on the port side, in the after end of No. 3 hold forward of the engine room. There was a dull explosion and a fair amount of water thrown up on the port side. No flash was seen. The ship rolled to starboard, then to port, but quickly righted herself, settling bodily. The engine room bulkhead was pierced, both boilers collapsed and the main steam pipe was fractured. A spray of oil and steam was thrown high into the air, which obscured the view from the bridge. The engines and dynamos stopped immediately and all lights went out. Ventilators were blown off, some of which landed on the after deck. Nos 2 and 4 lifeboats were destroyed. The deck did not appear to be torn or buckled. Although the ship settled several feet, she seemed to be in no immediate danger of sinking.
>
> After the signal for emergency stations was rung, the Third Officer went to the upper bridge to fire the rockets, but the portfire failed, the cap being lost in the darkness, so I switched on the red light. I collected the confidential books, etc., and sent the Chief and Second Officers to the boat deck to clear away the boats.

At no time did Captain Maley give the order to abandon ship. It was his intention to wait until the ship had stopped and then consider whether it was necessary to take to the boats. However, there were others on board who viewed the situation in a different light, and what had been a tightly controlled emergency turned into blind panic. It later came to light that when the *Fort Bellingham* was hit a rumour went round the ship that her cargo contained a large quantity of ammunition, sufficient to blow her and her crew into eternity. In fact, the only explosives in the holds were 5 tons of cordite, which without detonators was inert. DEMS gunners rushed to the boat deck, where they were joined by a number of the *Fort Bellingham*'s ratings and a few engineer officers. In the mistaken belief that they had only minutes to live, this confused throng, numbering around twenty in all, set about launching the lifeboats and rafts. As the ship was still making way through the water at some 4 knots, inevitable disaster followed. One lifeboat was lost, the other went away half-filled, and when Chief Officer Gourlay searched the main deck he found that all the life-rafts except two had been slipped and were floating astern.

Thirty-five men, including Captain Maley, his deck officers and Commodore Whitehorn and two of his staff, were still aboard the crippled ship. As there was no way of knowing how long the *Fort Bellingham* would stay afloat, Chief Officer Gourlay and a party of seamen attempted to put the two remaining life-rafts in the water, but both appeared to be jammed in the their cradles. Captain Maley's report explains the situation:

> The Chief Officer went round the decks and reported that all rafts, except one on the port side of the lower bridge and the one in the after rigging, had been slipped and were floating astern. One raft with a few men on it was seen near the lifeboat, whilst two others appeared to be empty. I gathered the remaining men together and finally freed the raft from the lower bridge, giving instructions that it was to remain alongside, but as it became water-borne, about eighteen men jumped on to it, cut the painter and it quickly drifted from the ship's side.
>
> The Chief Officer then took a party of men and endeavoured to release the raft from the after rigging. Meanwhile, with the First Officer and Fourth Engineer, I searched the accommodation, we found the Cabin Boy and turned him out. We then tried to enter the engine room, but found it completely flooded and filled with smoke and steam.
>
> As the raft on the port side aft was proving very difficult to free, the Chief and Second Officers went over the side to the waterlogged lifeboat in an attempt to make it serviceable. They were soon soaked in cold water and covered with oil fuel.
>
> At about 0130, about an hour and a half after the explosion, HMS *Offa* tried to come alongside, but owing to the heavy swell, her bows crashed against my ship. At this moment, the Commodore jumped on board the *Offa*, followed by his Yeoman of Signals and Telegraphist. All got aboard successfully. The Commodore had not told me that

he intended to make the attempt, but went off without saying a word. The destroyer then stood off and picked up survivors from the raft, also the Chief and Second Officers from the waterlogged lifeboat, which was still alongside. The Second Officer was immediately taken to the sick bay suffering from the effects of fuel oil.

Captain Maley and fourteen men remained on board with no means of abandoning the ship, until at 0230 HMS *Offa* lowered her whaler, which came alongside and took them off. In consultation with Captain Maley, *Offa's* commander, Lieutenant Commander R. F. Leonard, decided that there was no hope of saving the *Fort Bellingham*. Although she was not sinking noticeably lower in the water, her engine room was flooded and there was little possibility of towing her to Murmansk, so it was decided to sink her.

The British ship was reluctant to succumb to her wounds, and even though *Offa* used two torpedoes and eighteen 4-inch shells in an attempt to put her beyond reach of the enemy, she refused to sink. Lieutenant Commander Leonard could not waste any more time and ammunition on her, so left her to drift forlornly astern into the night. At about 0653 that morning Gerd Schaar in U-967 came across her and ended her agony with a single torpedo.

The *Fort Bellingham* was just five months old when she went to her lonely grave off Norway's North Cape. She took with her 4,900 tons of military equipment worth a king's ransom to the hard-pressed Russians. Of her crew, two men were believed to have been killed in the engine room when the German torpedo exploded in her bowels and two others jumped into the sea and were presumed lost, while thirty-five men were said to have abandoned their ship without orders. Captain Maley and the fifteen men who stayed aboard with him were rescued by HMS *Offa*, which also picked up another eighteen survivors from a life-raft. Commodore Whitehorn and two of his signals staff escaped by jumping aboard *Offa* when she was briefly laid alongside the *Fort Bellingham*.

The thirty-five men who prematurely abandoned the ship, eighteen of her crew, fifteen DEMS gunners and two of the Commodore's staff, were primarily responsible for the chaos that reigned when the *Fort Bellingham* was torpedoed. However, it must be borne in mind that the majority of them were very young and inexperienced. This was at a time when the heavy losses of British ships and men were beginning to take their toll. There was a serious shortage of trained seamen and gunners to man the ships, and men who had neither the aptitude nor the self-discipline to face up to the horrors of war were being sent to sea.

After he was rescued, Commodore Whitehorn said, 'Discipline in the ship was very lax and no attempt was made by the officers to take charge.' Examination of Captain Maley's account will show that this accusation against the *Fort Bellingham*'s officers was unfounded. Furthermore, Whitehorn's statement regarding discipline in the ship reveals how little he understood about how a merchant ship functioned. Unlike a Royal Navy captain, the commander of a merchant ship had no powers to hand out draconian punishments as per the King's Regulations; his only means of imposing discipline lay with the Log Book and the few totally inadequate fines it allowed him to levy for misdemeanours. He had a very thin tightrope to walk to keep an efficient and happy ship. It must also be remembered that, even in times of war, a merchant ship is still a commercial enterprise manned by civilians.

At the height of the attack on Convoy JW56A, the Isegrim pack grew to at least twelve U-boats, but in spite of the generally good weather prevailing, their success was not great. Only three ships were lost and the destroyer *Obdurate* was damaged. Equally, the convoy escorts did no better, for they failed to sink or damage a single U-boat. In fact, the only setback Isegrim suffered came late on the night of the 26th, when U-360 and U-601 were in collision and U-360 was forced to return to Narvik for repairs.

In the late morning of the 27th, with JW56A nearing Murmansk, its escort reinforced by three Soviet destroyers, U-boat Command in Norway decided to abandon the action and ordered the Isegrim boats to withdraw.

CHAPTER NINETEEN

Death on the Equator –
Khedive Ismail 12.02.44

The Indian Ocean was at its best, the sky a flawless blue, the sea mirror-calm, the wind a gentle breeze from the north-east. An eerie quiet lay over the ocean, with only the measured thump of the engines and the swish of the bow-wave disturbing the silence of the early afternoon. Lunch was over, and most of the passengers were below enjoying a concert party in the main lounge. On deck, a few dedicated sun worshippers were stretched out in steamer chairs. At any other time the *Khedive Ismail* might have been a cruise liner of the 1930s carrying the privileged to their next exotic destination. But the year was 1944, and the world was at war.

By December 1943, after a long and hard-fought campaign, British forces in Burma had at last turned the tables on the Japanese invaders, and a major offensive aimed at regaining lost territory was about to be mounted. Fresh troops were being brought in from bases around the Indian Ocean, among them 996 men of the 301st Field Regiment of the East African Artillery, who made up the majority of the *Khedive Ismail*'s passengers. Also on board were 271 Royal Navy personnel, 54 nursing sisters, 19 Wrens and 9 drivers of the Women's Transport Service. The ship's crew consisted of 22 British officers, 5 medical staff, 12 DEMS gunners and 144 Indian ratings. With a total of 1,536 passengers and crew on board, the ship's accommodation was fully occupied.

In her long life the *Khedive Ismail* had served many masters. Built on the River Clyde in 1922 for the Chilean Campania Sud Americana de Vapores for their Valparaiso to New York service, she had been launched as the *Aconcagua*, named for the highest mountain in the Andes. In 1931, following heavy losses sustained by CSVA in the depression years, she had been sold to Lithgows of Port Glasgow and returned to the land of her birth. A few years later, the Lithgow yard sold her on to another shipbuilder, William Hamilton of Belfast, who in turn found a buyer for her in Egypt, the Khedivial Mail Line of Alexandria. She was then renamed *Khedive Ismail* and employed ferrying cargo and passengers between Alexandria and ports in Greece and France. Egypt was then under joint British and French control, and in 1940 she was requisitioned by the Ministry of War Transport and converted for carrying troops in the Indian Ocean under the management of the British India Steam Navigation Company.

On Sunday, 5 February 1944 the *Khedive Ismail* sailed from Mombasa, East Africa with Convoy KR-8, bound for Colombo. The convoy consisted of five fast British troopships, Ellerman Line's 10,902-ton *City of Paris* and four others operated by British India, the *Ekma* (5,108 tons), the *Ellenga* (5,196 tons), the *Varsova* (4,701 tons) and the *Khedive Ismail*. Between them, the five ships were carrying a total of 6,311 military personnel.

Commanded by 49-year-old Captain Roderick Macaulay, who had been appointed convoy commodore, the *Khedive Ismail* led the way out of Mombasa, and once clear of Mackenzie Point the ships formed up in three columns abreast. At the head of the port outer column was the convoy's ocean escort, the heavy cruiser HMS *Hawkins*.

Built in 1917 and a veteran of the China Station, HMS *Hawkins* was a formidable looking warship armed with seven 7.5-inch and eight 12-pounders; but she was severely lacking in anti-submarine capability, which in this war was the main requirement of any convoy escort. She had no Asdic or any other underwater detecting equipment and was in reality far more vulnerable than any of the merchant ships she was charged with protecting. Fortunately, KR-8 also had a local escort comprising the Flower-class corvette *Honesty* and the two Banff-class sloops *Lulworth* and *Senna*, all fully equipped and well experienced in submarine warfare.

As the convoy formed up off the East African coast, 3,000 miles to the east the Japanese submarine I-27, which had sailed from Penang twenty-four hours earlier, was rounding the northern end of Sumatra and entering the Indian Ocean. In her conning tower was Commander Toshiaki Fukumura, who had orders to seek out and attack Allied shipping in the Gulf of Aden. The Suez Canal, which for some time had been inaccessible to the Allies, was once more in business, and it was reported that many ships were sailing unescorted in the Gulf.

I-27 was a 356ft-long cruiser-class submarine with a displacement on the surface of 2,584 tons, almost twice the size of the Type

IX, her German equivalent, and considerably larger than the average British destroyer. She was armed with six torpedo tubes in the bow, a 5.5-inch deck gun and a twin-barrelled 25mm AA gun in the conning tower. Housed in a hangar forward of the tower was a small reconnaissance seaplane, and she was also equipped to carry a midget submarine on deck when required. With a surface speed of 23 knots and an underwater speed of 8 knots, I-27 was undoubtedly fast, but she had an Achilles heel: largely because of her size, she was slow to manoeuvre and slow to dive, two characteristics that could prove fatal to a submarine at war.

Thirty-nine-year-old Toshiaki Fukumura was a long-serving member of the Imperial Japanese Navy, having entered the service as a midshipman in 1927. After sailing in the battleship *Matsu* he had joined the submarine arm in l933 as a navigator, advancing quickly through the ranks until in November 1939 he was given command of the small coastal submarine RO-34. Since taking command of I-27 in February 1943 he had had considerable success, sinking ten Allied ships of 54,453 tons and damaging three others. In the course of these sinkings he had earned the reputation of being a ruthless foe, prone to machine-gunning survivors in the water.

Four days after sailing from Mombasa, when crossing the Equator north of the Seychelles, KR-8's local escort returned to port, leaving the cruiser *Hawkins* in sole charge. The voyage so far had been without incident, and with the Admiralty reporting no German or Japanese submarines in the area, the indications were that it would continue so. Some forty hours later, on the morning of the 11th, HMS *Hawkins* was joined by the P-class destroyers *Paladin* and *Petard*, two of the Royal Navy's best. Less than three years off the stocks, they were 37-knotters equipped with the latest in anti-submarine gear. The two destroyers took up station 3,000yds on either bow and began zigzagging, their Asdics sweeping ahead for any sign of an underwater enemy. KR-8 was then only 270 miles west of the naval air base on Addu Atoll, and with air cover expected soon it seemed that, to quote an old adage, 'it was all over bar the shouting'.

Dawn on the 12th saw the convoy approaching the One and a Half Degree Channel, the 80-mile-wide gap in the Maldive archipelago, and making 13 knots. During the course of the morning, Captain Whitehorn, as convoy commodore, suggested to the

Senior Officer Escort, Captain Josselyn in HMS *Hawkins*, that the merchant ships should now commence zigzagging. His suggestion was noted, but no action was taken. No air cover had yet arrived, but with Addu Atoll only just over the horizon to starboard and Colombo less than two days steaming away, Josselyn appears to have been content to leave things as they were. The convoy continued on its serene way, seemingly oblivious to any dangers that might still lay ahead.

Aboard the *Khedive Ismail* noon sights had been taken and the course adjusted appropriately. Normal afternoon routine was being followed. Below decks, the concert party was in full swing, with Nursing Sister Edith Bateman giving a spirited rendering on the grand piano of the Warsaw Concerto, while on deck the sunbathers sipped their post-lunch gin and tonics contentedly. The war seemed to be on some far-off planet. Then, without warning, this peaceful scene was cruelly shattered.

I-27's periscope was sighted simultaneously by the leading ship of the starboard column, British India's *Varsova*, which was slightly ahead of her station, and the destroyer *Petard*. Aboard *Petard*, zigzagging on the starboard bow, the Officer of the Watch, Lieutenant R. de Pass, happened to be looking astern when he caught a glimpse of the periscope as Fukumura took a quick sweep around the horizon. At the same time, three DEMS gunners, standing to at the 4-inch on the *Varsova*'s poop, saw what they described as 'A dark green periscope protruding some 3ft above the water and travelling towards the *Khedive Ismail* at about 4 knots'. The gunners tried to bring their gun to bear, but it would not depress low enough.

Fukumura had been approaching the One and a Half Degree Channel from the east when he sighted the smoke of the convoy, which was then on a reciprocal course. Remaining on the surface until the sighting was confirmed by the appearance of mast and funnels on the horizon, Fukumura submerged and waited. KR-8 continued on course in complete ignorance of the danger it was steaming towards.

As the convoy drew nearer, Fukumura sank deep, and with motors stopped and observing silent routine, he allowed the two destroyers to pass over him. Once inside the convoy, he came back to periscope depth and took another quick look around. I-27 was then about 50yds astern of the *Varsova*, but Fukumura had eyes only for the cruiser *Hawkins*. He took careful aim and fired a spread of four torpedoes.

I-27's spread bracketed the British cruiser, one torpedo passing ahead of her, another astern. The *Khedive Ismail*, which at the time was partially overlapping *Hawkins*, was the unlucky recipient of the other two torpedoes. Second Officer Cecil Munday, who was on watch on the bridge of the troopship at the time, later stated:

> I am of the opinion the submarine fired a fan of torpedoes from the starboard quarter of the convoy; I was on watch at the time, talking to one of the signalmen, when I saw the wake of a torpedo pass our stern and miss the stern of HMS *Hawkins* by 50 feet. Immediately afterwards we were struck by a torpedo in No. 4 hold on the starboard side, followed five seconds later by a second torpedo, which struck in the boiler room, on the starboard side. No one saw the track of either of these torpedoes, but I sighted the U-boat's periscope about 400 feet away between the centre and starboard columns.
>
> There was a loud explosion with the first torpedo, which caused the vessel to list 12° to starboard; the second explosion, which was more violent than the first, may have caused one of the boilers to explode. There was no flash with either explosion, but I saw flames rising outside the funnel through the fidley gratings. No water was thrown up, but a great amount of debris was flung high into the air. The second explosion caused the main stairway and troop deck to collapse, thereby trapping a great number of people. The vessel continued to heel over to starboard, until she was on her beam ends, and then disappeared.

An unnamed eyewitness described how, when the first torpedo struck, he saw the mainmast collapse and much of the after part of the superstructure cave in, while the hatch covers of the after hold were blown high in the air. When, five seconds later, the other torpedo hit directly below the funnel, there was a major explosion inside the vessel, resulting in the *Khedive Ismail* breaking in two. The stern sank first, then the bow section up-ended and corkscrewed below the surface. One minute and forty seconds after she was first hit, the ship was gone.

Acting Petty Officer Percy Crabb, one of the Royal Navy contingent on board the *Khedive Ismail*, in later years recorded his experience:

> I was in the POs' mess with seven other petty officers when the troopship was torpedoed between 1400 and 1500 by, I believe, two tin fish, one in the engine room and one aft under the counter. I was asleep at the time. Immediately she listed over; everyone made a dash for the companionway except yours truly and PO Harper; we both made for the two portholes, which were open. I remember scrambling through and hobbling down the ship's side, stepping over the rolling chock and diving into the sea, by the time I surfaced the ship had gone. I swam to a green smoke canister some thirty yards away, hanging on to this I looked around me, there were several survivors either swimming or hanging on to whatever floated.

Soon after the second torpedo hit, Captain Whiteman, realizing that his ship was mortally wounded, gave the order to abandon ship, informing Second Officer Munday that he would remain on board until everyone else was off. This was a brave gesture that would cost Roderick Whiteman his life; the *Khedive Ismail* capsized and sank only seconds later.

Second Officer Munday later said:

> There was no time to launch any boats, but many rafts and four lifeboats broke away as the ship sank. The Chief Officer and the Troop Officer ordered everybody to jump overboard as the ship was turning over. The Chief Officer jumped, but fouled some ropes and was pulled under with the ship; he eventually came to the surface, found a raft onto which he climbed and managed to pull on board a Wren who was struggling in the water. He said that he felt no effect of suction on the low side of the ship as she sank. I went along to No. 2 boat and saw a Wren officer lying on the deck; as she was unconscious and frothing at the mouth, I did not consider anything could be done for her, so I climbed over the high side and walked down the ship's side into the water.

I swam some half dozen strokes from the ship when a big wave overtook me, and as I was drawn under I saw many bodies and wreckage floating past; I momentarily surfaced and managed to take a few deep breaths before being again drawn under. I was then on the port side of the ship, but on surfacing again I found myself off the starboard bow. I therefore must have passed completely under the ship.

The reaction of *Paladin* and *Petard* to the sighting of the periscope by Lieutenant de Pass was immediate. Both destroyers turned outwards under full helm and raced back to the rear of the convoy, where it was thought the attacker might be. Asdic contact was established, and with *Petard* directing, *Paladin* dropped two patterns of depth charges. There was no visible reaction, Fukumura having already moved out of range. Now the hunt had to begin in earnest.

At this point, as Senior Officer Escort, Captain Josselyn in HMS *Hawkins* intervened. Having in mind the possibility of more than one enemy submarine being involved, he called for one destroyer to return to the convoy, leaving the other to deal with the attacker. *Petard* being the senior ship, Commander Egan ordered *Paladin* to rejoin, after first picking up survivors sighted in the water. Among those survivors was Petty Officer Crabb, who later wrote:

The convoy had dispersed by this time and it seemed we were left to our own devices; some 200 yards away were two lifeboats from the ship, one upside down, survivors were all making for them so I decided to do the same.

I am almost certain the submarine passed under me, as there was quite a turbulence of water and a wake left behind. This was the scene when the destroyers *Petard* and *Paladin* arrived at high speed, the submarine must have been picked up on their Asdics, because they started depth charging some 300 yards away. I distinctly remember one charge from the thrower exploding just above the surface of the sea. It was a very strange experience to feel shock waves coming through the water and the almighty thump in the stomach. Luckily, I was still hanging on to the smoke float, which took most of the concussion.

> *Paladin* had dropped off a motor boat and sea boat to pick up survivors. I eventually made it to the troopship's lifeboat and got aboard, we managed to row towards *Paladin*, which was slowly circling us, while *Petard* was still depth charging further away. We got alongside *Paladin* and hastily scrambled aboard, among us three nursing sisters, two Wrens and one South African WTS; this was all that was left of their contingents. I remember a seaman throwing me a pair of sandals, as I was barefoot, because the steel decks of the destroyer were very hot.

HMS *Paladin* was in the act of sending away her boats to pick up survivors when I-27 appeared to give away her position. Commander Egan, on the bridge of *Petard*, saw a sudden eruption in the water about 1,000yds to the east which had the appearance of a submarine blowing its tanks. Egan carried out an Asdic sweep in the area but could get no contact. He then concluded that the disturbance must have been caused by a sudden rush of air escaping from the submerged wreck of the *Khedive Ismail* and decided to join *Paladin* in the more urgent business of rescuing people from the water. It soon became obvious that there were not many of them. To quote Commander Egan, 'Survivors were regrettably few and concentrated in a small area, with barely half a dozen up-turned boats and a few rafts.'

As *Petard* approached the survivors with her boats swung out ready to lower, another large bubble of air broke the surface close to the wreckage marking the last resting place of the *Khedive Ismail*. Egan immediately abandoned the rescue and made for the spot at full speed. Once again he was disappointed, for no Asdic contact could be made. He was about to rejoin *Paladin* when, to his great surprise, a submarine suddenly shot to the surface about 1½ miles on *Petard*'s starboard quarter. Egan's report reads:

> By this time *Paladin* had recovered all survivors and both ships turned simultaneously to the attack, firing with all weapons and scoring many hits. I then proceeded to pass as close astern of the U-boat as practicable, firing three depth charges from the port throwers and trap, set to 50 feet, when close aboard, which fell reasonably near but were not lethal.

Meanwhile the U-boat got under way but attempts by the crew to come out of the conning tower were frustrated by the combined fire of both ships. At least two of the crew were blown to shreds. *Petard* now opened from the target while *Paladin* closed at high speed to the attack, signalling that she intended to ram.

Although there was a possibility of the U-boat re-submerging, I did not wish to take this action, except as a last resort, I therefore ordered *Paladin* not to ram.

Egan's signal came too late. *Paladin* was then only 600yds from the surfaced submarine and bearing down on her at full speed. The *Khedive Ismail*'s second officer, Cecil Munday, who had been picked up by HMS *Paladin*, described the action:

All the survivors in the *Paladin* were ordered to lie flat on deck. We then proceeded at full speed and steamed straight for the submarine with the intention of ramming. When only a few feet away the Senior Officer in HMS *Petard* signalled, 'Don't ram'. Immediately the helm was put over in an attempt to clear, but as she shot past the submarine's hydroplane guard caught in the *Paladin*'s side, below water, and ripped her side from amidships as far aft as the 4″ gun. Water poured into the ship and everybody was ordered on deck.

Damage parties reported that the *Paladin*'s hull had been sliced open for some 80ft just below the waterline. Her engine room was awash, and two fuel tanks and the after magazine were flooded. The destroyer slowly lost way, until she was lying dead in the water and listing to starboard. *Paladin* was out of the fight.

Petard now took up the sword, and there followed a bizarre running action lasting nearly an hour, in which destroyer and submarine circled each other like two prize fighters in the ring, each looking for an opportunity to land the killer punch. I-27 appeared to be unable to dive, and because of the hail of machine-gun and cannon fire sweeping her decks her gunners were unable to man her 5.5-inch. However, her six torpedo tubes were a menace not to be ignored. If she were able to manoeuvre into a position to fire, *Petard* would be in great danger. As it was, the destroyer smothered the submarine with shot and shell, firing a total of 300 rounds of 4-inch and a constant stream of smaller shot. I-27's deck gun was blasted over the side and her conning tower riddled, but due to *Petard's* lack of armour-piercing shells, she failed to hole the submarine's hull. Commander Egan wrote in his report:

> The problem of tackling a U-boat under these conditions was vexatious. Gunfire inflicted no apparent damage to pressure hull and running up alongside sufficiently close to lob depth charges to a lethal distance, with the U-boat under helm, at the same time keeping clear of bow and stern tubes, was hazardous. These tactics were finally abandoned due to the danger of collision and it was decided to sink her by torpedo.
>
> Here again the target appeared simple, but only the seventh torpedo found its mark and she finally blew up at 1153 (GMT). When the column of water subsided, nothing was visible except an oil patch. Another violent underwater explosion occurred seven minutes later, which only brought more diesel oil and a few pieces of wreckage to the surface.

Paladin now reported she was in danger of sinking. Her engine room was flooded and it was feared that the forward engine room bulkhead would give way under the weight of water. Her remaining torpedoes were fired off, and everything moveable and not essential was thrown overboard, while her survivors were transferred to HMS *Petard*. Fortunately, by the time the sun went down *Paladin* had stopped taking on water and appeared to be out of danger. *Petard* then passed a tow line, and the two destroyers set off for Addu Atoll, leaving HMS *Hawkins* to look after the remaining four ships of the convoy. The destroyers arrived safely at the base at 0740 the next morning.

The sinking of the *Khedive Ismail* with the loss of 1,297 lives, including 77 women and 137 of her crew of 183, will go down in history as one of the worst shipping disasters of the Second World War. There are conflicting reports as to why so many people died, when the weather was so favourable and other ships were close by. It has been said, although never officially confirmed, that I-27 was hiding under the survivors in the water and that HMS *Petard* made at least one depth charge run through them, causing many deaths. If this was so, then Commander Rupert Egan was only following Navy protocol, the safety of the other ships in the convoy taking precedence over the lives of survivors in the water.

Kenneth Harrup, who was serving in the repair ship HMS *Lucas* at the time, in later years wrote:

> Our orders were to join the *Khedive Ismail* and convoy KR 8 but when they learned that our maximum speed was only 9 knots they departed without us at 15 knots on the 5th. We left on the 8th and sailed through the wreckage and empty lifeboats before arriving at the Maldives where we carried out first aid repairs to the damaged destroyer. Apart from this our voyage was completely uneventful, but only now do I realize how close we came to disaster.
>
> If that raider had not been disposed of in that terrible moment of decision by the *Petard* captain, my ship and the lives of some 500 navy men would almost certainly have fallen to that Japanese submarine. We had so little in the way of defences – just a 12 pounder gun and a few depth charges, we would have been a sitting duck. With that thought in mind, perhaps those dozens of poor souls did not die in vain on that most tragic day 61 long years ago, when swimming hopefully towards their rescuers only to find that they were their executioners.

Epilogue

The war in Europe officially ended at midnight on 7 May 1945. Hitler was dead, and his appointed successor, Grossadmiral Karl Dönitz, had signed the document of unconditional surrender. Three days earlier, in his capacity as C-in-C U-boats, Dönitz had sent the following message to his fleet: 'All U-boats cease fire at once. Stop all hostile activities against Allied shipping.'

News of the cessation of hostilities must have come as a great relief to Captain James Cushnie and his crew in the British ship *Avondale Park*, due to sail that night from Methil in the Firth of Forth. The threat of death they had lived with for six years had at last been lifted.

It had been a long and bloody war for British shipping, commencing with the sinking of the unarmed *Athenia* by U-30 just a few hours after hostilities began on 3 September 1939, and continuing without let-up for six long years. So many good ships had been lost, so many brave men had died. It would not have been surprising if there was a general feeling of quiet satisfaction, of a 'job well done', in the ranks of Convoy EN 491 as it prepared to sail from Methil to Oban, on the other side of Scotland, on a warm thundery evening in May 1945.

EN 491 consisted of just five merchant ships, two British and three Norwegian. At the height of the war, the short passage they were about to undertake, through the Pentland Firth and the Minch, had been considered a dangerous challenge, open to attack by both U-boats and the long-range Focke-Wulf bombers of the Luftwaffe. Now the risk was minimal, and consequently even the convoy's small escort of three armed trawlers seemed excessive.

The convoy left Methil at 2030 on 6 May, just as dusk was closing in. Leading the starboard column was the 2,878-ton *Avondale Park*, built for the Canadian Government in Nova Scotia in early 1944 and now on bareboat charter to the British Ministry of War Transport, who in turn had put her under the management of Witherington & Everett of Newcastle-upon-Tyne. Commanded by

Captain James Cushnie, she flew the Red Ensign and was manned by a British crew of thirty-eight, including four DEMS gunners. She had on board a full cargo for Belfast.

At that time, no one, whether sailing in EN 491 or ashore, was aware that Kapitänleutnant Emil Klusmeier, commanding U-2336, had either not received Dönitz's order to cease fire or had chosen to ignore it.

U-2336 had sailed from Larvik on her first patrol six days earlier, while Germany was still at war. She was a Type XXIII coastal submarine of an experimental design, small in comparison with the Type VII which had borne the brunt of the long campaign, being only 114ft long, less than 10ft in the beam and of 258 tons displacement when submerged. She was powered by a 575 h.p. diesel or a double-acting electric motor giving 572 h.p., both of which could be used underwater with her Schnorkel. The latter enabled her to remain submerged for long periods at a speed of 12½ knots, giving her the ability to stalk and outrun most Allied merchantmen. The Type XXIII did, however, suffer one severe disadvantage: due to lack of space in her hull she carried only two torpedoes, and when these had been fired, her tubes could only be reloaded externally in port. She also mounted no guns on deck, further restricting her attack capability.

Emil Klusmeier had served as watch officer in several conventional U-boats between 1937 and 1940, after which he joined Dönitz's staff at Lorient. He had not returned to sea until March 1945, when he took command of U-2336 after her then commander Jürgen Vockel had been killed in an air raid on Hamburg.

It is known that while stationed ashore Klusmeier had been involved with the design and building of the Type XXIII and had helped write the battle instructions for the experimental craft. It has been said that he volunteered to step into Jürgen Vockel's shoes solely to be able to test his contribution to the boat in action.

Shortly before midnight on 7 May, in the final hour of the war in Europe, Convoy EN 491 was passing 1½ miles south of the Isle of May, in the mouth of the Firth of Forth. The ships were not showing navigation lights, but in view of the relaxed atmosphere prevailing no one seemed particularly bothered about complete blackout. U-2336, lying in wait off the Isle of May, therefore had no difficulty in seeing the small convoy as it approached. Stealthily, Klusmeier moved in on the surface.

The *Avondale Park* was leading the starboard column of the convoy, closely followed by the small Norwegian coaster *Sneland I*, which was staggering under the weight of 2,800 tons of coal for Belfast. Neither ship saw Klusmeier's torpedoes heading their way.

The *Avondale Park* was first to be hit, one torpedo exploding in her engine room and blasting a great hole in her starboard side, through which the sea poured in. Chief Engineer George Anderson and Donkeyman William Harvey lost their lives in the blast. They were the last British merchant seamen to die by enemy action in the Second World War, and their ship, which sank in a few minutes, was the last British merchantman to go.

The numbers bear repeating: when the war in Europe ended and the blockade of the British Isles was finally lifted, 2,535 British merchant ships had been sunk by enemy action and 36,749 British merchant seamen had died as a result. To put this into its proper prospective, it must be remembered that sailing in Britain's Merchant Navy in time of war, despite the ships being armed and constantly under attack, was still classed as a civilian occupation. All those who manned the ships were volunteers, no man being forced to return to sea once his ship had been lost. It was not uncommon for a British merchant seaman to have five or six ships sunk under him in succession, especially at the height of the Battle of the Atlantic, when 200 ships a month were going down; yet there is no record of any British merchant ship being held up in port for lack of a crew. Those men always came back, no matter what perils they faced.

An article written by Dave Molyneux, Secretary of the Blue Funnel Association, says it all:

> I cannot say what drove these men and boys to return to face U-boats, Surface Raiders, Pocket Battleships, and dive bombers, then again, it was their living and livelihood to keep their wives and families. How did these merchant seamen sign articles time after time, and go back to sea when they had seen their brothers on other ships in convoy torpedoed, dive bombed and blown to pieces? Tankers carrying a time bomb in their holds, blown up in a ball of flame with very little chance of survival – if they did – only to be choked with burning oil in their lungs or on fire in the water?

The men working in the bowels of the ship, engineers, donkeymen, firemen, greasers, who were first to know of a torpedo exploding in the engine room, for a split second, and in that split second – oblivion. They knew no more. Those trapped in cabins – twisted metal and bulkheads – seeing the sea pouring in – unable to escape. Sheer terror – screaming, ripping flesh off their hands trying to get out – then finally and hopefully, peace as the waters closed over them.

Those who survived the explosion, after shock, lowering lifeboats, lucky in some respects if in daylight – but imagine the blackness of night. No lights – steam escaping, the ship listing, groaning as she protested against the violence of buckled steel and the cold seas pouring into the gaping jagged hole in her side. Their only chance now was a wooden lifeboat, open to all nature's violence that she could throw at them – those lucky enough to get into a lifeboat. There were those who clung on to pieces of wreckage for as long as they could – only to slip away into the depths with no trace. At first thankful for surviving - then wonder if the lifeboat would spot them.

> 'When we look at the restless sea – remember them,
> For they are not restless any more – they are at last
> At peace in the never ending restless sea.
> They gave so much.'

Prior to the outbreak of war in 1939 Britain topped the world's league of merchant shipping, with over 4,000 ocean-going ships sailing under the Red Ensign. On any one day, an average of 2,500 British merchant ships were at sea or in ports scattered across the globe. These ships dominated the ocean trade routes, carrying up to 50 per cent of the world's exports and imports. When war came, by their sheer numbers they were able to absorb the brutal assaults of a determined and highly efficient enemy for six long years.

Two generations on, this island nation has turned its back on the sea, with the result that its once great merchant fleet has shrunk to fewer than 400 ships, the majority of which are now manned by cheap foreign crews, who owe no loyalty to the flag they sail under.

Ninety per cent of Britain's exports and imports are still carried by sea, and the lack of a sizeable merchant fleet has resulted in a loss of revenue to the nation which runs into billions of pounds annually. Furthermore, in the event of a major war, without sufficient ships to supply her needs Britain would face starvation and surrender within weeks.

It is a matter of survival.

Bibliography

Books

Admiralty, *East of Malta, West of Suez*, HMSO, 1943

Banks, Arthur, *Wings of the Dawning*, Images Publishing, 1996

Blair, Clay, *Hitler's U-boat War*, Cassell, 2000

Blair, Clay, *Silent Victory*, Bantam Books, 1975

Bryant, Arthur, *The Turn of the Tide*, Collins, 1957

Carruthers, Bob, *The U-boat War in the Atlantic* Vols 1–2, Pen & Sword Books, 2013

Churchill, Winston, *The Second World War* Vols 1–6, Cassell, 1952

Course, Captain A. G., *The Deep Sea Tramp*, Hollis & Carter, 1960

Hecks, Karl, *Bombing 1939–45*, Robert Hale, 1990

Howarth, Stephen, *Morning Glory*, Hamish Hamilton, 1983

Laskier, Frank, *My Name is Frank*, George Allen & Unwin, 1941

Mallmann Showell, J. P., *U-boats under the Swastika*, Ian Allan, 1973

Montgomery, Michael, *Who Sank the Sydney?*, Leo Cooper, 1981

Padfield, Peter, *Dönitz – The Last Führer*, Cassell, 1993

Rohwer, Jürgen, *Axis Submarine Successes*, US Naval Institute Press, 1999

Ruegg, Bob and Arnold Hague, *Convoys to Russia*, World Ship Society, 1993

Slader, John, *The Fourth Service*, Robert Hale, 1994

Smith, Anthony, *Survived*, Quintin Smith, 1998

Terraine, John, *Business in Great Waters*, Leo Cooper, 1989

Thomas, David A., *The Atlantic Star*, W.H. Allen, 1990

Veranov, Michael, *The Third Reich at War*, Siena, 1998

Werner, Herbert A., *Iron Coffins,* Casell, 1999

Woodman, Richard, *The Real Cruel Sea*, John Murray, 2004

Other sources

National Archives, Kew
Imperial War Museum
BBC

Nautical Magazine
Sea Breezes
Ships Monthly
Ships and Shipping Today & Yesterday
uboat.net

Index